D1522748

Beyond Hofstede

Beyond Hofstede

Culture Frameworks for Global Marketing and Management

Edited by

Cheryl Nakata
Associate Professor of Marketing and International Business,
University of Illinois-Chicago

First published 2009 by
PALGRAVE MACMILLAN

Palgrave Macmillan in the UK is an imprint of Macmillan Publishers Limited,
registered in England, company number 785998, of Houndmills, Basingstoke,
Hampshire RG21 6XS.

Palgrave Macmillan in the US is a division of St Martin's Press LLC,
175 Fifth Avenue, New York, NY 10010.

Palgrave Macmillan is the global academic imprint of the above companies
and has companies and representatives throughout the world.

Palgrave® and Macmillan® are registered trademarks in the United States,
the United Kingdom, Europe and other countries.

ISBN-13: 978-0-230-20239-9   hardback
ISBN-10: 0-230-20239-X   hardback

This book is printed on paper suitable for recycling and made from fully
managed and sustained forest sources. Logging, pulping and manufacturing
processes are expected to conform to the environmental regulations of the
country of origin.

A catalogue record for this book is available from the British Library.

Library of Congress Cataloging-in-Publication Data

Beyond Hofstede : culture frameworks for global marketing and
    management / [edited by] Cheryl Nakata.
      p. cm.
    Includes index.
    ISBN 978-0-230-20239-9 (alk. paper)
  1. Marketing—Cross-cultural studies. 2. Management—Cross-cultural
    studies. 3. International trade—Social aspects. I. Nakata, Cheryl.
    HF5415.B4455 2009
    658.8'4—dc22   2009013619

10   9   8   7   6   5   4   3   2   1
18 17 16 15 14 13 12 11 10 09

Printed and bound in Great Britain by
CPI Antony Rowe, Chippenham and Eastbourne

Dedication

This book is the result of the collective efforts of many, beginning with the contributing authors: Wendi L. Adair, Eric J. Arnould, Søren Askegaard, Mary Yoko Brannen, Donnel A. Briley, Nancy R. Buchan, Xiao-Ping Chen, C. Samuel Craig, Claudia Dale, Susan P. Douglas, P. Christopher Earley, Elif Izberk-Bilgin, Dannie Kjeldgaard, Leigh Anne Liu, Fiona Moore, Piers Steel, Vas Taras. These leading management and marketing scholars from universities around the world were broached in October 2007 to write a research monograph on new frameworks and perspectives on culture, going beyond the dominant Hofstede paradigm. In the following spring, they generously provided chapters distilling their expertise and latest research.

To share and discuss these ideas, a symposium was held in Chicago on May 23–25, 2008 at the University of Illinois at Chicago (UIC). The authors, along with UIC faculty and students, came together in rich exchanges about culture and its implications for global marketing and management. Dean Stefanie Lenway, Associate Dean Abagail McWilliams, Department Head Mark Shanley, and Professor Thomas Murtha of UIC's College of Business Administration graciously supported the symposium. Professor Elif Izberk-Bilgin, Co-Chair of the symposium, as well as doctoral students Kelly Weidner and Esi Abbam Elliot, helped to organize and make the event a success. Faculty members Joseph Cherian, Benet DeBerry-Spence, and Jelena Spanjol facilitated the discussions.

Finally but no less important were friends, family, and supporters who cheered the book project from start to finish, including Adele, Angela, Barbara, Cindy, Estelle, Jim, Linda, Maisie, Pat, Phil, and Tami. To all authors, UIC faculty and students, and family and friends, the book is gratefully dedicated.

Contents

Figures

Tables

Acknowledgments

The New Yorker is acknowledged for copyright permission for cartoons appearing in Chapter 11 of this book.

Contributing Authors

Wendi L. Adair (wladair@watarts.uwaterloo.ca, Ph.D., Northwestern University) is Assistant Professor of Organizational Psychology at the University of Waterloo. Professor Adair's research and teaching focus on communication, negotiation, and teams in the global marketplace. Her research on reciprocity in cross-cultural negotiations received awards from the American Psychological Association and the International Association for Conflict Management. Professor Adair's research appears in journals including *Journal of Applied Psychology*, *Organization Science*, *International Journal of Conflict Management*, and *Negotiation and Conflict Management Research*, and in multiple edited volumes.

Eric J. Arnould (earnould@uwyo.edu) is Distinguished Professor of Sustainable Business Practices at the University of Wyoming. He holds a Ph.D. in cultural anthropology and worked as a consultant on economic development problems in many West African countries before becoming a full-time marketing academic in 1990. Eric has taught at the University of Nebraska; University of Colorado-Denver; Cal State University Long Beach; University of South Florida; University of Southern Denmark; University of Ljubljana, Slovenia; Bilkent University, Ankara, Turkey; and EAP-ESCP, Dauphine University, and IAE-Sorbonne all in Paris, France. Professor Arnould's research on consumer culture theory, economic development, services marketing, and marketing channels in developing countries appears in many social science and managerial periodicals and books.

Søren Askegaard (aske@sam.sdu.dk) is Professor of Marketing at the University of Southern Denmark. He has a postgraduate Diploma in Communication Studies from the Sorbonne University, Paris and Ph.D. in Business Studies from Odense University, 1993. He has been employed to teach at the following universities for shorter or longer periods of time: Bilkent University, Turkey; ESSEC, Université de Savoie, ESC Clermont-Ferrand, and Université de Lille 2, France; Lund University, Sweden; Suffolk University; and University of California, Irvine, USA. His research interests generally are in the field of consumer culture theory and commercial symbolism, and his research has been published in numerous international journals and anthologies. He is the co-author of a major European textbook on consumer behavior.

Mary Yoko Brannen (maryyoko@mac.com, branne_m@cob.sjsu.edu) is the Spansion Chair of Multicultural Integration at the Lucas Graduate School of Business, San José State University and Visiting Professor of Strategy and Management at INSEAD, Fontainebleau, France. She received her MBA with emphasis in International Business and Ph.D. in Management with a minor in Anthropology from the University of Massachusetts at Amherst, and a BA in Comparative Literature from the University of California at Berkeley. Her research focuses on ethnographic approaches to understanding the effects of changing cultural contexts on technology transfer, work organization, and multinational mergers and acquisitions. Her non-academic interests include dressage, Japanese brush painting, and Zen Buddhism.

Donnel A. Briley (D.Briley@econ.usyd.edu.au) is Professor of Marketing at the University of Sydney, Australia. His areas of expertise are consumer choice and international marketing, and his research has focused on understanding the influence of culture and ethnicity on consumers' judgments and decisions. He has published articles from this stream in top marketing and psychology journals, including *Journal of Consumer Research, Journal of Marketing Research* and *Social Cognition*; and he serves on the editorial board of *Journal of Consumer Research*. He has a Ph.D. from Stanford University, an MBA from University of California, Berkeley, and has studied at Institut d'Etudes Politiques de Paris, France.

Nancy R. Buchan (nancy.buchan@moore.sc.edu, Ph.D., University of Pennsylvania) is Associate Professor of International Business at the University of South Carolina. Professor Buchan's research focuses on the building and maintenance of trust and cooperation in cross-cultural relationships. Her research appears in outlets such as the *Journal of Consumer Research*, the *American Economic Review* and the *American Journal of Sociology* and in several edited volumes. She has received grants from the Russell Sage Foundation and currently heads a project funded by the National Science Foundation examining the influence of globalization on cooperation.

Xiao-ping Chen (xpchen@u.washington.edu) received her Ph.D. from the University of Illinois. She is currently a Professor of Management and Organization at the Foster School of Business, University of Washington. Her research interests include group dynamics, decision making, leadership, Chinese guanxi, and cross-cultural management. Professor Chen has published her research in top-tier journals such as

Academy of Management Review, Academy of Management Journal, Journal of Applied Psychology, Organizational Behavior and Human Decision Processes, and *Journal of International Business Studies.* She was on the faculty previously at Indiana University and Hong Kong University of Science and Technology.

C. Samuel Craig (scraig@stern.nyu.edu) is the Catherine and Peter Kellner Professor and Deputy Chair of the Marketing Department at New York University's Stern School of Business. Professor Craig co-authored *Consumer Behavior: An Information Processing Perspective, Global Marketing Strategy,* and *International Marketing Research,* 3rd edition. He is also the author of over 100 articles and technical papers, which have appeared in leading marketing journals. He received his Ph.D. from the Ohio State University. He has taught marketing for executive programs in the United States as well as France, the UK, Thailand, India, Singapore, Greece, and Slovenia.

Claudia Dale is a graduate student and research assistant at the Robinson College of Business, Georgia State University. She is formerly a business librarian at Georgia State University. Her research interests include knowledge management, organizational knowledge, and learning, particularly in an international context.

Susan P. Douglas (sdouglas@stern.nyu.edu) is Paganelli-Bull Professor of Marketing and International Business at New York University's Stern School of Business. She received her Ph.D. from the University of Pennsylvania. She is co-author (with C. Samuel Craig) of two books, *Global Marketing Strategy* and *International Marketing Research,* 3rd edition and has published over 80 articles in leading marketing and international business journals. Her research interests focus on global marketing strategy, cross-cultural consumer research, and methodological issues in international marketing research. She is a Fellow of AIB, and former Dean of the AIB Fellows, and a Fellow of EMAC and former Chair of EMAC Fellows.

P. Christopher Earley (chris.earley@business.uconn.edu) is the Auran J. Fox Chair in Business and the Dean of the University of Connecticut School of Business. His interests include cross-cultural aspects of organizations including the dynamics of multinational teams and motivation. Recent publications include *Cultural Intelligence: Individual Interactions Across Cultures* (with Ang Soon), *Multinational Work Teams: A New Perspective* (with Cristina Gibson), *The Transplanted Executive: Managing in Different*

Cultures (with Miriam Erez), and "Creating Hybrid Team Cultures: An Empirical Test of International Team Functioning" (with E. Mosakowski, *Academy of Management Journal*).

Elif Izberk-Bilgin (ebilgin@umd.umich.edu) is Assistant Professor, Marketing at the University of Michigan-Dearborn. Professor Izberk-Bilgin holds a BA in Sociology from Boğaziçi University in Istanbul, Turkey, an MBA with specializations in Marketing and International Business and a Ph.D. from the University of Illinois-Chicago. Her research focuses on globalization of consumer culture, consumer activism, cross-cultural consumption, branding, and sociological aspects of consumerism in emerging countries. Professor Izberk-Bilgin's research appears in *Consumption, Markets, and Culture*, *Advances in Consumer Research*, *Developments in Marketing Science*, and *Frontiers of Entrepreneurship Research*.

Dannie Kjeldgaard (dkj@sam.sdu.dk) is Associate Professor of Marketing at the University of Southern Denmark. He received his Ph.D. in Business Economics in 2003 from the University of Southern Denmark. Before joining academia he worked for four years in a London-based PR consultancy. Dannie's work primarily looks at the process of glocalization and its intersection with branding and consumer culture, and has been applied to a number of market place phenomena such as style consumption, place branding, brandscape glocalization, gender, media and identity construction, global consumer segments, body culture, ethnicity and qualitative methodology.

Leigh Anne Liu (iiblal@langate.gsu.edu) is Assistant Professor of International Business at the Robinson College of Business, Georgia State University. She received her Ph.D. in management from Vanderbilt University. Her research centers on social cognition in cross-cultural organizational behavior, negotiation, and conflict management.

Fiona Moore (Fiona.Moore@rhul.ac.uk) is an industrial anthropologist who received her D.Phil. from Oxford. Her research focuses on identity in MNCs, and she has conducted studies on the use of ethnic identity as a strategic resource by German expatriates in London, identity among workers and managers at an automobile plant, and the social adjustment of Korean labor migrants in London. She is currently researching hybrid identities among Anglo-Chinese managers. Recent publications include *Transnational Business Cultures* (Ashgate, 2005) and *Professional Identities: Policy and Practice in Business and Bureaucracy* with Shirley Ardener (Berghahn, 2007).

Cheryl Nakata (cnakat1@uic.edu) is Associate Professor of Marketing and International Business at the University of Illinois at Chicago. Her interests in culture center on its theoretical explorations and managerial applications in international business and marketing, including for innovation and strategy purposes. Her work has appeared in the *Journal of International Business Studies, Journal of Marketing, Journal of the Academy of Marketing Science* and edited volumes among others, and won overall conference and research track awards. She serves on several editorial boards, and prior to joining academia held managerial positions in Fortune 500 companies and operated an international marketing research consultancy performing studies in over 40 countries.

Piers Steel (piers.steel@haskayne.ucalgary.ca) is a University of Calgary associate professor at the Haskayne School of Business who studies culture, motivation, and meta-analytic issues. In particular, he has published several meta-analytic reviews, articles on meta-analytic methodology, and studies of subjective well-being and personality at both national and individual levels of analysis. His work has been reported in hundreds of media outlets around the world, including the *New York Times, CNN, USA Today, LA Times, Readers Digest, Scientific American,* and the *Discovery Channel.* Presently, he is writing a book on procrastination, which will be published worldwide, sooner or later.

Vas Taras (taras@ucalgary.ca) is Assistant Professor of International Management at the University of North Carolina at Greensboro. He received his Ph.D. in Human Resources and Organizational Dynamics from the University of Calgary, Canada. His research interests are in management and development of cross-cultural workgroups and in evaluation of training effectiveness. He is especially interested in diversity management in domestic organizations that employ immigrants. Vas has lived, worked and studied in half a dozen countries and has extensive experience as a manager, entrepreneur, and cross-cultural team coach and diversity management consultant. He is a member of the Editorial Board of the *International Journal of Cross-Cultural Management.*

Part I Introduction and Overview

1
Going Beyond Hofstede: Why We Need to and How

Cheryl Nakata

In 1980 Geert Hofstede published his landmark study, *Culture's Consequences: International Differences in Work Related Values*. The book described what has been the largest survey of work values, encompassing 88,000 employees in 72 countries. An updated version expanded the survey to an additional ten countries and three regions (Hofstede, 2001). Arguably more important than the scale of the study was the framework it introduced. Based on the survey data, Hofstede put forth a new and parsimonious conceptualization of culture, accompanied by measurements and indexes. He proposed that culture is the "collective programming of the mind which distinguishes the members of one human group from another" (1980, p. 13), and more specifically identified five universal values occurring to varying degrees in each country: individualism, masculinity, power distance, uncertainty avoidance, and long-term orientation. The framework translated the rather amorphous idea of culture into a tractable construct amenable to empirical research. Subsequently, the framework has been widely applied in various business disciplines, as well as spilling over into the social sciences.

Recent literature reviews point to Hofstede's framework as the dominant culture paradigm in business studies. In reviewing the international business literature, Kirkman and colleagues note that the work is more widely cited in the Social Sciences Citation Index than competing theories of culture, "inspiring thousands of empirical studies" (2006, p. 285). In an analysis of cross-cultural management studies Taras and Steele observe that the book is a "super classic," and conclude that nearly all cross-cultural studies have been influenced by its approach to culture (see their chapter in this book). Sivakumar and Nakata (2001) likewise comment that the paradigm has grown in impact, superseding other culture theories and catapulting Hofstede into the ranks of the top three referenced international business authors. And Nakata and Izberk-Bilgin (also in this volume) determine that marketing researchers have incorporated Hofstede's framework into their work with far greater frequency than any other culture concept.

What explains this popularity? There are several reasons. Hofstede's work first of all rests on a mammoth survey of thousands of respondents in a diverse array of countries and regions. The data collected was sufficient to derive statistically based insights into culture that had not been possible before. It would be difficult to replicate or improve upon this study even today, though the recent GLOBE project attempts to do so (House, Hanges, Javidan, Dorfman, and Gupta, 2004). Another reason is that the set of values—initially four, with a fifth added later—is collectively capable of describing all, not just a subset of, national cultures. So for researchers interested in explaining or describing any single culture or cluster of cultures, the framework is pliable for a range of needs. A third reason is that the dimensions have theoretical moorings. While the charge has been leveled that the framework is overly reductionist, a reading of Hofstede's work reveals some grounding in prior theoretical work done in anthropology, sociology, and psychology. The factor of individualism is a case in point. Hofstede anchors this dimension in conceptualizations offered by Kluckhohn and Strodtbeck (1961), Parsons (1937), and others. Finally, Hofstede's provision of a survey questionnaire and operationalization of culture into standardized scores facilitates application in quantitative research. Rival frameworks, even when more nuanced, such as Hall's high–low context concept, have not gained widespread acceptance in part because of the lack of instruments (see Adair, Buchan, and Chen in this book for a discussion of this issue).

Conditions ripe to look beyond

Nonetheless conditions have emerged indicating that the time is ripe to look beyond Hofstede. There is a need for new understandings of culture, especially in the fields of global marketing and management, the domains most concerned with the implications of culture for business. One indicative condition is the increasingly fluid nature of culture. In this age of globalization, cultures are traversing national borders, co-mingling, hybridizing, morphing, and clashing through media, migration, telecommunications, international trade, information technology, supranational organizations, and unfortunately terrorism. With interdependencies created through globalization, such as interlocking financial and banking systems, people—the carriers and possessors of culture—are interacting, confronting, and exchanging their diverse ways of life across geographies as well as in social and institutional settings at unprecedented rates and levels.

When Hofstede wrote his book in 1980, the world was a simpler place. Nations, his primary interest, were fairly bound, stable, and intact. In the nearly three decades that have passed, nations have become more permeable and heterogeneous, and are altering through dismantlement (e.g. the former Soviet Union) as well as integration (e.g. the European Union). Multinational firms, another of Hofstede's interests, in this period have increased in breadth, influence, and cultural complexity. Firms are hiring nationals in growing numbers, grooming personnel with transnational and not just home-country skills, and exploring ways of leveraging the cultural intelligence of an expanding corps of bi- and tricultural workers (see Brannen's chapter in this book).

Also, as these firms enter into new markets around the world, they face consumers who are far more familiar with and exposed to global brands and products than they were three decades ago. The Internet, among other means, is spreading the word about these offerings, along with a multiplicity of lifestyle and cultural images. Consumers are embracing, rejecting, and altering these products and messages, creating new cultural identities and cultural forms in the process. Confronted with this fluidity, practitioners and researchers of global marketing and management are seeking alternative paradigms of culture that will help them navigate the now more varied and dynamic terrains of markets, consumers, and organizations around the world.

Another condition that indicates a need to look beyond Hofstede is the state of scholarship on and theorization of culture. An examination of the contents of ABI-Inform, one of the largest business literature databases, shows interest in culture has grown dramatically since *Culture's Consequences* was published. The number of culture studies appearing in business journals totaled 575 from 1980 to 1990, grew to 1712 from 1991 to 2000, and then jumped to 2212 from 2001 to 2007. The figures amount to a nearly 300 percent increase in research output when comparing the first to the third decades. As suggested by reviews of the literature, the surge is tied to Hofstede, given the preponderance of culture studies using his framework (Kirkman et al., 2006; Sivakumar and Nakata, 2001).

While the trend is promising in that researchers are honing in on culture as a way of comprehending global economic and market transformations, it also points to a maturing line of inquiry that would benefit from an expansion of culture paradigms. The near-exclusive adoption of the Hofstedean view means that business researchers—intentionally or unintentionally, implicitly or explicitly—have agreed that it captures as a phenomenon all that culture is. Convergence on a single paradigm should signal arriving at the end of a journey of discovery, having examined competing or complementary perspectives and found them wanting. However, because few alternative views have been investigated, the journey has in fact just begun.

Business researchers owe much to Hofstede for pointing to the relevance and potency of culture as a theoretical lens through which the world is seen. Yet Hofstede never claimed that his is the one and only lens. Researchers have perhaps all too eagerly and persistently latched on to it for the reasons noted earlier, ignoring other possibilities to invigorate their work. Thought leaders repeatedly made the observation that non-Hofstedean interpretations of culture are required to move the fields of global marketing and management ahead (e.g. Earley, 2006; Kirkman et al., 2006; McSweeney, 2002). This situation does not suggest that Hofstede's perspective, which has produced significant understanding, should be completely abandoned. Instead, it suggests that it is time to widen the vista, so that other views are invited and considered, enriching the conversation about culture and leading to greater insights for business.

What this book aims to do

This book addresses the need to look beyond Hofstede. It may be the first attempt, hopefully with others that might follow, to generate more varied discourse about culture in relation to global marketing and management concerns. The book has two specific aims. The first is to describe and elaborate the importance and implications of pursuing culture theories other than Hofstede's. By taking stock of Hofstede's culture paradigm and what more of the same, that is, its almost exclusive application, will lead to, we can better understand where culture studies as a body of knowledge stands and the direction we need to move to. The second aim is to explore the development and use of new views and frameworks to expand insights on how culture matters in the international business setting. While cross-cultural management and marketing studies with non-Hofstedean outlooks have been produced, these have by and large been isolated, independent endeavors. By collecting such works in one place, this book informs readers of the existence, nature, and uses of culture concepts, along with methodological considerations, that are distinct from Hofstede's.

To fulfill these aims, a diverse approach was taken to assemble the book's contents. It is diverse first of all in being interdisciplinary: the two fields of global management and global marketing are represented.

Although the two fields share much in common, focusing on some of the same issues such as organizational dynamics in multinational firms, the research tends to be disseminated through separate outlets and rarely draws on the other. Kirkman and colleagues (2006, p. 286) make a similar point with respect to the large number of studies centered on Hofstede's paradigm, describing the research distributed across several disciplines as "fragmented," "redundant," and "unable to benefit from the cumulative knowledge." To avoid that end, this book brings together work from the two fields leading the charge on culture studies in business.

The book is diverse also in methodological and philosophical underpinnings. Research is included reflecting both quantitative and qualitative methods as well as positivist and interpretive philosophies. Methods and philosophies are often closely tied to theory. By deliberately broadening the first two, the book arrives at more variation in the third. One of the reasons the Hofstedean take on culture is deemed confining is that it assumes certain methods and philosophy (see Nakata's concluding Chapter 12). Finally, the book is diverse in that emergent as well as established scholars from several continents and cultures (e.g. Danish, Turkish, Chinese, Russian, Canadian, Japanese, American, British) contributed chapters. The authors' diverse backgrounds inform their work and thereby enrich discussion about culture's essence and ways.

How this book is organized

The remainder of the book is structured into five sections, labeled Parts II through VI. The first of these, Part II, is entitled "Reviews and Critiques of Culture Frameworks." In this section, three chapters describe the context and motivations for looking beyond Hofstede. Collectively, the chapters provide the necessary foundation for the book, helping the reader understand the premise for and value of exploring non-Hofstedean points of view.

P. Christopher Earley in Chapter 2 draws on past studies and expertise to describe (a) the nature of culture, its loose definition, and many uses; (b) several approaches to comprehending culture, along with coinciding issues such as ecological fallacies; (c) ideological similarities among these approaches, as well as their under-emphasis on theory and over-emphasis on differences; (d) the need for fresh approaches going beyond value typologies, as well as theory-building at the grand and mid-range levels; and (e) some possible candidates, including the concepts of universal work culture and cultural intelligence.

Vas Taras and **Piers Steel** in Chapter 3 provide an overview of the significant impact of Hofstede's work on cross-cultural business studies. Moreover, they analyze what they term the "Ten Commandments" of cross-cultural research, which are assumptions stemming from the use and misuse of Hofstede's theory. The assumptions have become pervasive in the literature. The authors discuss the viability of these assumptions as well as outline possible directions for future cross-cultural studies based on empirical research, including meta-analyses.

Cheryl Nakata and **Elif Izberk-Bilgin** in Chapter 4 review a decade of marketing studies to understand the use, role, and nature of culture theories. Using content analysis, they find that while culture theories are increasingly relied on to address international marketing issues, the theories are applied implicitly and informally, limiting potential insights. Additionally, the theories tend to follow double-empirical, analog structures, which are weaker knowledge-producing forms. Consistent with other reviews, they find that Hofstede's conceptualization surpasses all others in frequency of use. The authors conclude that culture knowledge faces the prospect of premature restriction, and recommend a broadening of approaches while the field is still maturing, such as through consumer culture theory.

The next section, Part III, is entitled "Conceptualizations of the Culture Problem." This section elaborates how culture has been problematized, surfacing traditional assumptions about the fundamental nature of culture. The contributors move past these assumptions by proposing new concepts of culture that account for dynamic conditions in firms and among consumers fostered by globalization.

Mary Yoko Brannen in Chapter 5 portrays the complex and shifting cultural landscape within and surrounding transnational firms. In so doing, she points out its contradiction with static, simplified renditions of culture, notably value-based interpretations such as Hofstede's, and offers the more compatible notion of culture as root metaphor for organizations. The author elaborates this idea by specifying the need for knowledge transfers across divergent contexts faced by organizations, and the potential role of biculturals or persons of mixed cultural identities to aid in this process. The author provides a model of culture as contextually negotiated content, wherein patterns of meaning and agency result from interactions among organizational members.

Søren Askegaard, Dannie Kjeldgaard, and **Eric J. Arnould** in Chapter 6 propose a new interpretation of culture that contrasts with its portrayal as a background variable influencing consumption and marketing practices. The authors begin by reviewing the legacies of Hofstede and Leavitt, who brought the concepts of globalization and culture into the marketing literature, and then deconstruct some of their assumptions (e.g. culture as essentialist) in light of recent globalization theory. The authors next offer a new view of culture as an organized network of principles of action and understanding reflexively and continuously negotiated. Accordingly, consumers and marketers are aware of cultures and cultural symbolism and modify their actions as a consequence, propelling culture change and globalization. This interpretation inverts the traditional culture–marketing relationship, and requires new language to talk about culture.

Part IV, "Extensions of and Advances in Culture Frameworks," furthers the discussion of culture by specifying ways in which culture has been typically framed, and how these ways ignore critical considerations affecting observed culture, such as context, implicit communications, and situational influences. Paths around these difficulties are presented, including methodological tools and theoretical solutions.

Susan P. Douglas and C. **Samuel Craig** in Chapter 7 describe how cultures exist within contexts and are thus shaped by them. In their review of culture concepts in marketing research, the authors find that the significant role of context is often not recognized, introducing confounds into comparative studies. To address this problem, they articulate the various types of context that can be incorporated into studies, such as ecological context, societal affluence, and religious context, and describe methods to allow direct examination of contextual influences. Among these methods are experimental design, use of country-level covariates in regression analyses, comparison of patterns within countries or between locations and groups, and application of hierarchical linear regression to parse out context effects.

Wendi L. Adair, **Nancy R. Buchan**, and **Xiao-Ping Chen** in Chapter 8 offer a theoretical solution to the Hofstede dilemma by exploring Edward Hall's culture context theory. Hall posits that culture is an adaptive system in which ways of communicating and doing things are internalized, contrasting with the cognitive, ideational, and inert qualities of culture propounded by Hofstede. The authors note widespread acceptance of Hall's theory but its limited use in management and marketing studies based on an extensive literature review. Thereafter they synthesize Hall's theory, describing its four components of communications, relationship, time, and spatial contexts, and delineate how future research may utilize the theory to generate global management and marketing insights. Among steps proposed for future research are the examination of antecedents and consequences of high–low context, and the development of context measures at the individual level.

Donnel A. Briley in Chapter 9 discusses the value dimensions approach that has dominated cultural analyses in marketing and other social sciences. A notable limitation of the approach is the imprecision of value dimensions such as individualism–collectivism, which encompass a broad range of specific concepts. Additionally, the dimensions are not as constant as presumed: an individual's values can change from moment to moment depending on situational conditions. To address these limitations, the author presents a dynamic view of cultural influence based on social cognition theory. According to this view, cultural influence arises from a loose network of knowledge structures such as norms, schemas, and motives. Preferences are constructed at the time judgments or decisions are made, rather than deterministically resulting from integrated worldviews. Briley presents empirical research demonstrating these effects, and concludes that cultural differences in behavior are changeable and situation-specific.

"Alternative Culture Frameworks and Perspectives" is the title of Part V of the book. This section provides understandings of culture that contrast with Hofstede's. Consistent with growing recognition of the interconnections and transformations resulting from globalization, these new understandings attempt to capture the fluid, multi-directional interactions, discourses, and influences experienced by organizations, subgroups, and individuals that are cultural in nature.

Fiona Moore in Chapter 10 addresses the need for a model of culture that reflects the complexity of culture while being in practice transferable across organizations. Based on a case study of an Anglo-German multinational automaker, Moore develops such a model, in which firms are conceived as nexuses of subgroups with multiple ties to one another and outside communities. Thus culture is neither an integrated nor a fragmented entity, such as a national or workplace culture characteristic of groups; rather, it is the product of subgroups engaging in discourses at organizational, local, and global levels, sharing and negotiating meanings over what it is to be a firm, an employee, British, German, working or middle class, and so on. The model is concretized by rich descriptions of the author's work on the automaker's assembly line as well as observations of and interviews with employees and managers in different sites.

Leigh Anne Liu and Claudia Dale in Chapter 11 expound on the diminishing relevance and utility of concepts where culture is depicted as independent, coherent, and stable. The authors recommend shared mental models as a framework that better captures the interactive and mutable nature of culture. Rooted in social construction theory, the shared mental models framework examines the degree of convergence between individually held mental models, which are cognitive networks of informational, relational, and emotional elements of knowledge. While this framework shares with Hofstede the notion of mental programs, it goes beyond by integrating context and situational dependence, along with adaptation to new conditions and environments. The authors illustrate the potential use of the framework in communications, conflict management, negotiation, and organizational theory research, among other possibilities.

In Part VI, the last section of the book, entitled "Reflexive Considerations," is presented. This section ties the individual parts and chapters together by reflexively examining the underlying assumptions about culture and how to study it, comparing approaches within business research with those beyond in the broader social sciences. On the basis of this examination, a research agenda is proposed to bring a more expansive view of culture theory into business research.

●Cheryl Nakata in Chapter 12 presents a reflexive study of classical and contemporary culture writings from the social sciences to enlarge the understanding of culture beyond interpretations dominant in marketing. The writings are analyzed for assumptions about the ontological traits, epistemological structure, and epistemological philosophy of culture, and juxtaposed against assumptions supporting theories such as Hofstede's. The analysis shows that culture is more widely and variously conceived in the social sciences. For instance, culture takes on the idealized–superorganic epistemology, where culture is an abstract causal force impacting people's lives, as well as the realist–organic epistemology, where culture is a social dialectic between people. This range is not well reflected in the marketing literature. The author advances a research agenda to improve the heterogeneity of culture ideas, termed Pure A, Pure B, and Hybrid theories, and provides examples of their application to marketing issues.

Moving beyond Hofstede: Key insights

While Hofstede's paradigm has brought needed attention to culture, it has also presented culture as more fixed and certain than conditions in

rapidly transforming markets and organizations around the world indicate. This book attempts to move beyond that paradigm by presenting
fresh frameworks and perspectives. In so doing, the book additionally
provides key insights on furthering the development of new understandings of culture. The insights are summarized here for the reader.

Insight #1: Enlarge the meaning of culture

Culture has taken on a singular meaning in the Hofstedean universe,
namely a cognitive construct expressed as five constant values shared
across a nation. In this book contributors offer rival definitions, which
collectively indicate that culture is far more encompassing. Among these
definitions are culture as meanings that people attach to the world
(Earley in Chapter 2); as root metaphors for organizations (Brannen in
Chapter 5); as networks of systematically diverse principles of action and
understanding (Askegaard and colleagues in Chapter 6); as artifacts or
communications (Douglas and Craig in Chapter 7); as adaptive systems
rooted in social context (Adair and colleagues in Chapter 8); as knowledge structures activated by situational factors (Briley in Chapter 9); as
continuously negotiated meanings of belonging (Moore in Chapter 10);
and as shared mental models or converging knowledge networks (Liu and
Dale in Chapter 11). The range of definitions breaks the boundaries of
Hofstede's conceptualization by acknowledging that culture lies at various levels (individual, group, organization, country, or between them)
and in diverse forms (meaning, metaphor, context, knowledge structures,
adaptive structures, principles of actions and understanding). Thus one
way to move past Hofstede is to enlarge the meaning of culture.

Insight #2: Identify the assumptions about culture

A related insight is that to arrive at new paradigms, base assumptions
about culture should be determined. It is at the level of assumptions that
paradigms take their structures. Several contributors explicate Hofstede's
assumptions, note their consequences, and comment on how assumptions influence culture theory formulation. Taras and Steel (Chapter 3),
for example, lay out the assumptions embedded in and surrounding use
of Hofstede's framework, and present empirical and theoretical evidence
that questions these assumptions. One such assumption is that cultures
are extremely stable. The authors point to well-acknowledged forces
that are altering culture (namely modernization and convergence), and
to data showing that significant cultural shifts are taking place in many
countries (Ronald Inglehart's global surveys). Askegaard and colleagues
(Chapter 6) present a similar line of argument. They discuss Hofstede

and Leavitt's influential culture and globalization theories, and in light of contemporary movements challenge some of their root premises, such as that culture is reducible to a background variable that effects change rather than being reflexively acted upon by social agents and consumers. Nakata (Chapter 12) expands the list of challengeable assumptions, including that culture is cognitive, bounded, immutable, coherent, and unified. The assumptions are then used to show how new culture theories can be built. In sum, by identifying the assumptions about culture, and checking them against realities within and outside businesses today, new theories of culture can be formulated and applied.

Insight #3: Embrace more complex forms of culture

As noted earlier Hofstede's framework gained popularity in part because of its parsimony. While this quality made culture tractable and amenable to survey research, it has been criticized for oversimplifying what is widely acknowledged as an inherently complex phenomenon (Kirkman et al., 2006; Sivakumar and Nakata, 2001). Thus a third way to move beyond Hofstede is to insert greater complexity into concepts of culture. Complexity can be pursued in many forms, as reflected in the range of interpretations of culture in this book. Among these interpretations is Brannen's concept of culture (Chapter 5) as negotiated meanings and actions by individuals in organizational contexts and exchanges. Individuals bring to organizations their diverse and embedded cultural profiles, including from bi- and multicultural histories. Once in their organizations, they negotiate stances with them, sometimes adhering close to and in other instances more distantly from their cultures of origin. In this regard culture is not an exogenous, monolithic force imprinting itself on society, but is constructed on a continuous basis as individuals navigate, understand, and act in organizations. This conceptualization of culture has subtleties not found in Hofstede's theory, and reflects the multiplex nature of culture formation.

Insight #4: Account for dynamism in culture

Another avenue for extending beyond Hofstede is incorporating more dynamism into ideas about culture. Hofstede maintained that culture undergoes barely perceptible change. As international trade increases, multinational businesses expand, and the World Wide Web extends, the notion of culture as an untouched, closed system becomes anachronistic and irrelevant. Hence, the contributors propose concepts where response, evolution, and transformation are part and parcel of the cultural landscape.

Adair, Buchan, and Chen (Chapter 8) delineate the utility of Hall's framework, which observes that multiple forms of context, such as communications and space, alter people's behaviors. Culture is thus an adaptive system. Briley (Chapter 9) posits that culture is composed of knowledge structures that are activated in different ways depending on situational factors. Individuals shift values on the fly and thus arrive at different judgments and decisions, contrary to the idea of culture as a fixed, irresistible force. Similarly, Liu and Dale (Chapter 11) insert dynamism into culture by offering a paradigm wherein individuals revise their mental models by interacting and forming shared representations that help them make sense of and respond to situations as they arise. At the organizational level, Moore (Chapter 10) depicts firms as nexuses of subgroups interlinked with one another and to external communities, near and far. Meanings are negotiated through these linkages and exchanges, generating a variety of discourses. Culture is thus not a static, fully formed entity, but instead evolves meanings of the organization, national identity, social class, work unit, and so on for groups and individuals. As such notions of movement and interaction are explored, advancements can be made in culture theory.

Insight #5: Take an interdisciplinary, multi-method, and complementary philosophical approach

A deliberately wide net was cast in this book in order to capture new understandings of culture. The wide net represents a fifth way forward, namely to take an interdisciplinary, multi-method, and complementary philosophical approach to studying culture. As elaborated by Nakata and Izberk-Bilgin in Chapter 4, as well as Nakata in Chapter 12, the Hofstede framework relies on a particular approach. That approach can be described as survey-based and statistically derived resulting in a double-empirical, analog theory. The approach is also firmly rooted in the modernist philosophy, where culture, operating according to universal laws across time and space, is a constant force affecting social behaviors.

However, as demonstrated in this book, considering other disciplinary, methodological, and philosophical vantage points can lead to an enriched conceptualization of culture. Among disciplinary vantage points explored here are those of consumer behavior, marketing strategy, international marketing, organizational culture, organizational development, organizational psychology, and cross-cultural management. In terms of methods, case study, ethnography, and other qualitative tools as well as survey, experimental design, and other quantitative techniques are reflected. With respect to philosophy, both modernist and interpretive traditions are represented. Together these perspectives present a fuller spectrum of possible cultural understandings. As observed by Douglas and Craig (Chapter 7), culture has been studied by diverse disciplines employing different research paradigms. Ignoring this diversity and being confined to one approach does a disservice to the research enterprise if the goal is indeed to know what this thing called culture is and does. Therefore, the last insight for extending past Hofstede is to embrace this diversity, which should reap the rewards of new knowledge.

References

Earley, P. C. (2006), "Leading Cultural Research in the Future: A Matter of Paradigms and Taste," *Journal of International Business Studies*, 37, 922–31.

Hofstede, G. (1980), Culture's Consequences: International Differences in Work Related Values. Newbury Park, CA: Sage.

Hofstede, G. (2001), Culture's Consequences: Comparing Values, Behaviors, Institutions and Organizations Across Nations. Thousand Oaks, CA: Sage.

House, R. J., Hanges, P. J., Javidan, M., Dorfman, P., & Gupta, V. (2004), *Culture, Leadership, and Organizations: The GLOBE Study of 62 Societies*. Thousand Oaks, CA: Sage.

Kirkman, B. L., Lowe, K. B., & Gibson, C. B. (2006), "A Quarter Century of Culture's Consequences: A Review of Empirical Research Incorporating Hofstede's Cultural Values Framework," *Journal of International Business Studies*, 37, 285–320.

Kluckhohn, F. & Strodtbeck, F. (1961), *Variations in Value Orientation*. Westport, CT: Greenwood Press.

McSweeney, B. (2002), "Hofstede's Model of National Cultural Differences and Their Consequences: A Triumph of Faith—A Failure of Analysis," *Human Relations*, 55, 89–118.

Parsons, T. (1937), *The Structure of Social Action*. New York, NY: The Free Press.

Sivakumar, K. & Nakata, C. (2001), "The Stampede Toward Hofstede's Framework: Avoiding the Sample Design Pit in Cross-Cultural Research," *Journal of International Business Studies*, 32, 555–74.

Part II Reviews and Critiques of Cultural Frameworks

2
So What Kind of Atheist Are You? Exploring Cultural Universals and Differences*

P. Christopher Earley

Nearly two decades ago, I had the occasion to spend a Fulbright sabbatical in Israel working with my long-time colleague and mentor, Professor Miriam Erez, at the Technion in Haifa, Israel. Coincidentally, this was the year of the Gulf War in 1990–1. During these tense times, we sought refuge in humor and distraction in daily ironies. A colleague described the experiences of a recent immigrant to Israel who had decided to become a naturalized citizen. In pursuing citizenship, the person completed an extensive interview form, after which she was called in for a personal interview with a government official. During the interview, the official looked at her form and asked her, "What religion are you?," to which she replied, "I'm an atheist." After a few moments of reflection, the immigration officer again repeated his question, "What religion are you?," and again, she answered, "I'm an atheist." Now showing some irritation, the officer demanded, "No, what RELIGION are you?" and she angrily replied, "Look, there wasn't a box for it on the form so I wrote in that I'm an atheist. . . . I don't believe in God, and I'm an atheist." The officer looked at her and said, with some frustration and bewilderment, "Fine—are you a Jewish Atheist, a Muslim Atheist, or a Christian Atheist?"

This incident conveys the underlying message of this chapter, namely, that people operate from a universal base of understanding, and they seek to reconcile differences into similarities through which they can interact with the world around them. Researchers have long sought to understand the nature of culture and its potential influence on human activity. When the first of our species crossed a desert or river and encountered neighbors who exhibited alternative ways of behaving, that was when the first cultural anthropologist emerged. Certainly, the formal study of groups of people by outsiders has been evidenced in Western and Eastern

19

civilizations for thousands of years (Mead, 1967). Of course, our fascination with cultural differences and similarities among people has been piqued again in the last and this century by the advance of business and economic transactions across national and geographic boundaries. It is with this spirit that we see modern-day cultural scientists who seek to understand the relevance of such differences among people working in an organizational or work context. Well beyond the scope of this particular chapter is a review of this vast literature, but I will focus on the task at hand—a brief review of major streams of cultural work, with some analysis of where we might wish to direct future efforts.

In my 2007 article in *Journal of International Business Studies*, I worked on a comparison of two general approaches of very significant scope and impact: Geert Hofstede's seminal work compared with the approach taken by Robert House and his colleagues in the GLOBE project. In this chapter, I will continue this discussion and supplement it with my own take on some new directions of the field, including some work by Miriam Erez on identifying a universal work culture, as well as my own work on cultural intelligence.

I begin my analysis by using these distinctions to describe the nature of "culture," how both camps define culture, and its relation to others' use of the term, including culture as an interpretation of meaning at a collective or individual level. In the next section, I follow with a brief discussion of the several approaches and their focus on the fundamentals, including the nature of the analysis used and the level of constructs, followed by a discussion of the underlying quagmire implied by such levels. In the third section, I address the ideological similarities of these approaches, as well as their theory-driven versus empirically derived nature. Many of the existing approaches entangle levels (individual, collective) for purposes of analysis, constructs, and application. I suggest that many existing approaches provide very important empirical assessments of current cultural conditions while they underemphasize substantive theoretical underpinnings and overemphasize differences at the cost of universals. That is, there needs to be a refocusing of scholars' efforts toward the development of key grand and mid-range theories that link nebulous assays such as these to organizational practices, activities, and outcomes.

How cultured do we need to be?

At least some of the confusion in the field of cross-cultural research stems from a loose and imprecise definition used of "culture." One must remember that the construct has become so disagreeable that some within the field of anthropology (e.g., Geertz, 1973) recommend that the concept be set aside for more concrete and manageable concepts.

Hofstede (1980) dealt with culture by focusing solely on societal cultures (differences between respondents from different countries). In a number of different points in his paper, Hofstede equates culture with measuring a value orientation characteristic of people from a given nation and this, of course, is consistent with Hofstede's original work on the topic (1980) and his more recent description of culture as the "software of the mind" (1991). Thus, one discusses the culture of the French versus the culture of the Canadians. A more detailed analysis of his position makes it clear that Hofstede does not limit the application of "culture" to a geopolitical boundary, as illustrated in his own comparison of organizational versus national cultures:

> After having done both a large cross-national and a large cross-organizational culture study, we believe that national cultures and organizational cultures are phenomena of different orders: using the term 'cultures' for both is, in fact, somewhat misleading.
>
> (Hofstede et al., 1990, p. 313)

But this quote illustrates that Hofstede considers "culture" to be different at a societal (national) versus organizational level. More recently, the GLOBE scholars have found little or no empirical justification for separating the two types of culture, and so they treat them similarly. In fact, GLOBE defines culture somewhat along the lines of Herskovits's (1955) view: pertaining to the human-made aspect of the world. That is, culture reflects artifacts of existence, such as iPods, computers, and water glasses.

But Hofstede's conceptualization of culture as the possession of a nation is unsatisfactory, because various "value dimensions" suggest such aggregations are contradictory with the constructs themselves. For example, how true does it ring for us to consider the power distance of a highly collective culture? By its axiomatic nature, a collective culture has a number of highly distinctive "in-groups" (Erez and Earley, 1993; Triandis, 1994) that may have very different characteristics. That is, one such in-group might be very low on power distance, while another might be quite high on it. Variability across subgroups may be overwhelmed by using an aggregate measure of culture at a societal level, but this fails to recognize that such within-society differences may flourish—a point raised by Martin (1992) in her analysis of culture. Martin argued that a focus on cultural similarities across people coming from a common grouping will mask important subgroup differences. Such differences are presumed to be less extreme in more individualistic cultures. So the very interaction among key cultural values suggests that a national or societal level of analysis, such as posed by Hofstede, is problematic as well (see Brett et al., 1997, for an excellent discussion of potential difficulties resulting from the interaction among cultural values).

My own view is that these various camps have chosen somewhat idiosyncratic views of "culture" as a construct, and they employ them somewhat inconsistently. For a group so concerned with Herskovits's definition, GLOBE does not focus strongly on actual artifacts that are present in the various societies in which they operate. A content and structural analysis of the tools employed in these various societies largely is absent from their research, so I don't believe that the Herskovits definition is fully exploited. Their adherence to this definition is a matter of practice, to justify why they separate their survey questions into the two forms of "should be" versus "actually is." Unfortunately, this is a rather artificial distinction that clearly is confounded by basic psychological processing. A much more compelling "actually is" definition might be derived from a true assessment of the artifacts of a society. (For example, one might look at the dispersion of income or proliferation of social programs in a society to assess the "actually is" of power distance or social concern rather than asking informants to make such a determination. If research on impression formation and judgment has taught us anything, it is that our underlying values and experiences influence social judgments of situation [Fiske and Neuberg, 1990].)

It is perhaps for this reason that my own work, developed with Erez and others, sidesteps this cultural quagmire; we operationalize culture purely as a psychological construct reflecting a multitude of influences on an individual (e.g., Earley, 1989; Erez and Earley, 1993). This practice might seem to take the "culture" out of culture (stripped of its collective nature), but if one looks at Rohner's (1984) oft-cited definitions of society, culture, and social systems, our approach is not inconsistent.

How do constructs such as "society" or "social system or social structure" differ from "culture"? Rohner (1984, p. 131) offers useful distinctions; he defines a society as "the largest unit of a territorially bounded, multigenerational population recruited largely through sexual reproduction, and organized around a common culture and a common social system." He defines a social system as the behavioral interactions of a multiple individuals who exist within a culturally organized population. Then, Rohner (1984, p. 119) defines culture as *"the totality of equivalent and complementary learned meanings maintained by a human population, or by identifiable segments of a population, and transmitted from one generation to the next"* [italics in the original].

Rohner thus acknowledges that the cross-generational transmission of cultural meanings within a society may be imperfect, such that over time individuals acquire variations of the cultural meanings held by their predecessors. Cultural meanings are typically not shared uniformly by an entire society, and they are not shared precisely. Any two individuals from a given culture may hold slightly different meanings for the same event or construct, and these two individuals may have shared meanings with other parties in the society but not with one another. Rohner further states:

> It is probable that no single individual ever knows the totality of equivalent and complementary learned meanings that define the "culture" of a given population, and it is therefore unlikely that the person is able to activate, at any given moment, the full range of meanings that define the "culture" of his or her people. But complementary meanings free one from the necessity of having to know all of one's "culture." For example, most persons do not need to know how to behave as a physician or shaman if they are ill, only how to behave properly as a patient.
>
> (Rohner 1984, p. 122)

Using Rohner's definitions, it is possible to distinguish the effects of culture, social system, and society on individuals' actions and behaviors. Rohner uses White's analogy of American football to describe the relationship of culture to social system: Knowing the rules of football does not imply that one can anticipate or predict the next play during a game. Cultural knowledge allows the observer to interpret the behavior and judge the appropriateness or legitimacy of a given play but not to predict a specific play or behavior.

In this sense, researchers have missed out on a more theoretically compelling view of culture. Instead, we are left with the frequently used approach of focusing on the values espoused by members of a given sample and aggregated to reflect the society (nation, or something somewhat similar to Rohner's view). But this means that we fall short of truly understanding culture because values (and an imperfect assessment of actual practices in the GLOBE context, or what Rohner would call an element of the social system) are only one contributor to the meaning a group of individuals might attribute to a given stimuli.

This last point is a very critical one that I made in my 2007 *JIBS* paper regarding this large-scale assessment approach to studying culture, and it presents two areas of potential contradiction with the existing views of culture. First, **culture is not a value (or set of values)**; culture is the meaning we attach to aspects of the world around us. As I will argue in the final section of this chapter, many of the shortcomings of current research on cross-cultural issues can be connected to an obsession we have with *values as culture* rather than *meaning as culture*. Even traditional scholars dealing with values (e.g., Kluckhohn and Strodtbeck, 1961; Mead, 1967; Parsons and Shils, 1951; Rokeach, 1973) did not fall into the trap that suggests values are culture; they merely suggested that cultures may vary in their value orientations, just as they may vary in their institutional practices. Second, meaning systems are imperfectly shared across individuals and/or segments (sub-populations) within the same society.

An example might help illustrate the point I'm making about culture as a meaning system versus culture as a set of values. Two people can witness the exact same event and interpret (gain meaning) it comparably but have completely different value-based evaluations of the valence of the event. It isn't that people are witnessing different events (or aspects of the event); rather, they employ different value systems to assess the event. There need not be any confusion about the meaning of the event; the differences in the value judgments about an event may differ a great deal. This example illustrates Rohner's point about meaning versus values, and it is a point that is overlooked by Hofstede, House et al., and many other organizational researchers focused overly on a values-based approach to their work. But even the meanings attached to an event may be imperfectly shared across individuals from the same society operating under the same social system, according to Rohner. The symbolic meaning of a trial has divergent interpretations for individuals within the same society.

Thus, a culture of study assessing "should be" versus "actually is" through individuals cannot be expected to provide convergence, particularly in highly diverse populations. I am not advocating any one approach to culture, but I am suggesting that researchers need to be very precise in how they use the construct as they engage in their research rather than employing a loose definition based on their operational intentions.

Methods of paradigm and other confusions

Before delving into the specifics of levels of analysis from an empirical view, it is important to discuss the nature and meaning of constructs across cultures. It is helpful to explore the terms coined by Berry and

Triandis, among others, to capture the folly of using constructs developed in one setting to apply to other settings without fully understanding the construct validity and generalizability of doing so. These concepts are captured in four research paradigms that Harbir Singh and I described a number of years ago (Earley and Singh, 1995). The four research design approaches depict distinct ways to study the mechanisms linking culture and behavior within organizations.

First is the unitary form that emphasizes a single instance of a phenomenon. This style of research is similar to what others have labeled as "emic" (e.g., Berry, 1990) or "pseudo-emic" (e.g., Earley and Mosakowski, 1996), which refers to understanding a single cultural group or nation on its own terms using its own constructs.

Second is the gestalt form, or an emphasis on examining a system as an intact system rather than through breaking it apart. The gestalt form has several features, such as examining relationships as they occur across different systems and developing system interpretations with reference to the specifics of the system.

The third approach is called the reduced form. The reduced form emphasizes the analysis of a system's constituent parts to understand the processes within the system. The characteristics of this form include several features: The system itself can be separated into components, and specific relationships in the system can be studied by focusing on them to the exclusion of other relationships in the cultural system. Also, constructs are drawn from other models of cultures, and relationships are interpreted using specific aspects of the cultural system.

Finally, the fourth form is referred to as the hybrid, or one that utilizes aspects of both a gestalt and a reduced perspective. First, in developing research questions with the hybrid form, gestalt systems are studied in order to identify important aspects of the systems. Second, hypothesized relationships in the hybrid form are derived across systems, and they are not necessarily unique to a given system. Third, constructs and relationships in this form are assumed to be separable from the system in which they are embedded, but the mapping back on to an existing system may not be linear or additive. Fourth, specific relationships are interpreted using reduced parts of the system but with reference to the general system. These interpretations can, in turn, lead to a further refinement of general principles.

The GLOBE research project on leadership adopts what Earley and Singh (1995) describe as a hybrid research design. The constructs were developed within cultures and subsequently generalized across cultures. House (pers. comm.) suggests that country practices, such as the average height of tombstones or the size and focus of national monuments, are country-level indicators of cultural values that were measured at an individual level of analysis. Multiple samples of nations and within-nation groups were used in the GLOBE project. Cultural values were linked to both industry-level outcomes, such as performance, and individual-level perceptions, such as leadership attributions. By linking these multiple levels, this project is able to observe how cultural values may be critical mechanisms connecting leadership characteristics to industry performance.

This example of a hybrid design illustrates some important facets of a sophisticated cross-cultural research design. First, the constructs are proposed, operationalized, and measured at different levels of analysis. For example, leadership is assessed as an individual-level construct (using two perceptual viewpoints) but related to macro outcomes, such as economic growth.

Second, constructs measured at different levels are linked with intermediate constructs. GLOBE's primary linking constructs operate at either the individual or country level of analysis, though there is no requirement that they be measured at one or the other level. It may be desirable to measure the linking mechanism at a third level of analysis (e.g., industry), because conceptually, any linking mechanism does not exist solely at the micro or macro level of analysis.

Third, a hybrid design permits an analysis of either how micro-level features affect macro-level outcomes or vice versa. Cultural constructs are measured at both micro and macro levels and therefore can be used at both micro and macro levels of analyses in a consistent fashion. The within-level analyses are then complemented by cross-level analyses to verify the logical consistency of the cross-level assumptions.

Fourth and finally, a hybrid design raises the question of sampling. Sampling across nations provides variability in a cultural construct at both individual and country levels. However, if the theoretical model only relates cultural constructs to individual-level processes, cross-national sampling is not required. In the case of GLOBE, the conceptual framework is a cross-level one that attempts to integrate individual, industry, and country effects to understand the universal aspects of leadership.

Mixing of levels; or, how do you get a nation to fill out a survey?

A great deal of debate and disagreement among cultural researchers focuses on survey data measured at an individual level but capturing (or intending to capture) collective-level constructs. As my former colleague Lyman Porter would say, "Organizations don't behave, people do." Although it is well beyond the scope of this chapter to debate this general point, there is clearly a great deal of confusion in the literature concerning the level measurement and construct in relation to cross-cultural and national research. This point is aptly made in Hofstede's (1980) original treatise through his description of the ecological fallacy. Since that time, many strong academics have attacked the level of analysis and grouping problem (for a very effective discussion, refer to Klein et al., 1994), with entire volumes focusing on the topic, such as F. Dansereau and F. Yammarino's annual *Advances in Cross-Level Organizational Research* series.

But in cross-cultural research, the debate continues unabated. My own practice has been to avoid the dilemma (with a few notable lapses) by assessing and analyzing constructs at a common level (individual), but with a caveat that such work is an individual-differences approach. Hofstede and the GLOBE researchers fall into a similar trap; item responses refer to an individual's perception of the surrounding world and, therefore, are contaminated with the person's unique experiences, biases, and so forth. How might one escape this dilemma and truly assess constructs at a "collective" or societal level? By abandoning values surveys asking individuals to assess their view of the world. If one wishes to measure an organization's "behavior," it is necessary to look at an outcome (action) that is uniquely defined by the entity. For example, one such outcome might be the reporting structure in an organization. Individual employees do not report structures, and so this is a construct that applies at one level but not another. However, taking individual assessments (perceptions) of reporting structures also does not average, sum, or interact to form a collective variable, and it has limitations for understanding culture (Klein et al., 1994). One simply needs to consult an organizational chart to understand the reporting structure in an organization. (Admittedly, this only captures a formal reporting system and not the nuances of the informal chart.)

My point is that Hofstede, GLOBE, and similar approaches fall into a similar trap of aggregation. And it is a trap that is inevitable if one uses values measured by individual perceptions as indicative of collective culture. As one example, take the three items Hofstede cites for measuring power distance in his original work:

(a) the preference for one style of decision making by one's boss over other styles, (b) the perception of the boss' actual decision making style, and (c, for non-managerial employees only) the feeling that employees were afraid to disagree with their manager (which I saw as an indirect way of stating that they themselves were afraid).

(Hofstede, 1980, p. 82)

As Hofstede points out, these items are unrelated at an individual level (unsurprisingly—(a) reflects a valence, (b) reflects a practice, and (c) reflects a subjective reaction to an implied practice). These are measures assessing three very different features of psychological perception, but Hofstede argues that they are related at an "eco-logic level," that is, at a country-level grouping. It is not clear why Hofstede would expect these three different psychological constructs to be related at an aggregate level. However, GLOBE posits why there well might be differences in the correlation patterns of their two measures (what should be versus what is), and they find pattern differences. In fact, I would suggest that Hofstede's lack of differentiation at a macro-level of analysis for such different measures as he employed may be more troublesome. That is, we do not know why Hofstede's items converge at a cultural level, but GLOBE offers an explanation for why their measures diverge at an individual (and cultural) level.

Haven't I heard this song before?

Stepping back a bit suggests a debate that has been ongoing for many years in the literature. Recall Kluckhohn and Strodtbeck's (1961) original values typology in relation to "country" or "region." In reality, Kluckhohn collected her data within a very small geographic area (less than 25-mile radius) but focused on distinct communities within that area that had some, but limited, interdependence. From this source, she developed a well-defined typology of values that served as the inspiration for a number of other frameworks, including Hofstede's (1991), Hampden-Turner and Trompenaars's (2000), Schwartz's (1992, 1994),[1] and GLOBE's (House et al., 2004). But what is the theoretical or applied base of such typologies?

Few anthropologists and psychologists have provided a theoretical frame-work for generating values typologies, though some of the very strongest situate values in a larger socio-economic-political-cultural framework (e.g., Berry's eco-cultural model, 1971; Parsons and Shils's value orientations, 1951; Triandis's subjective culture framework, 1972). In the field of cross-cultural organizational behavior, value orientations are adopted but not compelled theoretically. Neither GLOBE nor Hofstede (the two most common frameworks drawn upon by organizational researchers) provide such theoretical grounding and context, and I believe that this is an unfortunate consequence. Without a mid- or grand-level theory, we have yet another typology of values and more debate. Are there 12 core cultural values? Are there 10, 8, 5? Does it really matter for the organizations researcher who is interested in employee actions and outcomes across cultural settings? My answer is simply "no"—unless one is trying to understand macro-level outcomes based on a configuration of values taken together as some form of profile. Applying these values piecemeal to an individual in a particular setting puts us at danger of falling into real stereotyping or cross-level fallacies.

Are there theoretical contributions from GLOBE that are not already evident in Hofstede's or others' work? If one simply looks at GLOBE as a values assessment, then I would posit that it has little marginal value. The song of values has familiarity as well, because these typologies have been with us for a century (or longer). Mead provided us with guilt and shame, Parsons and Shils provided us with collectivity and power, Kluckhohn and Strodtbeck provided us with being-in-doing, and so on. My point is that the interesting part (to me, at least) of the GLOBE work was not the values typology alone but the universal assessment of a construct, such as leadership, but this part is lost in the commentary by most scholars in discussing GLOBE.

What are the attributes of a useful and fulfilling theory? No theory of organizational behavior today fully provides the conceptual framework for understanding how culture, managerial practices, and work behavior are interrelated, though this understanding was the purpose of the framework Erez and I proposed (1993). (The lack of an adequate theoretical framework for understanding the moderating effect of culture has led to our development of the cultural self-representation model.)

Campbell (1990, as cited in Erez and Earley, 1993) proposes that the development of a conceptual model can be achieved in three ways: It can be evaluated empirically; it can stem from the evaluations of experts in the field of study; and it can be derived analytically. Empirical confrontation is essential for testing the meaning and validity of scientific hypotheses. What happens to a theory when it is not supported by empirical findings? The answer to this question is guided by two different approaches. One approach represents the school of logical empiricism that asserts that some theories are right and others are wrong, and that empirical confrontation offers a test of whether a given theory is valid. The second approach represents a position of contextualism that maintains that all theories are right and that empirical confrontation involves a continuing process of discovery of the contexts in which hypotheses are true and those in which they are false. According to the constructivist paradigm, the role of the empirical side of science is to explore and discover the range of circumstances in which each of the opposite formulations holds.

The second criterion for evaluating the quality of theoretical models is by expert evaluation. Researchers in the field of cross-cultural psychology have admitted that their theoretical models are poorly developed. In particular, theories of organizational behavior have been criticized for lacking validity generalization across cultures (Boyacigiller and Adler, 1991). Thus, on the basis of peer evaluation, present models of organizational behavior fail to account for cultural moderators.

The third criterion of theory evaluation is analytic by nature. From an analytic perspective, several conventions in organizational behavior may be questioned: (1) mediating processes do not serve as the action lever of boosting employees' work motivation, (2) cognitive information processing inhibits the development of contextual models of organizational behavior, and (3) at present, there exist few ways to relate the individual-based explanations of individual behavior in micro research to the environment or context-based explanations of organizations in macro research (Erez and Earley, 1993).

What does Campbell's guidance suggest with regard to values-based approaches to understanding cross-cultural work? As values-based approaches, the work by Hofstede, Schwartz, Hampden-Turner and Trompenaars, GLOBE, and so forth satisfies Campbell's criteria of contextualism and peer review; after all, these approaches involve co-investigators, managers, and scientists from many countries. They provide local operationalizations of measures through decentering and related methods, so they recognize contextualism and empirical confrontation. At the same time, the peer network used in the GLOBE design or Schwartz's approach provides the internal critique advocated by Campbell for peer review. However, many cultural values studies fall short on Campbell's third criterion, namely, theory assessment through analytic means generated from a theoretical framework. That is, neither GLOBE nor Hofstede provide a coherent and tight conceptual model linking individual assessments to more macro ones (they do provide some guidance along these lines, but their frameworks are largely exploratory rather than confirmatory). Schwartz's values approach is a counter-example that was both theoretically based and analytically tied to the theory orientation.

But as a **leadership study**, GLOBE provides our first pseudo-etic (and perhaps truly etic) glimpse of leadership, and it is the first of its type (i.e., large-scale values study) to generate a universal framework of an organizational behavior theory. Against the backdrop of Campbell's criteria, I believe that GLOBE has moved toward a strong model of global leadership. They have tackled all three criteria with reasonable success; their approach has been tested empirically across many cultures, their approach has withstood the scrutiny of their peer network, and their approach has provided analytic links between the constructs of leadership, context, and culture. So perhaps the song has finally changed. Against the background of Hofstede's criticism that the GLOBE work represents a US-centric approach, though this claim seems somewhat untenable given the decentering and multiparty assessments undertaken by the GLOBE team, I am aware of no other study having achieved this level of collaboration across researchers and regions.

As I turn to in the next section, I think that this contribution of a GLOBE-type study is particularly important now, as in the future of cross-cultural work.

To be (similar) or not to be?

There are four general propositions that I will use to complete my analysis and the body of work that constitutes much of what we see in cross-cultural organizational behavior. Put succinctly: (1) stop doing "grand" values assessments; (2) develop some mid- and/or grand-level theories that link culture to action; (3) consider alternatives for values as a basis for exploring culture in relation to action; and (4) refocus attention on similarities rather than differences. The first three of these points were made in my *JIBS* article, but I've added an important fourth point.

Enough is enough

My first point is self-evident: We have enough of these values-based, large-scale surveys, and it just isn't terribly useful to have more of them. In my own career, I have seen the Hofstede, Schwartz, GLOBE, Meaning of Work, and Chinese Values Survey, to name a few of the prominent assessments. Just as I argued nearly a decade ago that it was time to move away from studies focusing on individualism–collectivism (Earley and Gibson, 1998), I would now suggest that scholars refocus their attention away from any more of these values surveys and focus on developing theories and frameworks for understanding the linkages between culture, perceptions, actions, organizations, structures, and so forth.

The problem with values-based approaches is not an inherent one. The difficulty is that researchers feel compelled to use the resulting typologies as a means of explaining any and every "difference" they find across samples. This dilemma reminds me to a large extent of the problem faced in large-scale correlational medical research, telling us to drink more red wine one month and then to pour it down the drain the next! Finding that Japanese are more "risk averse" (higher in uncertainty avoidance) and less innovative than Americans doesn't help us understand and explain why the number of patents per scientist is higher in Japan than in the United States. (Nor would it explain had the correlation run in the anticipated direction, for that matter.) Associations are exactly that, associations and not causal explanations.

Proposition 2; There Is Nothing So Practical as a Theory

There are a number of very strong examples of the type of theory-building that I would suggest is needed in the literature. I begin by citing two "grand theories" (meaning that they relate very macro-level constructs to meso- and micro-level ones) and two "mid-range theories" (meaning that they deal with contiguous constructs across closely related levels of analysis or within the same level). For a nice example of a grand theory, Berry (1971) proposed an ecological–cultural theory that updated and expanded upon Whiting's model. According to Berry's approach, culture develops within a specific ecological environment. The adoption of cultural content is selective and adaptive, and, therefore, different ecological environments modify different cultures. Adaptation to the environment requires different levels of sophistication and cognitive complexity. As a result, we find that cognitive schemas vary across cultures in both their complexity and content parameters, and this influences various forms of social behavior. For example, Berry argues that conformity and other social behaviors are tied to a society's economic and ecological systems, though the evidence for his model is mixed.

Triandis (1972) presents another cross-level approach to culture in his book, *The Analysis of Subjective Culture*, which is notable for its breadth in linking physical and social environments, individual values, and psychological processes. This model addresses how people in different cultures perceive their social environment and how environmental factors influence these processes. In Triandis's (1972) model, the distal antecedent of subjective culture is the physical environment, which includes resources and historical events. The physical environment has a direct impact on a society's economic activities, which, in turn, influence more proximal antecedents, such as occupations and labor structure. Historical events have an impact on the social and political organizations that evolve in a society and on more proximal aspects of culture, including language, religion, location, and feedback from own behavior. The impact of basic psychological processes such as learning (cognitive and instrumental), categorization, and conditioning on subjective culture is illustrated through a variety of more specific sociological and psychological constructs including roles, tasks, norms, cognitive structures, values, affect, behavioral intentions, habits, and utilities. The determinants of action in Triandis's model are an individual's behavioral intentions and habits. Patterns of action are a function of behavioral intentions, which are influenced by subjective culture. It is the relation between subjective culture and behavioral intentions that provides the explicit link lacking in many other models. In a subjective culture approach, values influence behavioral intentions through an individual's affective states and cognitive structures (though values are reciprocally determined by cognitive structures).

More recently, Nisbett and colleagues (e.g., Nisbett et al., 2001; Sanchez-Burks et al., 2000) have sought to integrate concepts of culture and cognitive process through a mid-range theory focusing on cognitive styles. They propose a theory of how systems of thought differ according to cultural context, focusing on differences between East Asian and Western thinkers. They suggest that East Asians tend to think more holistically, attending to the entire field and relating causality to it as an entirety, whereas Westerners use a more analytic style and pay attention to objects and the categories to which they belong. They trace the origin of these thinking patterns to differences in the social and cultural systems underlying the societies. Although this might sound as if it were a grand theoretic approach, their very extensive analysis of the social and cultural milieu provides a backdrop for cognitive and social information processing, and the specific linkages found, for example, in the Triandis model are lacking in Nisbett and colleagues' work.

Proposition 3: Here are a few of my favorite things

In the past decade, there have been a number of scholars who have taken up a call to focus on alternatives to a values-based approach to studying culture. One such approach is called "cultural intelligence," and it has been a focus of my own work for quite some time. A number of researchers, including myself, Soon Ang, Kok-Ye Ng, David Thomas, and Kerr Inkson, to name a few, have undertaken a very different approach to studying cultural differences through this construct (see Earley and Ang, 2003; Ng and Earley, 2006; Thomas and Inkson, 2004). Cultural intelligence focuses on understanding an individual's capacity to adapt to varying cultural settings based on facets of cognitive and metacognitive processing, motivational mechanisms, and behavioral adaptation. Rather than using exogenous and contextual factors shared in a society (values, meaning) as drivers of behavior, cultural intelligence focuses on an individual's capabilities to adapt in a cultural setting as a driver of behavior. Although this work is nascent, it provides a very different avenue for studying cultural effects and influences on individual action.

Another interesting avenue that is being explored by Erez and her colleagues is a universal approach to global organizations (e.g., Erez and Gati, 2004; Erez and Shokef, in press). Erez and her colleagues have focused on the identification of a global work culture. Employees of global companies need to communicate and coordinate their activities with others, thus bringing in a mosaic of cultures with no one common shared meaning system that enables them to understand one another and correctly interpret fellow employees' actions. Sharing common meanings, values, and codes of behaviors can facilitate their communication and improve the coordination of their activities. Erez and her colleagues propose that one such form of a macro-level shared meaning system, formed superordinate to that of national culture, is a global work culture. They define a global work culture as the shared understanding of the visible rules, regulations, and behaviors, as well as the deeper values and ethics, of the global work context (Shokef and Erez, 2006).

What is important, from my perspective, about their work is that they have identified a universal, or generalist, approach to how individuals define themselves in a global organization that transcends national boundaries. Their thesis is that in global companies, there are similarities of structure, functioning, and practices that are universal, and it is important to focus on such general levels to understand individual employees in these terms. Core features of employees include a competitive performance orientation, quality emphasis, customer orientation, and innovation and change. This suggests that at a very general level and regardless of national origin individuals working at global companies share these common value orientations. Given the mobility of employees working in most developed and developing countries, this alternative approach of Erez has great potential to refocus the research debate.

These are just a few illustrations of the alternative approach that a scholar can take in conducting cross-cultural research through the use of mid-level and grand theory but without focusing on a values typology.

We have excellent work on a values approach to human behavior by Hofstede and House et al. (2004), as well as Kluckhohn and Strodtbeck,

Parsons and Edward, Rokeach, and Schwartz, just to name a few. Indeed, the GLOBE and Hofstede projects have been very important for providing a glimpse of the contextual backdrop in which mid-range theories operate. For example, Nisbett's work on cognitive styles (Nisbett et al., 2001) or Sternberg and Grigorenko's (2006) work on intelligence across cultures represent the integration of cultural milieu with specific psychological processes. GLOBE's additional contribution is the proposal of a pseudo-etic construct of leadership and associated mid-range theory relating it to various organizational outcomes. Perhaps now our attention and focus should be on leveraging these values studies and other forms of assessments (Leung and Bond, 1989) and rethinking our approach to studying culture and international variation on behavior based in organizations.

Proposition 4: People are people, so why can't we just set aside our differences?

One of the key points I raise when I consult with companies and talk about creating effective global teams, as well as exploring cultural intelligence, is that the key to success in understanding the role of culture in organizational behavior is not focusing on differences but on similarities. The analogy is use to stimulate this thinking begins with asking a group of managers to add together two numbers: $1/2 + 1/3$. After a few moments, someone says "5/6ths," and then I ask how this answer was determined. Of course, the process requires determining the lowest common denominator and converting what was dissimilar to what is now similar. This is the key to creating an effective global team as well; not determining how people differ from one another but focusing on similarity and building from it. I emphasize that a global team must have well-established common goals (focus of effort and direction), roles (enablers to coordinate action), and rules (for conduct in an ambiguous context).

In work with Gibson (Earley and Gibson, 2002) and Mosakowski (Earley and Mosakowski, 2000), we have found that globally diverse teams (those with members from varying countries of origin and cultures) require a strong emphasis on commonality to be successful. Indeed, our evidence shows that highly homogeneous teams (with respect to national composition) are just as effective as highly diverse ones provided the characteristics of homogeneity (nationality, in our work) are uncorrelated with the task to be performed by the team. Our empirical observation across a wide range of teams and tasks is that such an assumption (uncorrelated) is a fair and justified one. The key for a successful but highly heterogeneous team is the formation of a common social structure, emphasizing universally held goals, roles, and rules.

My point in discussing this work is that too much emphasis has been placed on identifying differences between cultures and people rather than focusing on the universals that bind people together. In Erez's recent work, as well as my own, our approach has been to set aside a differences orientation in favor of one looking to universals. But therein lies the rub: By focusing on similarities rather than differences, our standard positivist approach of rejecting a null hypothesis becomes problematic. Rather than seeking to demonstrate differences attributable to culture, I advocate a refocus of attention, showing similarities and universals. Returning to Herskovits's (1955) definition of culture from a slightly different viewpoint, my suggestion is that we focus on that very fact that all people have "man-made objects" in their environment, rather than attributing excessive and sporadic interpretations to the shape and manifestation of these objects. Similarly, an emphasis on higher-level cognitive functioning, such as meta-cognition (used as a core element in cultural intelligence work), is more interesting than the fact that Asians and Westerners might "think and reason" differently. I posit this because there may be many contextual influences not attributable to culture per se that explain differences we observe and prematurely claim are cultural effects. Take, as an example, the point made by Peterson and Smith (1997) in their study of temperature, role stress, and culture. They originally looked at the relationship of national culture to role stress and found what appeared to be a substantive pairing of the two. However, after discussion and debate in the literature, they reexamined this notion and found that ambient temperature actually appeared to drive the effects on role stress across nations, though this effect was mediated by the historical influence of temperature on cultural values. That said, the strong statement made by their critics (Van de Vliert and Van Yperen, 1996) that the relationship is a spurious one, best described as a simple influence of ambient temperature on role stress (more stress is associated with more heat), suggests that the heavy reliance on culture (and associated values) is limiting, and more parsimonious explanations may be justified.

As we proceed in our work, we need to shift our attention away from idiosyncratic or spurious differences that are both elusive and hard to replicate and toward the universal aspects of what makes people more effective in various social circumstances.

Notes

* This chapter is an elaboration and extension of an earlier article of mine, "Leading Cultural Research in the Future: A Matter of Paradigms and Taste," *Journal of International Business Studies*, 2007.
1. I note that among these typologies, the work of Schwartz stands out from a theory-driven perspective, in that his original approach used core psychological theory in generating his framework on values.

References

Berry, J. W. (1971) "Ecological and Cultural Factors in Spatial Perceptual Development," *Canadian Journal of Behavioral Science*, 3, 324–36.

Berry, J. W. (1990) "Imposed-Etics, Emics, and Derived-Etics: Their Conceptual and Operational Status in Cross-Cultural Psychology," in T. N. Headland, K. L. Pike, & M. Harris (eds) *Emics and Etics: The Insider/Outsider Debate.* Newbury Park, CA: Sage Publications.

Boyacigiller, N. & Adler, N. J. (1991) "The Parochial Dinosaur: Organizational Science in a Global Context," *Academy of Management Review*, 16, 262–90.

Brett, J. M., Tinsley, C. H., Janssens, M., Barsness, Z. I., & Lytle, A. L. (1997), "New Approaches to the Study of Culture I/O Psychology," in P. C. Earley & M. Erez (eds) *New Perspectives on International/Organizational Psychology*. San Francisco, CA: Jossey-Bass.

Earley, P. C. (1989) "Social Loafing and Collectivism: A Comparison of the United States with the People's Republic of China," *Administrative Science Quarterly*, 34, 565–81.

Earley, P. C. & Ang, S. (2003) *Cultural Intelligence: Individual Interactions Across Cultures*. Palo Alto, CA: Stanford University Press.

Earley, P. C. & Gibson, C. B. (1998) "Taking Stock in our Progress of Individualism and Collectivism: 100 Years of Solidarity and Community," *Journal of Management*, 24, 265–304.

Earley, P. C. & Gibson, C. B. (2002) *Multinational Work Teams: A New Perspective*. Englewood Cliffs, NJ: Lawrence Erlbaum Associates.

Earley, P. C. & Mosakowski, E. (1996) "Experimental International Management Research," in B. J. Punnett & O. Shenkar (eds) *Handbook of International Management Research*. London, UK: Blackwell Publishers, Inc., 83–114.

Earley, P. C. & Mosakowski, E. (2000) "Creating Hybrid Team Cultures: An Empirical Test of International Team Functioning," *Academy of Management Journal*, 43, 26–49.

Earley, P. C. & Singh, H. (1995) "International and Intercultural Research: What's Next?" *Academy of Management Journal*, 38, 1–14.

Erez, M. & Earley, P. C. (1993) *Culture, Self-Identity, and Work*. New York, NY: Oxford University Press.

Erez, M. & Gati, E. (2004) "A Dynamic, Multi-Level Model of Culture: From the Micro Level of the Individual to the Macro-Level of a Global Culture," *Applied Psychology: An International Review*, 53, 583–98.

Erez, M. & Shokef, E. (2008) "The Culture of Global Organizations," in P. Smith, M. Peterson, & D. Thomas (eds) *Handbook of Cross-Cultural Management Research*. Thousand Oaks, CA: Sage Publications, 285–300.

Fiske, S. T. & Neuberg, S. L. (1990) "A Continuum of Impression Formation from Category-Based to Individuating Processes: Influences of Information and Motivation on Attention and Interpretation," *Advances in Experimental Social Psychology*, 23, 1–74.

Geertz, C. (1973) *The Interpretation of Cultures*. New York, NY: Basic Books.

Hampden-Turner, C. & Trompenaars, F. (2000), Building Cross-Cultural Competence: How to Create Wealth from Conflicting Values. New York, NY: John Wiley & Sons.

Herskovits, M. J. (1955) *Cultural Anthropology*. New York, NY: Knopf.

Hofstede, G. (1980), Culture's Consequences: International Differences in Work-Related Values. Newbury Park, CA: Sage.

Hofstede, G. (1991) Cultures and Organizations: Software of the Mind. London, UK: McGraw-Hill.

Hofstede, G., Neuijen, B., Ohayv, D. D., & Sanders, G. (1990) "Measuring Organizational Cultures: A Qualitative and Quantitative Study Across Twenty Cases," *Administrative Science Quarterly*, 35, 286–316.

House, R. J., Hanges, P. J., Javidan, M. Dorfman, P., & Gupta, V. (2004) *Culture, Leadership, and Organizations: The GLOBE Study of 62 Societies*. Thousand Oaks, CA: Sage Publications.

Klein, K., Dansereau, F., & Hall, R. (1994) "Level Issues in Theory Development, Data Collection, and Analysis," *Academy of Management Review*, 19, 195–229.

Kluckhohn, F. & Strodtbeck, F. (1961) *Variations In Value Orientation*. Westport, CT: Greenwood Press.

Leung, K. & Bond, M. (1989) "On the Empirical Identification of Dimensions for Cross-Cultural Comparison," *Journal of Cross-Cultural Psychology*, 20, 133–51.

Martin, J. (1992) *Cultures in Organizations: Three Perspectives*. New York, NY: Oxford University Press.

Mead, M. (1967) Cooperation and Competition Among Primitive People. Boston: Beacon.

Ng, K. Y. & Earley, P. C. (2006) "Culture + Intelligence: Old Constructs, New Frontiers," *Group and Organization Management*, 31, 4–19.

Nisbett, R. E., Peng, K., Choi, I., & Norenzayan, A. (2001) "Culture and Systems of Thought: Holistic vs. Analytic Cognition," *Psychological Review*, 108, 291–310.

Parsons, T. & Shils, E. A. (1951) *Toward a General Theory of Action*. Cambridge, MA: Harvard University Press.

Peterson, M. F. & Smith, P. B. (1997) "Does National Culture or Ambient Temperature Explain Cross-Cultural Differences in Role Stress? No Sweat!" *Academy of Management Journal*, 40, 930–46.

Rohner, R. P. (1984) "Toward a Conception of Culture for Cross-Cultural Psychology," *Journal of Cross-Cultural Psychology*, 15 (2), 111–38.

Rokeach, M. (1973) *The Nature of Human Values*. New York, NY: The Free Press.

Sanchez-Burks, J., Nisbett, R. E., & Ybarra, O. (2000) "Cultural Styles, Relationship Schemas, and Prejudice Against Outgroups," *Journal of Personality and Social Psychology*, 79, 174–89.

Schwartz, S. H. (1992) "Universals in the Content and Structure of Values: Theoretical Advances and Empirical Tests in Two Countries," in *Advances in Experimental and Social Psychology*. San Diego, CA: Academic Press.

Schwartz, S. H. (1994) "Beyond Individualism and Collectivism: New Cultural Dimensions of Values," in H. C. Triandis, U. Kim, C. Kagitcibasi, S.-C. Choi, & G. Yoon, (eds) *Individualism and Collectivism: Theory, Method and Applications*. Newbury Park, CA: Sage Publications, 85–122.

Shokef, E. & Erez, M. (2006) "Global Work Culture and Global Identity, as a Platform for a Shared Understanding in Multicultural Teams," in E. A. M. Mannix, M. Neale, & Y. Chen (eds) *Research in Managing Groups and Teams: National Culture and Groups*. Oxford, UK: Elsevier, 325–52.

Sternberg, R. J. & Grigorenko, E. L. (2006) "Cultural Intelligence and Successful Intelligence," *Group Organization Management*, 31, 27–39.

Thomas, D. C. & Inkson, K. (2004) *Cultural Intelligence: People Skills for Global Business*. San Francisco, CA: Berrett-Koehler Publishers.

Triandis, H. C. (1972) *The Analysis of Subjective Culture*. New York, NY: John Wiley & Sons.

Triandis, H. C. (1994) *Culture and Social Behavior*. New York, NY: McGraw-Hill.

Van de Vliert, E. & Van Yperen, N. W. (1996) "Why Cross-National Differences in Role Overload? Don't Overlook Ambient Temperature!" *Academy of Management Journal*, 39, 986–1004.

3
Beyond Hofstede: Challenging the Ten Commandments of Cross-Cultural Research

Vas Taras and Piers Steel

Culture is a pervasive construct. A Google search for "culture" provides over half a billion hits, while the Yahoo! search engine generates a figure over two billion, which is more than for other such popular terms as politics, war, the environment, or sex. As for academic sources, the construct of culture has enjoyed immense interest from the scholarly community; major social science electronic databases provide links to 100,000–700,000 scholarly articles when "culture" is used as the search keyword.

While cultures have been explored for centuries by anthropologists, the phenomenon had been largely ignored in other fields of research until several decades ago. The explosion of interest in cross-cultural issues in management, psychology, and education was triggered by Hofstede's (1980) *Culture's Consequences*. Although a number of similar studies had been conducted before (e.g., Haire, Ghiselli, and Porter, 1966; Kluckhohn and Strodtbeck, 1961; Kuhn and McPartland, 1954; Rokeach, 1973), Hofstede was the first to offer a model of culture derived from a large international sample with fairly advanced, for its time, research design and data analysis techniques. The outcome of what is now known as the IBM study described and ranked countries along several cultural dimensions with a concise set of quantitative indices. The study provided an elegant model of cultural differences and made it easy to operationalize culture and include it as a variable in various models.

The need for quantitative culture indices became evident through its popularity. Hofstede's *Culture's Consequences* is a "super classic," having been cited about 5000 times. Interest in Hofstede's model remains very high even decades later, cited on average 288 times each year in 2000–7 according to the Web of Science; Google Scholar indicates twice as many citations. Furthermore, Hofstede's cultural indices have been used in over 500 empirical studies.

The effect of Hofstede's (1980) *Culture's Consequences* on the field of cross-cultural studies has been tremendous. By and large, all subsequent research in the area has been based on a Hofstedean approach to studying culture. Even though Hofstede never claimed that his approach was the only right way, and in fact was very explicit about possible alternatives, subsequent research generally did not deviate from the paradigm he described.

Several postulates, generally derived from Hofstede's work, have dominated the field of cross-cultural studies in the past three decades: (1) cultures are values; (2) values are cultures; (3) cultures are extremely stable; (4) culture is the cause, not an effect; (5) a cross-level analysis of culture leads to the ecological fallacy; (6) cultures cluster within geographic boundaries; (7) mean scores and ranking sufficiently quantify culture; (8) matched samples should be used to study cultural differences; (9) self-response questionnaires adequately measure culture; and (10) the Hofstedean framework is unique and the only viable framework for studying culture.

Even though Hofstede never explicitly stated some of these assumptions, and even warned against some of them, his thoughts and propositions expressed in his publications have often been misapplied, generalized to an extreme, or simply misinterpreted, leading to a crystallization of these ten "commandments" of cross-cultural research. The limitations of these assumptions have been increasingly recognized and highlighted. Nevertheless, these concerns have been relegated primarily to review pieces, whereas the vast majority of empirical cross-cultural comparison studies automatically took the traditional assumptions for granted, never straying far from the dominant paradigm.

The present chapter examines the ten assumptions, explicates their meaning, discusses their viability, and outlines possible alternatives and directions for further research. We support our arguments with the results of numerous empirical studies, including some of our own.

Traditional assumptions in cross-cultural studies

Assumption 1: Cultures are values

In *Culture's Consequences*, Hofstede (1980) discussed in detail the multi-level nature of culture. Using an "onion" diagram, he suggested that values represent the core of culture, while practices, expressed in rituals and symbols, represent the outer layer. Even though Hofstede acknowledged that culture is by no means limited to values, the sole focus of his four-factor (later, five-factor) model and instrument for quantifying culture, the Value Survey Module, is values.

Following Hofstede's approach, scholars commonly limit their analyses solely to values. Even though the existence of other layers of culture is usually discussed in the literature review sections of many cross-cultural empirical papers, the variables included in the analyses are virtually always limited to the measurement of values. Our analysis of 136 publicly available instruments for measuring culture (for details see Taras, 2008a; Taras, Rowney, and Steel, forthcoming) revealed that almost all existing instruments and their underlying models of culture are preoccupied with values and overlook other attributes of culture. Virtually all items included in the culture measurement instruments are attitudinal statements about various norms and beliefs. Furthermore, our review of the dimension definitions included in the underlying models confirmed that almost all existing culture measures, much like Hofstede's Value Survey Module, were specifically designed to quantify values and not other aspects of culture.

Even the few models and their corresponding instruments that were designed to go beyond values did not appear to provide a clean measure of other attributes of culture. For example, the model used in the GLOBE project (House, Hanges, Javidan et al., 2004) differentiates between cultural values and practices. However, any careful inspection of the instrument used in the GLOBE study reveals that items designed to measure practices were often referring to perceptions about existing values and norms, rather than practices per se (e.g., In this society: "it is worse for a boy to fail in school than for a girl to fail in school"; "being accepted by the other members of a group is very important").

It is ironic that despite the general agreement that values could be observed "only through behavior" (Hofstede, 2001, p. 10), most scholars chose to operationalize culture via self-reported values and not via directly observable practices. This choice is partly understandable, as cross-cultural samples are uniformly difficult to obtain under the best of conditions, making the more easily obtained attitudinal value surveys very tempting, aside from also being the traditional method for quantifying cultures. Unfortunately, due to the focus on values, to the exclusion of other aspects of culture, in the empirical literature, the nature and magnitude of the relationship between different layers of culture remains unknown, and it is still uncertain whether measuring solely values adequately captures the construct of culture.

Assumption 2: Values are cultures

The popularity of the assumption that cultures are values leads to an assumption that all values are cultural. That is, it has become common to attribute any value difference to cultural differences. Hofstede never argued that all values are cultural; rather, he selected the values that he believed were determined by cultural background. However, the popularity of his value-based model of culture has been so enormous that it has, unfortunately, overshadowed alternative views. As Stephen Jay Gould (1996, p. 57) states, "The most erroneous stories are those we think we know best – and therefore never scrutinize or question." When great ideas are raised to the status of unquestionable truth, devoted followers stop noticing important nuances, even those specifically pointed out by the originator. Over time, it became common to assume not only that cultures are values but also that all values are cultural.

To clarify the issue, we composed a comprehensive list of 27 cultural value dimensions used in 136 instruments to quantify culture and their underlying cultural models. The list included attitudes toward achievement, ambiguity avoidance, assertiveness, ritual suicide, believing in evil/good and changeable/unchangeable basic human nature, conformity, conservatism, determinism, family, gender equality, pleasure-seeking, humane orientations, teamwork, independent/interdependent self-perceptions, emotions, Machiavellianism, personal independence, power distance, relationship depth, views of the environment, risk avoidance, self-identity, self-reliance, time perception and orientation, status attribution, and rule application (for details, see Taras, 2008a; Taras et al., forthcoming). We sent the list to 36 leading cross-cultural management scholars and asked them to evaluate, based on their experience, the extent to which each of the dimensions was determined by culture. Close to 80 percent of the scholars anonymously responded to our call. The results were surprising: only a few types of values commonly used in cross-cultural studies scored as being highly related to culture. The majority of the dimensions were rated as unaffected or marginally affected by cultural background, including most facets of the extremely popular construct of individualism–collectivism.

It is possible to dismiss these results as an opinion. The respondents, however, were renowned experts in international management and demonstrated very high inter-rater reliability. If we give credence to experience and consensus, the findings of the survey strongly suggest that not all values are cultural, not even many of those that are commonly used in cross-cultural comparison studies. Many types of values seem to be culture-free and determined by personality, experiences, or even temporal states or emotions. As noted by Durvasula and colleagues (2006), simply finding a mean difference between two countries along a value dimension does not automatically make the dimension cultural. The mean difference may be due to various reasons other than culture, including differences in question interpretation, response styles, sample characteristics, or survey administration.

Assumption 3: Cultures are extremely stable

Although Hofstede never empirically tested hypotheses about culture change, in his publications, he expressed a series of assumptions about cultural change. Essentially, he believed in extreme cultural stability. Hofstede (2001) saw theories of culture change as "naïve" (p. 34) and predicted that national cultures should not change substantially "until at least 2100" (p. 36). As for individuals, he assumed that individual cultural values were formed in early childhood and remain unchanged throughout one's life. As Hofstede and colleagues (1990, p. 312) state, "by the time a child is ten, most of his or her basic values are probably programmed into his or her mind."

Following publication of Hofstede's (1980) *Culture's Consequences*, cultures have been traditionally viewed as unchanging. Hofstede's original, decades-old indices, derived using data from the IBM study of 1967–73, are still frequently used in secondary empirical analyses, even in the most recent years (e.g., Lim, Leung, Sia et al., 2004; Litvin and Kar, 2003; Metcalf, Bird, Peterson et al., 2007; Newburry and Yakova, 2006). Nevertheless, there is a good reason to believe that cultures can change more rapidly than Hofstede's adherents would believe. As far back as Marx's (1867) *Das Kapital*, there have been theories of cultural change. Today, two theories of cultural change are typically espoused: modernization and convergence. They indicate that societies will converge around some set of values as they modernize, usually those associated with Western, free-market economies. Considerable support for modernization or convergence has been found both theoretically (e.g., Bell, 1973; Eisenstadt, 1973; Kerr, Dunlop, Harbison et al., 1960; Webber, 1969) and empirically (Adams, 2005; e.g., Inglehart and Welzel, 2005; Ralston, Pounder, Lo et al., 2006).

Based on an analysis of World Value Survey data from 81 societies, Inglehart and colleagues find evidence of "massive cultural change" (Inglehart and Baker, 2000, p. 19) and that "cultural values are changing in a predictable direction as socioeconomic development takes place" (Inglehart and Welzel, 2005, p. 1). Similarly, American cultural dimensions, from authority and individuality to sexism and risk preference, have been measured by Adams (2005) every four years since 1992. He found repeated evidence of significant change, most notably from the apparent impact of the 9/11 attacks on the World Trade Center. This act of terrorism reversed what had been a steady decline in authoritarian values. Many other regions provided similar evidence of rapid cultural change (Fernandez, Carlson, Stepina et al., 1997; Ralston et al., 2006). In particular, based on meta-analytic data covering a 35-year period, Taras and Steel (2006) found a significantly persistent change toward lower power distance and higher individualism and achievement orientation worldwide, especially in countries that experienced dramatic economic and political changes, such as China or the former USSR republics. Another good example is Hofstede's own work. A portion of his sample was assessed twice with a hiatus of six years. As he admitted, "from a comparison between the two survey rounds, it became clear that there had been a worldwide shift on some questions" (Hofstede, 2001, p. 53). Regretfully, this finding was greatly downplayed, and instead, the author went on to defend extreme cultural stability.

Furthermore, extreme cultural stability belies cohorts. Cohorts are a well-established construct in which people develop common character-istics as a result of a shared social history. They are explicitly cultural, that is, "a property of cultures themselves, and as something that can be compared across historical periods or between nation-states" (Settersen and Mayer, 1997: 235). Cohorts are consequently a product of history, and new ones should be generated regularly, such as "Baby Boomers" or "Generation X," with at least 28 of them created in America over the past 300 years. In this context, cultural stability is an extremely aggressive position, as it implicitly rejects cohorts and emphasizes an unchanging uniformity of culture.

Finally, generational cohorts themselves have been observed to change. Using the General Social Surveys from the National Research Center, T. W. Smith (2000) summarized over 100 attitudes and values from 1973 to 1997. The general trend was change along with a dimin-ishing generation gap (i.e., increased homogeneity across all cohorts) for topics ranging from social welfare to sexual permissiveness. Others report a similar change within the relatively brief span of a generation (e.g., Brewster and Padavic, 2000; Smola and Sutton, 2002).

These theoretical and empirical conclusions clearly show that either what Hofstede labeled cultures is not culture, assuming culture is extremely stable, or that culture can change much faster than pos-tulated by Hofstede. If the former is true, we need to reevaluate if Hofstede's approach to operationalizing culture is valid. Otherwise, we have to reconsider our assumptions about the extreme stability of culture at both the national and individual levels.

Assumption 4: Culture is the cause, not an effect

Numerous studies, including Hofstede's (1980) IBM project, have found a strong relationship between cultural values and various individual- and national-level phenomena. For example, Hofstede reported correlations of up to .85 between cultural values and wealth, economic growth, economic inequality, and other country characteristics, as well as with such individual characteristics as socio-economic status, education, or profession. Similar findings have been reported in numerous subsequent studies. In terms of causality, culture traditionally is seen solely as the cause, while the other variables in the equation are "culture's consequences" (e.g., Franke, Hofstede, and Bond, 1991; Hofstede, 1980; Offermann and Hellmann, 1997).

Cultural determinism has dominated cross-cultural research for several decades. As evident from numerous reviews of cross-cultural research (Gelfand, Erez, and Aycan, 2007; Kirkman, Lowe, and Gibson, 2006; Ricks, Toyne, and Martinez, 1990; Sondergaard, 1994; Tsui, Nifadkar, and Ou, 2007; Werner, 2002), culture as a cause has been the almost exclusive focus of cross-cultural scholars. In a pair of comprehensive reviews by Kirkman and colleagues (2006) and Tsui and colleagues (2007), cross-cultural studies were classified into Type I and Type II. Type I represented studies that explored culture as a main effect on various outcomes. Type II represented studies that explored culture as a moderating effect. There was no Type III category that explored predictors of culture, an absence that strongly reflects the general trend in the field of cross-cultural research.

Cultural determinism largely stems from the cultural stability paradigm. If culture does not change for generations, then culture must be the cause and cannot be the effect. For example, the relationship between individualism and wealth for China and the United States has been traditionally assessed from the culture-as-a-cause point of view. That is, America is wealthier because it is more individualistic. However, considerable empirical evidence clearly indicates that cultures do change much more often and rapidly than previously thought (e.g., Adams, 2005; Inglehart and Welzel, 2005; Taras and Steel, 2006), and it is becoming evident that the recently well-documented rise of individualism in China is due to economic growth and not vice versa.

Unfortunately, establishing causality is extremely difficult in any relationship, especially when phenomena as complex as culture are involved. However, the Hofstedean paradigm of cultural determinism and culture's consequences can and should be questioned. It is plausible to expect that as countries, such as China or India, continue to experience economic and political changes, the values of the people in these countries will be changing as a result.

The same is true at the individual level; individual maturation and changes in the level of education and socio-economic status affect individual values. This development leaves many previous correlations with culture open to debate regarding causation. The causal arrow may well be reversed for many observed relationships, making culture a consequence, not a cause, or as Erez and Gati (2004) suggest, the relationship may be bi-directional.

Assumption 5: A cross-level analysis of culture leads to the ecological fallacy

Since *Culture's Consequences* and other publications authored by Hofstede, there has been an unwritten rule in the field of cross-cultural studies: "Never Mix National and Individual Levels of Analysis." Hofstede consistently warned against using his model with individual-level data and about the fallacy of making generalizations from his national cultural averages to individuals (Hofstede, 1995, 2001, 2002b). We do not question his logic, as indeed his instrument and model were obtained using aggregated data and designed for the national level of analysis. However, his repetitive warnings about the pitfalls of cross-level generalizations of his specific data set formed a perception that any cross-level analysis would lead to the ecological fallacy. As a result, multilevel models have become taboo in cross-cultural studies, and papers attempting to bridge national and individual cultures still tend to be red-flagged by reviewers.

There are two basic forms of cross-level inference error. Wrongly generalizing relationships observed at the group to the individual level is the ecological fallacy, which has a long history. Although it was mentioned earlier by Thorndike (1939), the researcher most remembered for his critique is Robinson (1950). The second type, wrongly generalizing relationships from the individual to the group, is known as the atomistic, the individualistic, or the reverse ecological fallacy (Diez-Roux, 1998), which is Hofstede's primary concern. The fear of these fallacies is so ingrained in our minds that any attempt at ecological inference—that is, bridging levels of analysis by going from the group to the individual level or vice versa—generates a predictable, negative, knee-jerk reaction.

Fortunately, we have progressed considerably since Robinson (1950), whose own examples were shown, ironically, to represent model mis-specification and not ecological fallacy at all (Hanushek, Jackson, and Kain, 1974). In the words of Jargowsky (2004, p. 721), "the 'ecological fallacy' has lost some of its sting, and should not cause researchers to abandon aggregate data." Ecological fallacy is simply a *threat* to valid-ity, one of several (e.g., differential attrition, self-selection, maturation), and not a necessary or perhaps even common confound. We need to stop dysfunctionally elevating its status to an absolute and consider the few situations in which it is of concern. As Steel and Ones (2002) review, misleading results originating in the ecological fallacy are rare, as individual and group analyses typically provide substantially similar results.

Furthermore, there are many times when ecological inference is the preferred manner to investigate. For example, Jargowsky (2004, p. 721) states, "aggregate data may be better than individual data for testing hypotheses, even if those hypotheses are about individual behaviour." Similarly, Schwartz (1994a, pp. 819–20) concludes, "as a result of the grouping operation, one may have controlled for the effects of other variables, making the ecological estimate less biased than the individual estimate." In other words, a reflexive terror of ecological inference tars the times when it can be equivalent to an individual-level analysis, or even superior. For example, the ecological fallacy should not occur, given a properly specified model, if the grouping is based on random sampling or a predictor (Jargowsky, 2004). Consider an investigation of the effects of sex using two groups that consist exclusively of men and women. Range restriction may still occur, as the variance may be smaller at the group level, but this issue is easily correctable. We do this type of group-level analysis regularly when we conduct t-tests, one of the most basic of statistical procedures. Using group-level summary statistics, means, and standard deviations, we draw conclusions about average differences between individuals within these groups.

However, as Hofstede (2001) correctly contends, ecological fallacy is more of a concern at the national level, where we are grouping by geography. Specifically, cultural stability arises from institutions, in particular "the family, educational systems, political systems, and legis-lation" (Hofstede, 2001, p. 11). Any national-level average will be due to both individual effects and the effects of national institutions. This combination *potentially* makes it difficult to generalize from the group to the individual, as these national institutions *may* obscure individual effects, *possibly* enhancing, erasing, or reversing them. Again, as per the words italicized in the previous sentence, the possibility of a threat is not the same as its realization.

Finally, recent progress in data analysis techniques has offered some great solutions for cross-level research. For example, hierarchical linear modeling (HLM) provides a formal way of achieving ecological inference with data representing multiple levels of analysis. Essentially, HLM allows us to determine statistically how variance is accounted for at the micro (individual), the meso (group or organization), and the macro (nation) levels, as well as the interactions between levels (Raudenbush and Bryk, 2002). Already a staple in the study of health and disease (Blakely and Woodward, 2000), HLM is becoming increasingly popular for cross-cultural research (e.g., Cheung and Au, 2005; Fischer, Ferreira, Assmar et al., 2005).

Assumption 6: Cultures cluster within geographic boundaries

Hofstede (2001, p. 9) defined culture as "the collective programming of the mind that distinguished one group or category of people from another." In his work, these "groups or categories" were countries, and their cultures were described by national averages. As Hofstede (2002a) noted in his response to McSweeney's (2002) remarks about the inappropriateness of national averages: "[nations] are usually the only kind of units available for comparison" (p. 1356). The research that followed did not deviate from the Hofstedean paradigm, and the outcome of subsequent cross-cultural comparison studies has traditionally been a set of national cultural averages. Although many scholars recognized substantial within-country variation in cultural values (e.g., Au, 1999; Huo and Randall, 1991; Smith and Bond, 1999; Taras et al., forthcoming; Steel and Taras, forthcoming), the issue of subcultures usually has been addressed by refining geographic borders and offering separate scores for different geographic regions within countries (e.g., House et al., 2004; Huo and Randall, 1991; Maznevski and DiStefano, 1995; Ralston, Kai-Cheng, Wang et al., 1996; Vandello and Cohen, 1999).

The dominance of the geography-based clustering of cultures has led to some potential misuse. In particular, assumptions about cultural values frequently have been made based on country of origin. Reviewing 210 cross-cultural studies published between 1995 and 2001, Schaffer and Riordan (2003) found that in 79 percent of the cases, nationality or country of residence was used as a proxy for culture. For example, Offermann and Hellmann (1997, p. 346) state that "cultural background was measured by the current citizenship (passport status) of each of the managers," and Eylon and Au (1999, p. 378) report, "participants were divided into high and low power distance groups by county-of-origin." This pervasive methodology is troubling, as Oyserman et al. (2002, p. 7) conclude: "Lack of empirical support for these assumptions [that national averages represents the individual] makes this approach vulnerable to criticism."

Within-country variations in cultural values have been well documented (e.g., Au, 1999; Huo and Randall, 1991; Smith and Bond, 1999). Although cultural regions are common in many countries, such as Anglophone and Francophone parts of Canada, it is very questionable that geographic boundaries are optimal for clustering cultures. A characteristic is justified as a clustering dimension only if it can effectively predict membership in target groups. Simply finding a significant mean difference for different regions is not sufficient to confirm discriminant validity of geographic boundaries (Durvasula et al., 2006). We are not aware of any studies that directly address this issue, but a study by Steel and Taras (forthcoming) may shed some light on the problem. One of the findings of this meta-analysis of 508 empirical studies was that, depending on the value dimension, a hefty 81–92 percent of the variation in cultures resides within countries. This result strongly suggests weak discriminant validity of geographic boundaries. Consequently, at least for the work-related cultural values as defined in Hofstede's model, it appears that socio-economic and demographic factors are much more relevant dimensions for clustering cultures and subcultures.

Years ago, area of residence (i.e., a country or region within a country) probably was a much better predictor of cultural values. In today's "global village," geographical boundaries are becoming less relevant in studies of culture and national, or even regional, averages. Analyses of cultures of socio-economic classes, professions, or generational cohorts are probably much more meaningful than analyses of national or regional cultures, at least within the framework of Hofstede's model, with its dimensions of individualism, power distance, uncertainty avoidance, and masculinity. It is time to reexamine the boundaries of cultural clusters.

Assumption 7: Mean scores and ranking sufficiently quantify cultures

The most important categories of information in the over 300 pages of Hofstede's (1980) *Culture's Consequences* are the tables providing the national cultural statistical averages and rankings. Although Hofstede raised a number of other issues in his numerous publications, the national averages are the cornerstone of his work. Such is Hofstede's emphasis on averages that his result tables did not offer any information about score dispersion within groups (e.g., variance).

Following Hofstede's path, most of the subsequent research focused on cultural means, be it national or group averages. The mean comparisons, typically using t-tests, have been the main tool for studying and describing cultures. Taras and Steel (2006) conducted a meta-analytic review of 532 empirical studies that involved culture measurement. Although all the reviewed studies reported sample means along cultural dimensions, less than half of the papers contained information about the dispersion of cultural scores within groups, such as standard deviations or ranges, and only about 2 percent of the studies explicitly referred to the measures of dispersion in their discussions. We found no study that analyzed cultural score dispersion within groups at a more advanced level, such as by considering skewness or kurtosis.

Although a mean provides important information about the culture of a group, it is certainly not sufficient to understand the phenomenon fully. Focusing solely on means may create a false perception of cultural homogeneity within a group, obstructing the detection of subcultures. For example, a statistical average provides no meaningful description of scores within groups with bimodal or otherwise non-normal distributions. At the same time, measures of value dispersion and skewness could provide useful information about the cultural composition of the group. After all, cultural diversity may be an important characteristic of a group and perhaps even a facet of culture.

Furthermore, cultural diversity or cultural homogeneity could be an important predictor of attitudes and behaviors. For example, it could be hypothesized that culture has a stronger effect on individual attitudes and behaviors in culturally homogeneous societies or groups. Unfortunately, with the focus solely on cultural means, many important issues could not be addressed or have been overlooked.

Assumption 8: Matched samples should be used to study cultural differences

Hofstede's IBM study was based on a uni-organizational design. While some criticized him for this approach (e.g., McSweeney, 2002; Schwartz, 1994b), Hofstede repeatedly argued that matched sampling was what allowed him to detect systematic *differences* in cultural values across countries and isolate effects of other factors, such as organizational culture, demographics, or economy (e.g., Hofstede, 1980, 2001, 2002a). Hofstede's argument is well taken. Indeed, it would be inadvisable to contrast national cultures by comparing samples of wealthy people from one country with a sample of relatively poor people from another country, as it would be difficult to determine whether the differences in cultural values are due to national or socio-economic differences.

Following in Hofstede's footsteps, later scholars have tried their very best to conduct their cross-cultural research using matched sampling. Traditionally, between-sample inconsistencies and within-sample het-erogeneity have been seen as limitations. Unfortunately, matched sampling, while indeed minimizing some threats to validity, greatly obstructs progress in cross-cultural research. First of all, matched sam-ples limit generalizability and often provide results that are not useful for many intended purposes. For example, as noted by Schwartz (1994b, p. 91), "highly educated well-paid IBM employees' ability to represent the general population likely differs from country to country, with the discrepancy probably being greater, for example, in the Third World nations (e.g., El Salvador, Pakistan) than in industrialized Western nations (e.g., Switzerland, United States)." In other words, most research-ers are looking for indices that represent the entire nation, not just a sub-culture of that nation (e.g., technology professionals), which may have only the most tenuous of connections to the general population.

Second, the use of matched samples obstructs the detection of subcultures. Ironically, matched sampling is an implicit acknowledge-ment of the existence of subcultures, yet decades of having strived to make "clean" comparisons using highly homogeneous matched samples greatly limits the diversity of data available for their analysis. Consequently, we have very limited knowledge about how individual characteristics, such as age or gender, affect cultural scores, despite implicitly acknowledging that they should have a significant effect.

Assumption 9: Self-response questionnaires adequately measure culture

While many scholars have explicitly voiced concerns and pointed out limitations of self-response attitudinal surveys (Harzing, 2006a, 2006b; Hui and Triandis, 1989; Johnson, Kulesa, Cho et al., 2005), the review of hundreds of studies in the area clearly confirms that Hofstede's approach (i.e., self-report questionnaires) has traditionally been almost the only way to quantify culture (Taras et al., forthcoming). Starting with Hofstede's IBM study, data in all major culture comparison projects have continued to be collected this way. However, we have made considerable psychometric progress since Hofstede's original Value Survey Module instrument. For example, Hofstede (2008) himself recently announced the release of a new and improved version of his instrument. Still, the improvements in the area of culture measurement have remained within the ubiquitous self-response questionnaire paradigm and have been limited to developing better item sets, improving scale reliabilities, and refining scoring schemes.

Limitations of self-report attitudinal surveys have been widely recognized and discussed in detail in various fields, in particular in personality and attitude psychology (Funder, 1995; Ozer and Reise, 1994; Schwarz, 1999). Some of the commonly cited limitations are the difficulties of giving accurate self-reported numerical assessments of the constructs encapsulated by the questionnaire and the subjectivity of responses.

Furthermore, the validity of self-reported questionnaires is likely reduced in cross-cultural settings as several problems, such as translation, cross-cultural differences in response styles, and differences in interpretation of the scale anchors, are exacerbated (Harzing, 2006a, 2006b; Hui and Triandis, 1989; Johnson et al., 2005). As a result, the degree to which the responses represent true scores (i.e., culture) is not known, and thus, it is not known whether score differences across countries indeed indicate cultural differences or are simply due to, for example, differences in the propensity for extreme responses in some cultures.

A number of methods have been suggested to control and correct for cross-cultural differences in response styles and response biases in international surveys (Hofstede, 1980; Leung and Bond, 1989; McCrae and Costa, 1997; Spector, Cooper, and Sparks, 2001). Unfortunately, these methods are rarely utilized and, in any case, are not without limitations (P. B. Smith, 2004). Future research should find ways to minimize these sources of self-report data contamination as well as explore alternative approaches to data collection, such as observations and experiments. At the very least, alternative assessment procedures can provide convergent validity for self-reported measures.

Assumption 10: The Hofstedean framework is unique and the only viable framework for studying culture

Although cross-cultural research was conducted before Hofstede, his 1980 *Culture's Consequences* marked the beginning of the research field of cross-cultural business and management, one that has developed fairly independently ever since. Rather young areas of research at that time, cross-cultural management, business, and marketing studies firmly embraced Hofstede's cultural framework. His numerous devoted followers, captivated by the novelty and apparent comprehensiveness of his model, did not actively seek and at times fiercely denied the viability of alternative solutions.

As a result of this entrenchment, the interaction between international business scholars and those representing the older but related fields of cultural psychology, sociology, and anthropology was drastically curtailed. Scholars from these different fields tend to present their findings at different conferences, publish in different journals, and neglect one another's work. As a result, cross-cultural management and marketing scholars, as well as those interested in cross-cultural issues in education, business strategy, and I/O psychology, embraced and started building upon Hofstede's framework without much consideration for the existence of alternatives in related fields. For example, published research on acculturation (for reviews, see Berry, 1994; Berry, 2003; Rudmin, 2003), a closely related field by definition, has virtually zero overlap with cross-cultural research literature that relies on Hofstede's framework. Similarly, empirical research on personality that relies on a very similar theory and methodology had been virtually unknown to cross-cultural management scholars until fairly recently. Only recently have calls for a closer look at the similarities and attempts to merge the bodies of research on cross-cultural management and acculturation (Taras, 2008b) and personality (e.g., Hofstede and McCrae, 2004; McCrae and Terracciano, 2005; Wallace and Fogelson, 1961) become more frequent.

While some sociologists and psychologists often referred to Hofstede's models in their work (e.g., McCrae, 2001; Smith, Peterson, Schwartz et al., 2002; Van de Vijver and Leung, 2000), cross-cultural business researchers tended to overlook the research in other fields. The lack of cross-pollination and interaction with other fields formed a perception among many cross-cultural business scholars that Hofstede's framework is the only, or at the very least the only viable, framework for studying culture. The lack of knowledge about existing relevant methodologies and models often leads to stagnation or needless duplication. For example, Mesoudi and colleagues (Mesoudi, Whiten, and Laland, 2006) argue for unification, particularly noting that the study of culture would greatly benefit from adopting principles from biological evolution. We agree. It is time to start exchanging ideas and build upon one another's experience.

Conclusions

The present chapter has reviewed the unofficial yet firmly institutionalized assumptions about what culture is and how culture should be studied. The ten "commandments" of cross-cultural research, at least to some extent, are all rooted in Hofstede's work, though most of them arose from misinterpretations of Hofstede's statements or the reification and improper extension of his propositions. While these traditional assumptions certainly have some merit, their validity is often greatly exaggerated, far beyond what considerable theoretical and empirical evidence would suggest. With the over-adoption of these assumptions, many previous studies were based on flawed logic and questionable research designs. The taboos imposed by this dominant paradigm greatly obstruct progress in cross-cultural research by limiting the scope of data and types of analyses that are "welcomed" in the field.

The future of cross-cultural research begins with the need for establishing and communicating under which circumstances these assumptions hold water, where they leak, or even when they sink completely. Only with this understanding will new research that breaks free from the currently dominant Hofstedean paradigm be conducted in any quantity and, importantly, be rewarded by publication. As we have discussed here, such research should consider which values are indeed cultural, what is significantly cultural aside from values, and how best either should be measured. How stable are the different dimensions of culture, and how often do they need to be updated? What is the relationship between different layers of culture? What are the meaningful boundaries of cultural entities? What theories and methodologies could be borrowed from other fields of research to study culture? Answers to these questions would provide the foundation for future research beyond Hofstede's framework.

The world has a need for increasingly sophisticated cultural advice on a multitude of fronts. Headline news stories cover issues, such as immigrants' assimilation problems, the difficulty of transferring democratic values to countries with authoritarian traditions, and the cultural problems that transnational or global companies have in implementing their business models around the world. Given the seriousness of these issues, we should not bypass any avenues that promise an improved quality in our results. Rather, to the degree we address any weaknesses in our field, we would be rewarded with a concomitant increase in the practical relevance and adoption of our findings.

References

Adams, M. (2005) *American Backlash: The Untold Story of Social Change in the United States*. New York, NY: The Penguin Group.

Au, K. Y. (1999) "Intra-Cultural Variation: Evidence and Implications for International Business," *Journal of International Business Studies*, 30 (4), 799–812.

Bell, D. (1973) *The Coming of Post-Industrial Society*. New York, NY: Basic Books.

Berry, J. W. (1994) "Acculturation and Psychological Adaptation: An Overview," in A.-M. Bouvy & van de F. Vijver, (eds), *Journeys into Cross-Cultural Psychology*. Lisse, Netherlands: Swets & Zeitlinger Publishers, 129–41.

Berry, J. W. (2003) "Conceptual Approaches to Acculturation," in K. M. Chun & P. Organista Balls (eds), *Acculturation: Advances in Theory, Measurement and Applied Research*. Washington, DC: APA, 17–37.

Blakely, T. A. & Woodward, A. J. (2000) "Ecological Effects in Multi-Level Studies," *Journal of Epidemiology and Community Health*, 54, 367–74.

Brewster, K. L. & Padavic, I. (2000) "Change in Gender-Ideology, 1977–1996: The Contributions of Intracohort Change and Population Turnover," *Journal of Marriage and Family*, 62 (2), 477–87.

Cheung, M. W. L. & Au, K. (2005) "Applications of Multilevel Structural Equation Modeling to Cross-Cultural Research," *Structural Equation Modeling*, 12 (4), 598–619.

Diez-Roux, A. V. (1998) "Bringing Context Back into Epidemiology: Variables and Fallacies in Multilevel Analysis," *American Journal of Public Health*, 88 (2), 216–22.

Durvasula, S., Netemeyer, R. G., Andrews, J. C., & Lysonski, S. (2006) "Examining the Cross-National Applicability of Multi-Item, Multi-Dimensional Measures Using Generalizability Theory," *Journal of International Business Studies*, 37 (4), 469–81.

Eisenstadt, S. N. (1973) *Tradition, Change and Modernity*. New York, NY: John Wiley & Sons.

Erez, M. & Gati, E. (2004) "A Dynamic, Multi-Level Model of Culture: From the Micro Level of the Individual to the Macro Level of a Global Culture," *Applied Psychology: An International Review*, 53 (4), 583–98.

Eylon, D. & Au, K. Y. (1999) "Exploring Empowerment: Cross-Cultural Differences Along the Power Distance Dimension," *International Journal of Intercultural Relations*, 23 (3), 373–85.

Fernandez, D. R., Carlson, D. S., Stepina, L. P., & Nicholson, J. D. (1997) "Hofstede's Country Classification 25 Years Later," *Journal of Social Psychology*, 137 (1), 43–54.

Fischer, R., Ferreira, M. C., Assmar, E. M. L., Redford, P., & Harb, C. (2005) "Organizational Behaviour across Cultures: Theoretical and Methodological Issues for Developing Multi-Level Frameworks Involving Culture," *International Journal of Cross Cultural Management*, 5 (1), 27–48.

Franke, R. H., Hofstede, G., & Bond, M. H. (1991) "Cultural Roots of Economic Performance: A Research Note," *Strategic Management Journal*, 12 (1), 165–73.

Funder, D. C. (1995) "On the Accuracy of Personality Judgment: A Realistic Approach," *Psychological Review*, 102 (4), 652–70.

Gelfand, M. J., Erez, M., & Aycan, A. Z. (2007) "Cross-Cultural Organizational Behavior," *Annual Review of Psychology*, 58 (20), 1–35.

Gould, S. J. (1996) *Full House: The Spread of Excellence from Plato to Darwin*. New York, NY: Harmony Books.

Haire, M., Ghiselli, E. E., & Porter, L. W. (1966) *Managerial Thinking: An International Study*. New York, NY: John Wiley & Sons.

Hanushek, E. A., Jackson, J. E., & Kain, J. F. (1974) "Model Specification, Use of Aggregate Data, and the Ecological Correlation Fallacy," *Political Methodology*, 1, 89–107.

Harzing, A.-W. (2006a) "Response Styles in Cross-National Survey Research," *International Journal of Cross Cultural Management*, 6 (2), 243–66.

Harzing, A.-W. (2006b) "Response Styles in Cross-National Survey Research: A 26-Country Study," *International Journal of Cross Cultural Management*, 6 (2), 243–64.

Hofstede, G. (1980) *Culture's Consequences: International Differences in Work-Related Values*. Beverly Hills, CA: Sage Publications.

Hofstede, G. (1995) "Multilevel Research of Human Systems: Flowers, Bouquets and Gardens," *Human Systems Management*, 14 (3), 207–18.

Hofstede, G. (2001) *Culture's Consequences: Comparing Values, Behaviors, Institutions, and Organizations across Nations* (2 edn). London, UK: Sage Publications.

Hofstede, G. (2002a) "Dimensions Do Not Exist: A Reply to Brendan Mcsweeney," *Human Relations*, 55 (11), 11355–61.

Hofstede, G. (2002b) "The Pitfalls of Cross-National Survey Research: A Reply to the Article by Spector et al. On the Psychometric Properties of the Hofstede Values Survey Module 1994", *Applied Psychology*, 51 (1), 170–3.

Hofstede, G. (2008) "For the Value Survey Module" from http://feweb.uvt.nl/center/hofstede/VSMChoice.html (accessed March 20, 2008).

Hofstede, G. & McCrae, R. R. (2004) "Personality and Culture Revisited: Linking Traits and Dimensions of Culture," *Cross-Cultural Research*, 38 (1), 52–89.

Hofstede, G., Neuijen, B., Ohayv, D. D., & Sanders, G. (1990) "Measuring Organizational Cultures: A Qualitative and Quantitative Study across Twenty Cases," *Administrative Science Quarterly*, 35 (2), 286–316.

House, R. J., Hanges, P. J., Javidan, M., Dorfman, P. W., & Gupta, V. (eds) (2004) *Culture, Leadership, and Organizations: The Globe Study of 62 Societies*. Thousand Oaks, CA: Sage Publications.

Hui, C. H., & Triandis, H. C. (1989) "Effects of Culture and Response Format on Extreme Response Style," *Journal of Cross-Cultural Psychology*, 20 (3), 296–309.

Huo, Y. P., & Randall, D. M. (1991) "Exploring Subcultural Differences in Hofstede's Value Survey: The Case of the Chinese," *Asia Pacific Journal of Management*, 8 (2), 159–73.

Inglehart, R., & Baker, W. E. (2000) "Modernization, Cultural Change, and the Persistence of Traditional Values," *American Sociological Review*, 65 (1), 19–51.

Inglehart, R., & Welzel, C. (2005) *Modernization, Cultural Change and Democracy: The Human Development Sequence*. New York, NY: Cambridge University Press.

Jargowsky, P. A. (2004) "The Ecological Fallacy," in K. Kempf-Leonard (ed), *The Encyclopedia of Social Measurement*, Vol. 1. San Diego, CA: Academic Press, 715–22.

Johnson, T., Kulesa, P., Cho, Y. I., & Shavitt, S. (2005) "The Relationship between Culture and Response Styles: Evidence from 19 Countries," *Journal of Cross-Cultural Psychology*, 36, 264–77.

Kerr, C., Dunlop, J. T., Harbison, F. H., & Myers, C. A. (1960) *Industrialism and Industrial Man: The Problems of Labor and Management in Economic Growth*. London, UK: Heinemann.

Kirkman, B. L., Lowe, K. B., & Gibson, C. B. (2006) "A Quarter Century of Culture's Consequences: A Review of Empirical Research Incorporating Hofstede's Cultural Values Framework," *Journal of International Business Studies*, 37 (3), 285–320.

Kluckhohn, F. R. & Strodtbeck, F. L. (1961) *Variations in Value Orientations*. Evanston, IL: Row, Peterson.

Kuhn, M. H. & McPartland, R. (1954) "An Empirical Investigation of Self Attitudes," *American Sociological Review*, 19, 68–76.

Leung, K. & Bond, M. H. (1989) "On the Empirical Identification of Dimensions for Cross-Cultural Comparisons," *Journal of Cross-Cultural Psychology*, 20 (2), 133–51.

Lim, K. H., Leung, K., Sia, C. L., & Lee, M. K. (2004) "Is Ecommerce Boundary-Less? Effects of Individualism-Collectivism and Uncertainty Avoidance on Internet Shopping," *Journal of International Business Studies*, 35 (6), 545–60.

Litvin, S. W. & Kar, G. H. (2003) "Individualism/Collectivism as a Moderating Factor to the Self-Image Congruity Concept," *Journal of Vacation Marketing*, 10 (1), 23–32.

Marx, K. (1867) *Das Kapital: Kritik Der Politischen Oekonomie*. Hamburg, Germany: O. Meissner.

Maznevski, M. L. & DiStefano, J. J. (1995) "Measuring Culture in International Management: The Cultural Perspectives Questionnaire," *The University of Western Ontario Working Paper Series*, 95–139.

McCrae, R. R. (2001) "Trait Psychology and Culture: Exploring Intercultural Comparisons," *Journal of Personality*, 69, 819–46.

McCrae, R. R. & Costa, P. T., Jr. (1997) "Personality Trait Structure as a Human Universal," *American Psychologist*, 52 (5), 509–16.

McCrae, R. R. & Terracciano, A. (2005) "Personality Profiles of Cultures: Aggregate Personality Traits," *Journal of Personality and Social Psychology*, 89 (3), 407–25.

McSweeney, B. (2002), "Hofstede's Model of National Cultural Differences and Their Consequences: A Triumph of Faith - a Failure of Analysis," *Human Relations*, 55 (1), 89–118.

Mesoudi, A., Whiten, A., & Laland, K. N. (2006) "Towards a Unified Science of Cultural Evolution," *Behavioral and Brain Sciences*, 29 (04), 329–47.

Metcalf, L. E., Bird, A., Peterson, M. F., Shankarmahesh, M., & Lituchy, T. R. (2007) "Cultural Influences in Negotiations: A Four Country Comparative Analysis," *International Journal of Cross Cultural Management*, 7 (2), 147–68.

Newburry, W. & Yakova, N. (2006) "Standardization Preferences: A Function of National Culture, Work Interdependence and Local Embeddedness," *Journal of International Business Studies*, 37 (1), 44–60.

Offermann, L. R. & Hellmann, P. S. (1997) "Culture's Consequences for Leadership Behavior: National Values in Action," *Journal of Cross-Cultural Psychology*, 28 (3), 342–51.

Oyserman, D., Coon, H. M., & Kemmelmeier, M. (2002) "Rethinking Individualism and Collectivism: Evaluation of Theoretical Assumptions and Meta-Analyses," *Psychological Bulletin*, 128 (1), 3–72.

Ozer, D. J. & Reise, S. P. (1994) "Personality Assessment," *Annual Review of Psychology*, 45 (1), 357–88.

Ralston, D. A., Kai-Cheng, Y., Wang, X., Terpstra, R. H., & Wei, W. (1996) "The Cosmopolitan Chinese Manager: Findings of a Study on Managerial Values across the Six Regions of China," *Journal of International Management*, 2 (2), 79–109.

Ralston, D. A., Pounder, J., Lo, C. W. H., Wong, Y.-Y., & Egri, C. P. (2006) "Stability and Change in Managerial Work Values: A Longitudinal Study of China, Hong Kong, and the US," *Management and Organization Review*, 2 (1), 61–97.

Raudenbush, S. W. & Bryk, A. S. (2002) *Hierarchical Linear Models: Applications and Data Analysis Methods* (2 edn). Thousand Oaks, CA: Sage Publications.

Ricks, D. A., Toyne, B., & Martinez, Z. (1990) "Recent Developments in International Management Research," *Journal of Management*, 16 (2), 219–54.

Robinson, W. (1950) "Ecological Correlations and the Behavior of Individuals," *American Sociological Review*, 75, 351–7.

Rokeach, M. (1973) *The Nature of Human Values*. New York, NY: Free Press.

Rudmin, F. W. (2003) "Critical History of the Acculturation Psychology of Assimilation, Separation, Integration, and Marginalization," *Review of General Psychology*, 7 (1), 3–37.

Schaffer, B. S. & Riordan, C. M. (2003) "A Review of Cross-Cultural Methodologies for Organizational Research: A Best-Practices Approach," *Organizational Research Methods*, 6 (2), 169–215.

Schwartz, S. (1994a) "The Fallacy of the Ecological Fallacy: The Potential Misuse of a Concept and the Consequences," *American Journal of Public Health*, 84 (5), 819–24.

Schwartz, S. H. (1994b) "Beyond Individualism/Collectivism: New Cultural Dimensions of Values," in U. Kim, H. C. Triandis, C. Kagitcibasi, S. C. Choi & G. Yoon (eds), *Individualism and Collectivism: Theory, Methods and Applications*. London, UK: Sage Publications, 85–119.

Schwarz, N. (1999) "Self-Reports: How the Questions Shape the Answers," *American Psychologist*, 54 (2), 93–105.

Settersen, R. A., Jr. & Mayer, K. U. (1997) "The Measurement of Age, Age Structuring, and the Life Course," *Annual Review of Sociology*, 23, 233–61.

Smith, P. B. (2004) "In Search of Acquiescent Response Bias," *Journal of Cross-Cultural Psychology*, 35 (1), 50–61.

Smith, P. B. & Bond, M. H. (1999) *Social Psychology Across Cultures* (2nd edn). Boston, MA: Allyn and Bacon.

Smith, P. B., Peterson, M. F., Schwartz, S. H., Ahmad, A. H., Akande, D., Andersen, J. A., Ayestaran, S., Bochner, S., Callan, V., Davila, C., Ekelund, B., Francois, P.-H., Graversen, G., Harb, C., Jesuino, J., Kantas, A., Karamushka, L., Koopman, P., Leung, K., Kruzela, P., Malvezzi, S., Mogaji, A., Mortazavi, S., Munene, J., Parry, K., Punnett, B. J., Radford, M., Ropo, A., Saiz, J., Savage, G., Setiadi, B., Sorenson, R., Szabo, E., Teparakul, P., Tirmizi, A., Tsvetanova, S., Viedge, C., Wall, C., & Yanchuk, V. (2002) "Cultural Values, Sources of Guidance, and Their Relevance to Managerial Behavior: A 47-Nation Study," *Journal of Cross-Cultural Psychology*, 33 (2), 188–208.

Smith, T. W. (2000) *Changes in the Generation Gap, 1972–1998: Gss Social Change Report*. (Vol. 43). Chicago, IL: National Opinion Research Center, University of Chicago

Smola, K. Y. & Sutton, C. D. (2002) "Generational Differences: Revisiting Generational Work Values for the New Millennium," *Journal of Organizational Behavior*, 23, 363–82.

Sondergaard, M. (1994) "Research Note: Hofstede's Consequences: A Study of Reviews, Citations and Replications," *Organizational Studies*, 15 (3), 447–56.

Spector, P. E., Cooper, C. L., & Sparks, K. (2001) "An International Study of the Psychometric Properties of the Hofstede Values Survey Module 1994: A Comparison of Individual and Country/Province Level Results," *Applied Psychology: An International Review*, 50 (2), 269–81.

Steel, P., & Ones, D. S. (2002) "Personality and Happiness: A National-Level Analysis," *Journal of Personality & Social Psychology*, 83 (3), 767–81.

Steel, P., & Taras, V. (forthcoming) "Culture as a Consequence: A Multilevel Multivariate Meta-Analysis of the Effects of Individual and Country Characteristics on Work-Related Cultural Values," *Journal of International Management*.

Taras, V. (2008a) "Culture Survey Catalogue: Original Items, Scoring Keys and Psychometric Properties of 134 Instruments for Measuring Cultural Values and Behaviors," from http://ucalgary.ca/~taras/_private/Culture_Survey_Catalogue.pdf (accessed September 1, 2008).

Taras, V. (2008b) *Work-Related Acculturation: Change in Individual Work-Related Cultural Values Following Immigration.* Unpublished doctoral dissertation, University of Calgary, Calgary, Canada.

Taras, V., Rowney, J., & Steel, P. (forthcoming) "Half a Century of Measuring Culture: Approaches, Challenges, Limitations, and Suggestions Based on the Analysis of 112 Instruments for Quantifying Culture," *Journal of International Management*, 15 (4).

Taras, V. & Steel, P. (2006) *Improving Cultural Indices and Rankings Based on a Meta-Analysis of Hofstede's Taxonomy.* Paper presented at the Academy of International Business Annual Meeting, Beijing, China.

Thorndike, E. (1939) "On the Fallacy of Imputing the Correlations Found for Groups to the Individuals or Smaller Groups Composing Them," *American Journal of Psychology*, 52 (1), 122–4.

Tsui, A. S., Nifadkar, S. S., & Ou, A. Y. (2007) "Cross-National, Cross-Cultural Organizational Behavior Research: Advances, Gaps, and Recommendations," *Journal of Management,* 33 (3), 426–78.

van de Vijver, F. J. & Leung, K. (2000) "Methodological Issues in Psychological Research on Culture," *Journal of Cross-Cultural Psychology*, 31 (1), 33–51.

Vandello, J. A. & Cohen, D. (1999) "Patterns of Individualism and Collectivism across the United States," *Journal of Personality and Social Psychology*, 77 (2), 279–92.

Wallace, A. F. C. & Fogelson, R. D. (1961) "Culture and Personality," *Biennial Review of Anthropology*, 2, 42–78.

Webber, R. A. (1969) "Convergence or Divergence?," *Columbia Journal of World Business*, 4 (3), 75–84.

Werner, S. (2002) "Recent Developments in International Management Research: A Review of 20 Top Management Journals," *Journal of Management*, 28 (3), 277–306.

4
Culture Theories in Global Marketing: A Literature-Based Assessment

Cheryl Nakata and Elif Izberk-Bilgin

As the body of international marketing research expands, periodic reviews are helpful for assessing the state of knowledge and identifying future courses of action. Particularly useful are efforts to examine theories, which reflect a field's most fundamental concerns and contemplated solutions. One set of theories garnering current attention centers on culture. Culture theories, such as Hofstede's (1980, 2001) universal values of individualism, masculinity, power distance, and uncertainty avoidance, help explain and predict a host of market and marketing behaviors within and across countries, including consumer innovativeness, brand credibility, and global advertising effectiveness (Alden et al., 1993; Erdem et al., 2006; Steenkamp et al., 1999). As Clark (1990) notes, culture theories offer a versatile means to study both managerial and buyer issues in global marketing. Moreover, they promise coherence and make sense of the interesting, yet detached, fragments of the many existing multicountry studies. As an integrating framework, culture offers a means to strengthen the theoretical underpinnings of global marketing, a discipline that repeatedly has been criticized as conceptually shallow (Albaum and Peterson, 1984; Sheth 2001; Wang, 1999).

In view of this significant interest in and potential contributions of culture theories to global marketing, it may be time to consider their application in scholarly research. Two other examinations of culture theories appear in international marketing: One evaluates a specific pair of culture paradigms (Steenkamp, 2001), and the other provides critical perspectives on culture (Clark, 1990). However, neither is based on a systematic assessment of culture studies in global marketing, leaving a noticeable and important gap in the literature. Several specific questions thus are worth exploring. Specifically, with regard to culture studies, we ask: What is the prevalence of culture theories in global marketing, and how has that prevalence changed over time? How are these theories used? What types of theories get applied, and are these theories likely to promote cumulative learning? What is the nature and structure of these theories? Are certain theories explored more than others? What do the answers to these questions suggest about the value and contribution of culture theories to global marketing knowledge?

With this study, we attempt to understand the use, role, and nature of culture theories in global marketing. In turn, we employ a content analysis of global marketing studies published from 1990 to 2000 in leading scholarly international business and marketing journals. These years offer a complete decade of work to review, a period of time long enough to identify trends, as well as being subsequent to other major reviews of global marketing literature (Albaum and Peterson, 1984; Aulakh and Kotabe, 1993; Li and Cavusgil, 1995). We begin by defining key constructs in the study, then describe the method for assessing international marketing literature. After we present the findings of the content analysis, we draw some conclusions and implications about culture theories in global marketing.

Definitions of key constructs

We begin by defining three key terms to circumscribe our study: culture, theory, and global marketing. One of the most widely discussed definitions of culture is Hofstede's "the collective programming of the mind which distinguishes the members of one human group from another" (1980, p. 25). In effect, culture is thoughts, often abstracted further as values, writ large across an entire social system. However, this definition limits culture to a mental good, diminishing the role of traditions, social arrangements, language and symbols, and collective behaviors, which other researchers deem as parts of culture (see Earley's chapter earlier in this book as well as Geertz, 1988; Shweder, 1984). To encompass the range of interpretations, we use the definition given by anthropologist Tylor (1958, p. 1): "that complex whole which includes knowledge, belief, art, morals, law, custom, and any other capabilities and habits acquired by man as a member of society." First proposed in 1871, Tylor's definition continues to be heavily referenced in culture studies, reflecting its enduring relevance.

Perhaps the best-known articulation of theory in marketing is that by Hunt (1990), who argues that a theory has three distinctive elements: a systematically related set of statements, law-like generalizations, and empirical referents. The three elements result in a structure "capable of both explaining and predicting phenomena" (Hunt, 1990, p. 149), and though not all structures are directly open to testing, they nonetheless possess empirical referents and predictive statements to qualify as theories. This requirement does not restrict the methodologies used to construct or test a theory. Others have offered similar definitions (for example, Whetten, 1989). Hence, we adopt Hunt's definition, noting that it accommodates a range of theories (grand, middle, lower range) and methods, while insisting on conceptual rigor.

The final term we specify is international marketing. Researchers have proffered a variety of definitions for global marketing (Keegan and Green, 2008), many of which focus on marketing processes in the international context, such as strategic marketing management (for example, regional branding) or marketing mix decisions (for example, export advertising). Consistent with this focus, we use an expanded definition derived from Albaum and Peterson's work: "Global marketing is marketing activities directed toward buyers and relevant to products or services that directly or indirectly cross national borders" (1984, p. 162).

Methodology

Because our primary interest centers on understanding culture theories in global marketing, we examine academic journals devoted to marketing, international marketing, and international business. We further narrow the set to leading scholarly periodicals, reasoning that the forefront of theoretical developments should appear in those outlets. To identify the outlets, we first consider prominent evaluations of marketing, international marketing, and international business journals. Hult, Neese, and Bashaw (1997) and, more recently, Baumgartner and Pieters (2003) have conducted evaluations in which they survey marketing faculty and citation analyses of marketing journals. Their works identify a small group of scholarly periodicals as the most influential and well regarded in marketing: *Journal of Marketing, Journal of Marketing Research, Journal of Consumer Research, Marketing Science, Journal of the Academy of Marketing Science, Journal of Retailing,* and *Journal of Business Research.* Dubois and Reeb (2000) undertake a similar analysis of international business and international marketing journals and identify the top journals in terms of quality and impact as *Journal of International Business Studies, Management International Review,* and *International Marketing Review.* To augment these lists, we performed a citation analysis of marketing, international business, and international marketing outlets using the Institute for Scientific Information (ISI) or Web of Science database.

The top journals in terms of impact and immediacy closely mirrored the previous results, with the notable exception of the appearance of the *International Journal of Research in Marketing*, which ranked first in immediacy and fifth in impact.

These 11 journals constitute our literature set. Both US- and non-US-based journals are included, consistent with the international nature of this study. We then identified all international marketing articles that appeared in these outlets from 1990 to 2000, using the definitions previously discussed and including both conceptual and empirical papers. Next, we content-analyzed the resulting 587 articles, which provides an appropriate method for assessing states of scholarship (Aulakh and Kotabe, 1993; Li and Cavusgil, 1995). Two raters performed independent analyses, and the interrater reliability is satisfactory (89 percent). When discrepancies occurred, the raters discussed the issues to resolve them. Although the literature examined is limited for practical reasons, the surveys and the ISI database provide objectivity in the article selection process.

Findings

Presence and use of culture theories

The first questions we sought to answer pertain to the prevalence of culture theories in global marketing research and the degree to which this prevalence has changed over time. Guided by our definitions, we classify each of the 587 studies according to whether it incorporates one or more culture theories. Culture theories appear in only a minority (24 percent) of studies ($\chi^2 = 156.40$, $p < .001$). An additional analysis also shows, however, that the inclusion of culture theories increases significantly in the second half of the decade, according to a chi-square analysis. One-fifth (20 percent) of the research incorporated culture theories from 1990 to 1995, whereas this proportion rose to more than one-quarter (28 percent) from 1996 to 2000 ($\chi^2 = 5.22$, $p < .05$). These frequencies indicate that culture theories have a fair though not pervasive presence in the literature and increasingly are relied on as underlying explanations for observed cross-national markets and marketing behaviors.

Next, we sought to determine how culture theories are applied and, specifically, the extent to which they are sufficiently elaborated and deliberately structured into these studies' conceptual foundations. Whereas implicit applications briefly discuss a culture theory, almost in passing, or introduce a theory at the end of a paper as a post hoc explanation for unpredicted results, other applications present a culture construct in more detail but again use it post hoc to explain unpredicted results or pre hoc to provide context and background. In these cases, the culture construct is not systematically integrated into the conceptual framework nor is it used to structure a set of tested hypotheses or literature-based propositions. In either case, we argue that the explication of the culture construct, from start to finish, is implicit. In contrast, explicit applications specify a theory at the start, then integrate it into their propositions or hypotheses, with careful notation throughout of culture's nature and dimensions, as well as predictions of its outcomes. If empirical work is involved, the results get discussed in relation to the theory, noting its support or lack thereof. Explicit applications are of greater value because they involve more rigorous examinations of a theory's utility and value. For example, Steenkamp and colleagues (1999) hypothesize that uncertainty avoidance, masculinity, and individualism have attenuating or mitigating effects on consumer innovativeness, then use measures of the three culture dimensions and a cross-national survey of consumers in 11 countries to examine those hypotheses.

Of the 141 studies that incorporate culture theories, approximately two-fifths (42 percent) use them explicitly, and the remainder (58 percent) employ them implicitly ($\chi^2 = 4.056$, $p < .05$). These proportions do not shift over the decade ($\chi^2 = .136$, $p < .10$), which suggests that culture theories, though increasingly popular, generally are referred to or used vaguely, which inhibits their contribution to the knowledge base. Knowledge advancement is arguably constrained by the predominance of implicit applications of culture theories. Generally in research, it is not sufficient to mention theories; rather, researchers must apply them in structured ways to maximize learning of the subject phenomenon.

Another indication that the use of culture theories tends to be loose and informal is our finding that the majority of studies (85 percent) have no explicit measure of culture, and only a minority apply an explicit measure (15 percent) ($\chi^2 = 67.63$, $p < .001$). Without an explicit measure, many studies revert to implying culture in their design by using country as a proxy (64 percent) rather than circumscribing culture deliberately (36 percent) ($\chi^2 = 10.17$, $p < .001$). For example, a study might conduct a survey in Japan and assume that respondents, given their national origin, represent collectivism. However, this approach ignores that other factors or even levels of culture, above or below that of the nation, may cause the observed effects. Any attribution of effects may erroneously be assigned to national culture. The flaws of the country-as-surrogate-for-culture assumption have been noted repeatedly in major reviews of global marketing literature, yet culture studies still do not fully reflect this understanding (Saimee and Jeong, 1994; Sekaran, 1984; Sivakumar and Nakata, 2000).

We also examined the use of culture theories in terms of geographic scope, which implies the nature of culture proposed by the theories. Culture can be defined at any geographic level at which a collective of people exists. For example, in the single country of the United Kingdom, there are distinctive cultures by region, such as Wales versus Northern Ireland. Similarly, culture can move up in the unit of analysis and refer to the nation (United Kingdom), trading bloc (European Union), group of contiguous nations (Western and Eastern Europe), cluster of shared religious and political histories (Western Hemisphere), or, largest of all, the world (global culture). Social scientists have formulated and studied culture across this range, as in Anderson's (1991) study of nationalism, which uses a country-level construct; Fukuyama's (1995) treatise on social capital, which considers culture a supranational construct; and Putnam and colleagues' (1993) examination of northern versus southern cultures in Italy, in which culture is a regional phenomenon.

To understand whether this range is reflected in the literature, we classify each of the articles with culture theories into five possible geographic scopes: world, regional, national, subnational, and trading zone. Nation is far and away the most popular geographic scope (70 percent), consistent with the previous finding that country often serves as a surrogate for culture. After nation, the most common scope is subnation (6 percent), followed by region (2 percent) and trading bloc (1 percent). In an example of a study that defines culture by trading bloc, Dawar and Parker (1994) investigate culture according to the trading region and culture cluster in consumer assessments of price and quality. However, we find no studies that define culture as a world-wide phenomenon (0 percent) ($\chi^2 = 10.17$, $p < .001$) (consistent with Earley's point earlier in this book about the lack of universal interpretations of culture). One-fifth of the culture studies (20 percent) are sufficiently vague about the geographic expanse of culture that we cannot classify them.

The distribution of studies by geographic scope changes significantly over the decade, with a notable increase in the number of studies circumscribing culture by national borders ($\chi^2 = 20.86$, $p < .05$). The percentage rises from 63 percent of all studies to 79 percent. Clearly, an understanding of cultural formulations beyond the nation-state is lagging. By comparison, just 3 percent of studies examine culture as a regional entity in the first half of the decade, dropping to 0 percent in the second half. This lack of studies represents a curious deficit in light of the increasingly crucial role of regional trade agreements, such as the EU, NAFTA, Mercosur, and ASEAN, in the global economy. Businesses are scrambling to understand the implications of evolving market federations like the EU, yet research is all but absent regarding their cultural dynamics and marketing implications.

In addition to examining geographic scope according to these five classifications, we consider it in terms of another typology: single country, comparative (more than one country), regional, or global. This alternative schema helps us determine if culture theories may be used in a narrower (single country or comparative) or broader (regional or global) way, or else more or less evenly across this spectrum of possibilities. Our analysis shows that culture theories tend to be construed and applied narrowly, with 22 percent of studies investigating one country and 43 percent addressing several countries (mostly two countries), though one-third (32 percent) apply culture theories in a global framework. Again, regional interpretations of culture are relatively rare (3 percent) ($\chi^2 = 49.94$, $p < .001$). These proportions do not alter significantly over the course of the decade. Therefore, though the country-level, and notably single- and dual-country–level construals of culture predominate, we find some indication of broadening global culture frameworks, a promising sign that culture occasionally is being interpreted in a more complex and encompassing fashion.

Nature and structure of culture theories

We next sought to answer questions about what types of culture theories have appeared in the literature, as well as what this finding suggests about the ability of those theories to promote learning. We approach these issues by applying a schema that describes the nature and structure of theories in international marketing, as initially presented by Clark (1990) with regard to the value and validity of culture theories in international marketing. Having reviewed the historical development of schools of thought about culture, Clark developed a typology of culture theories based on the nature of culture and the means of deriving theories. He outlines four types: culture-centered/theoretical, culture-centered/empirical, personality-centered/theoretical, and personality-centered/empirical. He also terms the first type "double theoretical" and the last "double empirical" (Clark, 1990, p. 72). Double-theoretical frameworks assume that culture expresses itself in the full scope of human practices and beliefs and may be arrived at deductively from intuitive insights, as is Barker's (1948) theory of heredity and environment. The antipode, the double-empirical framework, is wholly empirically driven, such that theory is generated as a post hoc explanation for data, often with the assistance of factor analyses. These frameworks are "devoid of substantial theory where it counts" (Clark, 1990, p. 72). For example, with his universal culture values, Hofstede was interested in profiling worker attitudes in a firm's international subsidiaries; he did not seek at the outset to find, nor did he theorize beforehand, the dimensions of culture.

Neither the double-theoretical nor the double-empirical form is recommended. Instead, Clark promotes the culture-centered/empirical and personality-centered/theoretical forms as preferable, because they offer both a rigorous empirical basis and a rich theoretical rooting. In a culture-centered/empirical theory, culture represents a complex societal-level phenomenon, and naturalistic inquiry, such as ethnography, should be used to determine its features. In the personality-centered/theoretical theory, culture is formulated inductively and crucially *a priori* as a modal personality. Subsequent tests of such theories use statistical analyses of aggregated, individual-level personality data. Examples of the two types are Hall's (1976) context conceptualization and Triandis's (1989) individualism–collectivism notion, respectively.

Using Clark's schema, we classify previous studies that have explicitly incorporated culture theories. Most (70 percent) fall into the double-empirical category, whereas approximately one-fifth use culture-centered/empirical (18 percent). The least frequent are double-theoretical (7 percent) and personality-centered/theoretical (5 percent) frameworks ($\chi^2 = 64.05$, $p < .001$). The dominance of the double-empirical variety indicates a general weakness in culture papers. As noted by Clark (1990, p. 72), such paradigms at best "represent a good starting point for richer, more interpretive assessments," but at worst "run the risk of degenerating into 'fishing expeditions' in which fortuitously discovered patterns in the data are given meaning no *a priori* theory would allow." In summary, our analyses of the nature and structure of culture theories point to rather significant shortcomings in the paradigms most frequently applied—shortcomings related to the possession of a desired theoretical richness and empirical foundation.

Another way of examining the nature and structure of culture theories applies the method for classifying theories developed by Sullivan (1998), who observes that theories can be divided into three groups on the basis of their complexity: analog, composite, and propositional. Analog theories are the most basic, representing phenomena with unidirectional, determinate effects. These theories frequently are represented by box-and-arrow diagrams, with the arrows moving in one direction to imply the main effects of one set of variables on another. Propositional theories in contrast represent phenomena with influences in multiple directions simultaneously and sometimes recursively. Constructs may be dependent variables in one rendition of the theory but act as independent, interactive, or mediating variables in another. Composite theories fall between analog and propositional in complexity, in that they reflect both linear and hierarchical relations between some constructs, as well as moderated relations between others. Complexity increases when moving from analog to composite to propositional theories. Generally, more structurally elaborate theories are preferable, insofar as they more comprehensively and accurately depict the well-known intricacies of culture and the contingent, contextualized nature of global marketing (McSweeney 2002; Sheth 2001). On the basis of this typology of theories, we classify those studies with explicit culture theories.

The overwhelming majority (91 percent) of studies use analog culture frameworks, whereas a handful presents composite and propositional theories (2 and 7 percent, respectively) ($\chi^2 = 145.05$, $p < .001$). Over the ten-year period, no significant shift occurs in these proportions ($\chi^2 = .85$, $p < .10$). Thus, the culture frameworks that continue to predominate in the literature take the simplest, unidirectional form and ignore the multiplex nature and effects of culture. This finding suggests that the theoretical development of culture knowledge within global marketing remains at an early stage, not yet progressing to capture more nuanced but critical dimensions of culture and its relations with other key phenomena.

A third way of understanding the nature and structure of culture theories is to examine the way in which culture is positioned in relation to other constructs. As implied by the analog form, the most basic positioning figures culture as an independent construct with one or more main effects on another construct. An example would be proposing that culture directly influences consumer receptivity to certain forms of advertising, such as greater individualism leading to more positive responses to individualistic advertising appeals. Yet composite and propositional theories assume that culture has more complex ties to other constructs, including its roles as a mediator, moderator, or even dependent construct. An illustration of the latter concept might theorize that global media and the standardization of marketing mixes across countries increase the homogeneity of cultures worldwide, along the thrust of Theodore Levitt's (1983) famed globalization argument. In this case, culture appears as a dependent construct, influenced by two other constructs, namely, global media and standardized marketing mixes.

To assess the degree to which culture has been positioned as an independent versus a mediating, moderating, or dependent construct in culture theories, we further classify existing literature into these four groups. A majority of theories consider culture to be an independent force or variable (55 percent), a minority imagine it as a mediating or moderating influence (6 percent), and none include it as a dependent element (0 percent) ($\chi^2 = .006$, $p < .001$). A comparison of the first half of the decade with the second indicates no change in these proportions. In other words, as noted by Taras and Steele's chapter in this book, culture is almost always a causal force rather than effect or something in between. Thus, the literature as a whole has maintained culture theories of the simplest variety, not examining culture as potentially more complex or with intervening, interactive, or recursive effects. This finding is consistent with the results we obtain using Clark's and Sullivan's schemas.

Specific culture theories

Finally, we set out to determine which specific culture theories systematically are integrated more often and how this occurrence changes over time. As suggested by the popularity of double-empirical models, Hofstede's universal culture paradigm is the most ubiquitous, appearing in more than two-thirds (68 percent) of the culture papers with explicit theories ($\chi^2 = 54.69$, $p < .001$). Its frequency increases over the course of ten years, from 60 percent to 75 percent. Through a series of cross-cultural surveys of IBM employees, Geert Hofstede identified four independent bipolar values that, in composite, represent national culture. Standardized indices for these values in more than 60 countries enable researchers to make direct cross-national comparisons, undoubtedly contributing to the utility and pliability of the theory. Another indication of its popularity is the finding that Hofstede's work, *Culture's Consequences* (1980, 2001), has been cited almost 5000 times according to the ISI database, making it one of the most referred manuscripts across the social sciences (see Taras and Steel in this book as well as Taras and Steel, 2006). Others have concluded that Hofstede's paradigm, given its widespread and growing use, is the most influential culture theory (Kirkman et al., 2006).

After Hofstede, the most frequently used culture framework is that of Hall (1976). With a frequency of just 14 percent, however, Hall's method falls in a far secondary position relative to Hofstede, and its usage drops over time from 24 to 6 percent. Hall's theory predates Hofstede's and uses secondary data, personal interviews, and direct observations of group and individual behaviors in Japan, the United States, England, and other countries. An anthropologist, Hall posited that societies could be divided into two groups, high and low context. High-context groups prefer complex, embedded, indirect forms of messaging (e.g., silence), whereas low-context persons emphasize direct, expressive, and transparent styles (e.g., verbal repartee). Beyond communications, he refers to aspects of time and space, such as chronicity and proxemics, resulting in an arguably more nuanced theory than Hofstede's. The intuitively appealing framework commonly appears in international marketing and business textbooks.

Triandis's (1989) theory of individualism–collectivism ranks third in frequency at 3 percent. Triandis argues that cultures reflect the dominant individual personality in a society, specifically preferences for sampling information. If most individuals prefer to sample informa-tion about themselves, the group has an individualistic culture; if most attend to information about others or the self in relation to others, the society is a collectivist culture. Finally, we find a few other culture theories, but they appear so infrequently that we grouped them in the category 'others.' Among them are theories of linguistic relativity by Whorf and cultural categories by McCracken (e.g., Applbaum and Jordt, 1996; Schmitt and Zhang, 1998).

The popularity of Hofstede's conceptualization appears to be behind the rise of culture theories in the global marketing studies we review. The theory has been used to understand a wide range of phenomena in the global context, including service tipping, branding imagery, emotional advertising appeals, and product diffusion (e.g., Ganesh et al., 1997; Lynn et al., 1993). Perhaps scholars have converged on Hofstede's work because it presents a practical and powerful theory that in a Darwinian fashion eliminates weaker, competing ideas; in effect, it has thus proven to be the best culture theory. However, there is reason to question this conclusion. As observed by McSweeney (2002), Taras and Steel (2006), and others, the theory has critical lapses, including a limited charac-terization of culture (e.g., national culture as static, homogeneous) and methodological flaws (e.g., survey of work, not culture, values and all in one company). Moreover, per our preceding analysis, Hofstede's paradigm falls in the double-empirical category, which is useful but not preferable in terms of its capacity to generate substantive learning.

Several observations also emerge about the role of Hofstede's theory in global marketing. Its wide and sustained popularity suggests that researchers have found it very valuable for investigating cultural effects in global markets and marketing. It has thus undeniably made significant contributions to the knowledge base. However, from another vantage point, this situation raises the question of whether the paradigm's dominance is entirely positive or healthy for knowledge production. As noted previously, Hofstede's framework is of the double-empirical variety. The mammoth studies conducted by Hofstede were designed to understand workplace values among IBM employees dispersed across more than 60 international subsidiaries. Hofstede did not intend nor expect to find culture or a culture model in the data prior to engaging in its collection. Factor analysis, followed by post hoc review of culture studies, enabled him to label and provide a theoretical basis for the four universal values he discovered. Although the framework has now gained a fairly solid theoretical girding, it was erected after the data were analyzed. The empirically driven nature of the theory makes it less than ideal.

A second observation about Hofstede's theory suggests that it has low structural complexity, subjecting it to further criticism. It is an analog theory, the simplest kind. Each of the four values—individualism, power distance, uncertainty avoidance, and masculinity—is proposed to affect another variable autonomously, as typically used in global marketing studies; for example, power distance influences managerial decision-making style (e.g., more authoritative rather than participatory). Yet certain values are highly correlated (e.g., collectivism and power distance), though interactions are rarely specified. In essence, the factors are treated discretely, each with highly deterministic effects (McSweeney, 2002). The good news is that this atomistic structure enables taking the factors independently and investigating their impact on focal variables. The downside is that this approach, well tried, is unlikely to capture subtleties and myriad influences moving concurrently, combinatorially, or in multiple directions, as is said to be characteristic of culture (Crane, 1994; Sowell, 1994). With this perspective, Hofstede's formulation can be viewed as excessively reductionist. In summary, Hofstede's theory, though a significant contributor to advancing knowledge in global marketing, on its own and through its heavy usage by researchers, is unlikely to produce all the required or desired learning about culture in global marketing.

Conclusions

The purpose of this study has been to understand the use, role, and nature of culture theories in global marketing. We address this purpose with a literature-based assessment of prior studies in leading scholarly global marketing journals. We draw several conclusions from this assessment. In particular, given their fair and increased presence in published research (more than one-quarter of all studies in the second half of the decade examined), culture theories over time claim a clear stake in the field and thus warrant serious consideration. They are not peripheral but provide significant knowledge that can be applied by practitioners to guide decision-making and by researchers to fathom the role of culture in global marketing phenomena.

At the same time, our assessment indicates that the promise of culture theories to strengthen the conceptual girding of global marketing studies might not be fulfilled or at least not as well as it could be. As we examined how theories were used, we found that most were applied implicitly, with a bit of hand-waving that acknowledges culture as a factor but fails to investigate its role formally with respect to the subject under study. The majority of studies use country as a surrogate for culture and do not apply an explicit measure of culture. Furthermore, nation and a single country or multiple countries specifically serve as the predominant geographic focus, ignoring the possibility that culture might be interpreted as occurring at levels above or below that of the nation state, as has been widely acknowledged among culture theorists (Crane, 1994; Sowell, 1994). All these approaches to culture necessarily limit learning about culture and how it matters to global marketing.

More indicative of the limitations of culture theories in previous literature is the dominance of a certain kind of and specific paradigm: double-empirical, analog models. And among those specifically used, Hofstede's looms large, responsible for more than two-thirds of culture studies. This paradigm is beguilingly parsimonious, highly functional for quantitative manipulation, and repeatedly supported through empirical testing, all of which may explain its frequent usage. Nonetheless, as pointed out by Clark (1990), double-empirical culture theories are less than ideal owing to their narrow conceptual moorings, and, as noted by Sullivan (1998), analog models are rudimentary and do not accurately capture the complex, dynamic nature of international business settings. Culture is acknowledged as multiplex and evolving, and double-empirical theories may minimize these realities (Kluckhohn and Kluckhohn 1973).

In addition, as per Sullivan (1998) and Sullivan and Weaver (2000), a discipline is better served and knowledge is more clearly advanced when there are a variety of and multiple theories and theory types competing for influence rather than a single or handful of theories. Our interest is not to engage in a discussion of the merits and detractions of Hofstede's theory; others can and have done a far better job (e.g., McSweeney, 2002; Steenkamp, 2001; Taras and Steel, 2006). Instead, we explore the issue of how culture theories may best contribute to global marketing knowledge. We posit that there is something to be gained by stepping back from research endeavors, noting that though the discipline of international marketing is still evolving, now is an opportune moment to widen the field of vision on culture.

Broadening the horizons of our understanding of culture requires us to engage in interdisciplinary research as well as to inquire, welcome, and utilize alternative conceptualizations of culture. One such conceptualization is recently offered by the burgeoning research stream within the marketing domain, Consumer Culture Theory (CCT), as

> the very fabric of experience, meaning, and action. . . . Rather than viewing culture as a fairly homogenous system of collectively shared meanings, ways of life, and unifying values shared by a member of society (e.g., Americans share this kind of culture; Japanese share that kind of culture), CCT explores the heterogeneous distribution of meanings and the multiplicity of overlapping cultural groupings that exist within the broader sociohistoric frame of globalization and market capitalism.
>
> (Arnould and Thompson, 2005, pp. 868–9)

This fragmented, plural, and fluid view of culture not only broadens our existing notions of culture and culture theories but enables researchers to investigate culture at micro-level social formations, such as subcultures and brand communities. One caveat of this perspective, however, is that its focus on individual-level meanings does not lend CCT studies to macro-level literature assessments such as ours.

Other alternative conceptualizations with application to global marketing are dynamic theories of culture, as explained hereafter in chapters by Briley as well as Liu and Dale. Unlike the Hofstede paradigm, where behaviors are said to be determined by membership in a national culture group, the dynamic view of culture posits that individuals' actions and decisions are governed by a complex constellation of factors, including situational ones. Hence individuals respond differently moment to moment depending on the context they find themselves in. This conceptualization does not deny the influence of national culture, but positions it as one of several determinants that interact with others to produce behavioral consequences. Marketers may find this view of culture to be a more powerful and comprehensive description of consumer as well as managerial behaviors, helping to explain what appears at times to be the idiosyncratic actions of people.

Although our analysis of culture theories in this chapter is limited, we encourage scholars to keep an open mind toward alternative definitions of culture; in a subsequent chapter, possible avenues are discussed for a broadening of culture theories gleaned through a reflexive reading of culture writings outside the global marketing domain. We are nonetheless hopeful that through the study presented in this chapter, which illuminates where we have been as a field of study and discipline, we can take the next step toward conceiving of culture outside of the dominant understanding. We take this step not for the sake of novelty, but in order to aid business practitioners and researchers in their quest to grapple with and manage the many profound implications of culture in today's global economy.

References

Albaum, G. & Peterson, R. A. (1984) "Empirical Research in International Marketing," *Journal of International Business Studies*, 15, 161–73.

Alden, D. L., Hoyer, W. D., & Lee, C. (1993) "Identifying Global and Culture-Specific Dimensions of Humor in Advertising: A Multinational Analysis," *Journal of Marketing*, 57, 64–75.

Anderson, B. (1991) Imagined Communities: Reflections on the Origin and Spread of Nationalism, 2nd edn. London, UK: Verso.

Applbaum, K. & Jordt, I. (1996) "Notes Toward an Application of McCracken's 'Cultural Categories' for Cross-Cultural Consumer Research," *Journal of Consumer Research*, 23 (December), 204–18.

Arnould, E. & Thompson, C. (2005) "Consumer Culture Theory (CCT): Twenty Years of Research," *Journal of Consumer Research*, 31 (March), 868–82.

Aulakh, P. & Kotabe, M. (1993) "An Assessment of Theoretical and Methodological Development in International Marketing: 1980–1990," *Journal of International Marketing*, 1, 5–29.

Barker, E. (1948), *National Character and the Factors in Its Formation*. New York, NY: Harper and Brothers.

Baumgartner, H. & Pieters, R. (2003) "The Structural Influence of Marketing Journals: A Citation Analysis of the Discipline and Its Subareas Over Time," *Journal of Marketing*, 67, 123–39.

Clark, T. (1990) "International Marketing and National Character: A Review and Proposal for an Integrative Theory," *Journal of Marketing*, 54, 66–79.

Crane, D. (1994) "Introduction: The Challenge of the Sociology of Culture to Sociology as a Discipline," in D. Crane (ed.), *The Sociology of Culture: Emerging Theoretical Perspectives*. Oxford, UK: Blackwell, 1–20.

Dawar, Niraj & Parker, P. (1994) "Marketing Universals: Consumers' Use of Brand Name, Price, Physical Appearance, and Retailer Reputation As Signals of Product Quality," *Journal of Marketing*, 58 (2), 81–96.

Dubois, F. L. & Reeb, D. (2000) "Ranking the International Business Journals," *Journal of International Business Studies*, 31, 689–704.

Erdem, T., Swait, J. & Valenzuela, A. (2006) "Brands as Signals: A Cross-Country Validation Study," *Journal of Marketing*, 70, 34–49.

Fukuyama, F. (1995) Trust: The Social Virtues and The Creation of Prosperity. New York, NY: The Free Press.

Ganesh, J., Kumar, V., & Subramaniam, V. (1997) "Learning Effect in Multinational Diffusion of Consumer Durables: An Exploratory Investigation," *Journal of the Academy of Marketing Science*, 25, 214–8.

Geertz, C. (1988) "Thick Description: Toward an Interpretive Theory of Culture," in P. Bohannan & M. Glazer (eds) *High Points in Anthropology*, 2nd edn. New York, NY: McGraw-Hill, 531–52.

Hall, E. (1976) *Beyond Culture*. New York, NY: Anchor Books.

Hofstede, G. (1980) Culture's Consequences: International Differences in Work-Related Values. Beverly Hills, CA: Sage Publications.

Hofstede, G. (2001) Culture's Consequences: Comparing Values, Behaviors, Institutions and Organizations Across Nations. Thousand Oaks, CA: Sage Publications.

Hofstede, G. & Bond, M. H. (1988) "The Confucius Connection: From Cultural Roots to Economic Growth," *Organizational Dynamics*, 16, 5–21.

Hult, G. T., Neese, W. T., & Bashaw, R. E. (1997) "Faculty Perceptions of Marketing Journals," *Journal of Marketing Education*, 19, 37–44.

Hunt, S. D. (1990) Modern Marketing Theory: Critical Issues in the Philosophy of Marketing Science. Cincinnati, OH: South-Western Publishing, 130–49.

Keegan, W. J. & Green, M. C. (2008) *Global Marketing*, 5th edn. Upper Saddle River, NJ: Prentice-Hall.

Kirkman, B. L., Lowe, K. B., & Gibson, C. (2006) "A Quarter Century of Culture Consequences: A Review of Empirical Research Incorporating Hofstede's Cultural Values Framework," *Journal of International Business Studies*, 37 (3), 285–320.

Kluckhohn, F., & Kluckhohn, F. (1973) *Variations in Value Orientations*. Westport, CT: Greenwood Press.

Levitt, T. (1983) "The Globalization of Markets," *Harvard Business Review*, 61 (3), 91–103.

Li, T. & Cavusgil, S. T. (1995) "A Classification and Assessment of Research Streams in International Marketing," *International Business Review*, 4 (3), 251–77.

Lynn, M., Zinkhan, G. M., & Harris, J. (1993) "Consumer Tipping: A Cross-Country Study," *Journal of Consumer Research*, 20, 478–88.

McSweeney, B. (2002) "Hofstede's Model of National Cultural Differences and Their Consequences: A Triumph of Faith–A Failure of Analysis," *Human Relations*, 55 (1), 89–118.

Putnam, R. B., Leonardi, R. & Nanetti. R. Y. (1993) *Making Democracy Work: Civic Traditions in Modern Italy*. Princeton, NJ: Princeton University Press.

Samiee, S. & Jeong, I. (1994) "Cross-Cultural Research in Advertising: An Assessment of Methodologies," *Journal of Academy of Marketing Science*, 22 (3), 205–21.

Schmitt, B. H. & Zhang, S. (1998) "Language Structure and Categorization: A Study of Classifiers in Consumer Cognition, Judgment, and Choice," *Journal of Consumer Research*, 25 (September), 108–22.

Sekaran, U. (1984) "Methodological and Theoretical Issues and Advancements in Cross-Cultural Research," *Journal of International Business Studies*, 14 (2), 61–73.

Sheth, J. (2001) "From International to Integrated Marketing," *Journal of Business Research*, 51, 5–9.

Shweder, R. A. (1984) "Preview: A Colloquy of Culture Theorists," in R. A. Shweder & R. A. Levine (eds) *Culture Theory: Essays on Mind, Self, and Emotion*. Cambridge, UK: Cambridge University Press, 1–26.

Sivakumar, K. & Nakata, C. (2000) "The Stampede Toward Hofstede's Framework: Avoiding the Sample Design Pit in Cross-Cultural Research," *Journal of International Business Studies*, 32 (3), 555–74.

Sowell, T. (1994) *Race and Culture: A World View*. New York: Basic Books.

Steenkamp, J. E. M. (2001) "The Role of National Culture in International Marketing Research," *International Marketing Review*, 18 (1), 30–44.

Steenkamp, J. E. M., Hofstede, F., & Wedel, M. (1999) "Cross-National Investigation into Individual and National Culture Antecedents of Consumer Innovativeness," *Journal of Marketing*, 63 (2), 55–69.

Sullivan, D. P. (1998) "Cognitive Tendencies in International Business Research: Implications to the Matter of a Narrow Vision," *Journal of International Business Studies*, 29, 837–63.

Sullivan, D. P. & Weaver, G. R. (2000) "Cultural Cognition in International Business Research," *Management International Review*, 40 (3), 269–97.

Taras, V. & Steel, P. (2006) "Culture as Consequence: A Multilevel Multivariate Meta-Analysis of the Effects of Individual and Country Characteristics on Work-Related Cultural Values," *Academy of Management 2006 Annual Meeting Best Paper Proceedings*.

Triandis, H. C. (1989) "The Self and Behavior in Differing Cultural Contexts," *Psychological Review*, 96, 506–52.

Tylor, E. B. (1958) *The Origins of Culture*, previously published as Chapters I–X of *Primitive Culture*, 1871. Gloucester, MA: Harper and Row.

Wang, C. C. L. (1999) "Issues and Advances in International Consumer Research: A Review and Assessment," *Journal of International Marketing and Marketing Research*, 24, 3–21.

Whetten, D. A. (1989) "What Constitutes a Theoretical Contribution?," *Academy of Management Review*, 14 (4), 490–5.

Part III   Conceptualizations of the Culture Problem

5
Culture in Context: New Theorizing for Today's Complex Cultural Organizations

Mary Yoko Brannen

As multinational companies (MNCs) race for the future while racing for the world motivated by the promise of scale economies in globalizing industries, they are doing so increasingly in the form of wholly integrated global firm structures in the wake of cross-border mergers, acquisitions, joint-ventures and alliances (Brannen and Peterson, 2009; Shimizu et al., 2004; Stahl and Mendenhall, 2005). In fact, today's economy is more globalized than it has ever been and, at least on the surface of it, the world looks more culturally integrated today than ever before as fast-paced, quick-to-market industries spread global trends like wild fire from East to West or West to East and back again. But, this is just a superficial impression. Just because schoolgirls throughout the world from California to Moscow are wearing Sanrio fashions and buying Gwen Stefani Harajuku Lovers perfume does not mean they know anything about what the life of one of those Japanese schoolgirls who rebelliously lets her hair down (figuratively, of course—more likely she puts it up in all sorts of creative, outrageous innovations) on the Harajuku overpass, joining her friends on Sundays, rain or shine. Likewise, just because corporate leaders of large MNCs have been managing across cultures for their entire careers and in many cases are managing across cultures daily right within the diverse cultural makeup of their own home organizations, does not mean that they have a sophisticated or even functionally agile understanding of how culture impacts the day-to-day enactment of their corporate strategy in their subsidiaries in Bangalore or Kunshan.

In fact, more than ever, what corporate leaders are discovering is that what they really lack is deep contextual understanding—specifically about culture in context. With little, superficial, or no training, today's time-pressed, multi-tasking, dislocated corporate leaders are finding themselves confronted with significant feelings of uncertainty and frustration as they struggle in real time through litmus-tests of deep contextual understanding. They find, for example, that differences in cultural sense-making in foreign subsidiaries curtail successful transfer of technologies and practices developed in the home cultural environment (Brannen et al., 1999; Fiss and Zajac, 2004) or act as barriers to strategic fit in knowledge-sharing across distance and differentiated contexts (Brannen, 2004).

Armed with only artifact-level understandings of cultural differences (cf. Schein, 1985) proliferated by easy-to-learn, fast-to-recall dimensions offered by Hofstede and other proponents of the aggregate values-based models of culture reviewed in earlier chapters of this book, global leaders find themselves stereotype rich and operationally poor where culture meets context. The fast-paced, interdependent, interactive nature of today's global economy has only pushed to the forefront what anthropologists and other close observers of culture have always known. From a distance, meanings and people's sense-making patterns might well be seen as commonly shared by a cultural group while differences across cultures are seen as great (Geppert and Clark, 2003; Zellmer-Bruhn, 2003). But, up close, when individuals with varying preconceptions (thanks to globalization) about each other's multiple cultures (national, regional, sub-organizational, etc.) and contexts (institutional, organizational, occupational, etc.) attempt to transfer, syncronize, learn from and even co-create, the use-value of these aggregate level cultural frameworks begins to seriously break down (Brannen and Salk, 2000; Brannen, 2004). As such, the culture construct in organization studies is at a pivotal crossroads. One could argue that the culture construct has always has been at a difficult juncture given the disparity between viewing culture "up close" versus "far and away." But, today the world economy is more globalized, interconnected, and co-arising than at any point in time, and what was once an occasional handicap in our understanding of culture and context is now at the least a significant missed opportunity and at the worst a major stumbling block. Given this pressing need to understand culture in context, this chapter zooms into this crossroads, focuses on the multi-faceted nature of the crossroads from complexities of the culture construct itself to tensions in the field exacerbated by the multiplicity of complexities facing today's global leaders, and concludes by outlining an alternative path toward conceptualizing culture for today's complex cultural organizations.

The crossroads

There are multiple forks in the crossroads faced by the culture construct, indeed so many that one might imagine rather an intricate topographical map in place of a simple Cartesian one as we navigate the complexities of understanding culture in context.

Complexities of the culture construct itself

Paradigmatic Appropriateness. Studies in cross-cultural management come predominantly from either what Burrell and Morgan term a "positivist" or "interpretive" paradigmatic orientation, with the former enjoying a certain hegemonic position in management studies (cf. previous chapter by Nakata and Izberk-Bilgin; also Lowe, 2001; Romani, 2008). As such, most research on global firms takes on a positivist ontology in which reality is seen as something "out there," measurable and objective, independent of the researchers themselves (Burell and Morgan, 1979). The dominance of the positivist paradigm in culture studies has thus led to a dominant epistemology in international management research characterized by a pursuit of causal relationships based on binary logic—a logic of "us"/"them" that maps nicely on to the aggregate value-based dimensions as put forth by Hofstede. The anthropologist Eric Wolf (1982, p. 34; cf. Brannen, 1994) calls such binary representations "two billiard ball" understandings of culture. National cultures are treated as monolithic entities (billiard balls) made up of fixed values that either collide, leading to unsuccessful ventures, or miss grazing each other rolling side by side, thus allowing the cultures to remain unscathed from the interaction. Clearly, when little was known about other cultures (especially in the field of management), something was better than nothing and having general guidelines for protocol helped expatriates and others crossing cultural boundaries to avoid getting off on the wrong path by inadvertently insulting their hosts or such. However, the positivist approach alone proves to be somewhat ineffective at dealing with the complex embedded, interconnected, and dynamic nature of today's contexts of cross-cultural management. The multifaceted ongoing contextually situated interactions that characterize today's complex cultural organizations demand a more nuanced interpretive paradigmatic approach (Redding, 1994 cited in Romani, 2008). Such an approach would go far in complementing positivist aggregate values-based views. Rather than treating culture as a variable to be measured and assessed, the interpretive approach essentially understands culture as a root metaphor for organizations (cf. Frost et al., 1985; Pondy et al., 1983; Smircich, 1983). The central features of the interpretive approach are laid out by Alvesson and Sköldberg (2000, pp. 58–66): namely, a search for tacit meanings rather than causal relationships (deep assumption-level cultural constructs following Schein, 1985); a view of organizational life as narrative or "text" replete with meaningful symbols rather than data and facts; an understanding of the subjective nature of research versus a purely objective view; and finally an understanding of the dynamic, interactive nature of culture. Such a paradigm shift (or complement as offered by the interpretive view) in the culture construct would go far to increase the efficacy of the culture construct in understanding pressing issues faced by today's complex cultural organizations. Further, such a paradigmatic shift would help open the way toward middle-range, process-based theories that might then lead to more dynamic models for understanding the interaction between global leaders, foreign managers and host country employees.

Level of Analysis Attentiveness.   Another theoretical fallout from generalizing to the aggregate whole is the propensity to ignore level of analysis appropriateness of the culture construct. In the organization studies literature this propensity was first exposed in the 1980s critique of the corporate culture literature in which organizations were treated as predominantly monocultural entities assuming a culturally homogeneous workforce (see Gregory, 1983; Martin and Siehl, 1983; Smircich, 1983; Van Maanen and Barley, 1984). These organizational culture scholars, following Whyte (1948) and Turner (1972), illuminated the co-existence of multiple frames of reference of the culture construct including national, organizational, occupational, as well as sub- and counter-cultures within them.

   Yet, nowhere is this inattentiveness to level of analysis more apparent than in the international management literature where the word "culture" is still, much more often than not, used synonymously with "nation," and national cultural traits are treated as systematically predictable behavioral patterns (Bhagat et al., 2002; Child, 1981; Roberts, 1970). The lack of cross-fertilization between organization studies and international management is unfortunate. US academe has been criticized for being sluggish in paying attention to even the most pressing domestic US cross-cultural issues such as cultural diversity, let alone to cross-cultural interactions between US and foreign parties (Adler, 1983; Boyacigiller and Adler, 1991; Gelfand et al., 2007). Further, the main framework for understanding such phenomena in international business has been Hofstede's cultural dimensions whose static, monolithic framework of national cultural differences does little to help explain how individuals embedded in multiple cultural spheres of reference from disparate national cultural systems are able to work together in an integrated fashion in today's complex cultural arenas. In sum, the international management literature continues to be unsophisticated in regard to the complexity of the culture construct while the organizational studies literature continues, for the most part, to be quite parochial.

The Nature of Culture Itself. Beyond the significant limitations of the positivist paradigm's penchant for fixing culture as static and monolithic, the lack of progress in conceptualization of a useful working understanding of culture as it impacts today's organizations stems largely from this level-of-analysis conundrum. This theoretical stagnation can be further traced to a fundamental misunderstanding of the nature of culture itself, namely that although culture is generally spoken of as a group level phenomenon, it is dynamically created and enacted by individual members (Van Maanen and Barley, 1984). As such there are significant differences within cultures that are overlooked when cultural elements are aggregated to the whole. Further, individuals are typically members of several sub-cultural groups at the same time. Therefore, an individual's cultural makeup is composed of a cross-section of traits from simultaneous memberships in several subcultures such as men, women, people from different regions, class, religion, and ethnicity, to name just a few subgroups. Thus, an individual's "culture of origin" does not necessarily neatly reflect the general attributes of her or his representative national cultural group.

Individuals exhibit a range of personal fit with their national cultures of origin, reflecting their ongoing particular cultural histories in various contexts and subgroup combinations (Brannen, 1994). Even within national cultural groupings, individuals exhibit national cultural attributes ranging from those that might be considered "marginal" within a given national culture to those that would be considered "hyper-normal" or embodying mainstream national cultural attributes to a very strong degree (Brannen, 1994). And so, in organizational settings, individuals tend to take on a plethora of different stances ranging from hyper-normal, normal to marginal-normal in relation to a given cultural dimension (Brannen, 1994; also Brannen and Salk, 2000). For these reasons, organizational cultures often are not representative of national cultures.

Nature of Cultural Knowledge. As organizational scholars, as opposed to anthropologists or sociologists who might study "culture" for culture's sake, we are interested in understanding "culture" as it impacts manage-ment. Nowhere is the impact of culture on management more appar-ent than when global firms attempt to transfer core competencies to or from new contexts. Technology is always coupled with social and cultural systems, and if these linkages are left unmanaged, unexpected outcomes occur, frustrating successful transfer (cf. Brannen et al., 1999; Brannen, 2004).

Knowledge transfer involves the movement of knowledge elements from one context to another. In order to transfer a knowledge element from one context so that it might be effectively used in another, man-agers need to identify the scope of its interdependencies as well as how it is known and understood both in its place of original residence and as much as they can about where they want to move it (Brannen et al., 2007). In other words, managers (and management scholars) need to deeply understand "knowledge contexts."

The contexts of a knowledge element are multifarious and comprised of the entire range of operational and epistemological interdependen-cies between that element and all other elements of knowledge in the local knowledge structure. As such, categories of context are difficult to fully and exclusively specify. This is perhaps why even though the importance of context has been recognized, researchers have defined its boundaries, dimensions, and categories very differently and have related context to the effectiveness of global operations in diverse ways (e.g., Gupta and Govindajaran, 2000; Inkpen and Dinur, 1998; Kostova, 1999; Kostova and Roth, 2002; Lane, Lyles, and Salk, 1998).

Unexpected changes in the nature and content of knowledge occur through the process of recontextualization—the transformation of the meaning of knowledge elements as they are uprooted from one context and moved to another (Brannen, 2004). Every knowledge context is the embodiment of its own system of signification, involving distinct work-related assumptions, behaviors, and practices ("culture"). Given this, transformations in meaning easily occur as what is sent from one site is received and perceived within the local cultural context. However, because such shared understandings are necessarily context-dependent and therefore embedded in organizational structures and processes that are often tacit, and therefore taken for granted, as in the case of Toyota's "kaizen" processes, even after rendering them explicit by language—i.e. "continuous improvement"—(and in some cases translating them into functional equivalents in yet another language), uprooting and mov-ing them from one location to another will always be vulnerable to recontextualization. Given the contextual embeddedness of knowledge, planning for and monitoring recontextualization is neither obvious nor simple. Further, due to the often-tacit nature of knowledge in the originating context, and to the impossibility of knowing fully the receiving context, the sender will always be challenged in understanding all but the most obvious, artifact-level aspects of potential recontextualizations in the receiving context, such as differences in organizational structures, shop-floor layout, and supplier relations. What managers engaged in such transfers need is comprehensive understanding of the interpretations of both the sending and receiving cultures in order to facilitate processes of sense making across cultures.

Complex Cultural Combinations at the Individual Level.   Whereas we have known for quite some time that MNCs need individuals with such capabilities as described above, we have not realized that there is a growing new workforce demographic with latent skills in this area. By 2020 America's largest ethnic group will be culturally mixed. Already in the state of California 25 percent of the population is foreign born, and in the Silicon Valley 53.3 percent of the population is already non-white. This trend is paralleled in Europe given the low birth rates of the established population and the concomitant increase in proportion of non-European born and second-generation immigrants.

Such people of mixed ethnicities carry with them not only racial variation but also mixed cultural sensibilities. Whereas the racial demographics are relatively simple to track, account for, and describe, the accompanying mixed cultural sensibilities are less obvious, relatively undocumented, and not understood. Organizational decision makers, HR directors and the like, typically assume that aggregate national cultural values data (such as Hofstede's dimensions) are useful predictors of individual behavior and, as such, fall into simplistic "two billiard ball" assessments of an employee's use-value in different cultural contexts.

However, many biculturals, especially immigrants, have been away from their culture of origin for so long that they are "no longer from there" and, owing to their immigrant status, are obviously "not from here," so they end up being neither/nor in regard to the two national cultures that define them. Their children are often even more distant from the national cultures their ethnicities belie and often do not even speak the languages of their parents' countries of origin. So, judging books by their cover, as it were, as in employing Hofstede's cultural dimensions to individuals on the basis of their ethnicity, is pretty much ineffective in these cases.

Whereas biculturals may not all bring the expected culture specific knowledge, in the same way as we know that people who have learned multiple languages in their childhood find it easier to keep learning new languages late in life, biculturals often bring latent abilities to understand and bridge cultures. Current research is showing that biculturals actually have significantly different skill sets that they bring to organizations than monoculturals and that certain types of biculturals bring critical cultural general knowledge such as cross-cultural adaptability skills and cultural metacognition (Thomas, Brannen, and Garcia, 2008). Cultural metacognition refers to an understanding of one's own cognitive behavior in the planning and monitoring of performance, and in the use of cognitive strategies in particular cultural domains. The more complex cognitive representations that biculturals and multiculturals develop as a result of internalizing more than one set of cultural schemas the more they develop higher-order cognitive processes required to manage complexity. Nissan's Carlos Ghosn is a good case in point. When asked by *Newsweek*, "How much do you think your own multicultural background has shaped your ability to move from culture to culture?" Carlos answered,

> [i]t's fundamental, like learning a language when you're a kid. You're going to have mastery when you're an adult that you'll never have for a language that you are learning as an adult. Being in a multicultural environment in childhood is going to give you intuition, reflexes and instincts. You may acquire basic responsiveness later on, but it's never going to be as spontaneous as when you have been bathing in this environment during childhood.
>
> *Newsweek*, June 30, 2008

As increasing numbers of organizational members find themselves in complex cultural settings the concomitant organizational challenges revolve around coordination and collaboration across multiple cultural contexts both internationally and increasingly within one's own work unit. In a globalizing world, more managers and professionals are required to interact with individuals from other cultures, make and maintain cross-cultural connections, work in culturally mixed environments, and perform tasks with counterparts in different countries that require an understanding and sensitivity to different cultural perspectives. In addition, management success is based more and more on the transfer of information, knowledge, and practices, of "soft" or "people-dependent" technologies and of whole systems of organization across cultural boundaries (Doz et al., 2001; Brannen, Doz, and Santos, 2007). As a result, global business success depends increasingly not only on understanding different cultures but on being able to bridge cultures and integrate within complex cultural organizations. As collaboration, communication and trust-building gain importance and as flows of knowledge and processes become increasingly more critical success factors for global firms, the role of individuals in mediating between and within cultures becomes a vital part for organizational performance.

Biculturals and individuals with mixed cultural identities bring an insufficiently recognized opportunity to today's global organizations that our current understanding of the culture construct does not encompass. However, most biculturals are unaware of the skills that they possess as they have generally have felt "neither/nor," and, organizations that employ them are just as naive as to their skill sets, confusing ethnicity with country-specific understanding. For example, a Vietnamese-American might be better at facilitating and melding together knowledge from a multiplicity of national contexts rather than representing an American firm in Vietnam, a country that he has either not been part of in a long time or has never experienced first-hand. Such typical misunderstandings make it difficult for bicultural employees to contribute their most valuable skills and, at the same time, reinforce the personal insecurities they feel as neither/nor.

As biculturals and hybrids with mixed cultural schemas like Nissan's Carlos Goshn become more and more common, national cultural attributes as indicators of individual behavior will become less and less useful.

Tensions in the field

In sum, the notion of national culture itself is at the crossroads as abstract value-based understandings of culture fail the acid tests of current complex cultural realities in today's global firms. The crossroads are further exacerbated by complexities of embedded contexts (home, host, global, virtual, etc.) and complex technologies—the commingling of cultures side by side, two in one, as well as multiple cultural identities. All of this results in complex leadership challenges. Today's global leaders need to be able to think globally as well as locally, possess cultural intelligence (general versus specific cultural knowledge), and, most critically, be able to leverage cultural metacognition by exercising mindfulness in mediating cultural knowledge and employing skillful bridging behaviors.

Going forward—A model for conceptualizing culture as contextually negotiated content

In response to the limitations of the management literature on culture in providing an adequate framework for understanding the cultural dynamics in today's complex cultural organizational settings, I propose a model of culture as contextually negotiated content. The model builds on the "negotiated culture" approach, which views organizations as settings where patterns of meaning and agency arise from the ongoing interactions and exchanges of its members in particular organizational contexts (cf. Brannen, 1994; Brannen and Salk, 2000; Ong, 1987; Salk and Brannen, 2000). The concept of negotiated order is a related concept in sociology following Anselm Strauss's articulation of the approach (1978, 1982), which was founded on earlier theory development in cultural dynamics in the field of sociology (cf. Mead, 1934; Hughes, 1958; Dalton, 1959; and Goffman, 1961). For Strauss the structure of an organization and the micro politics of its negotiated order are closely tied:

> The negotiated order on any given day could be conceived of as the sum total of the organization's rules and policies, along with whatever agreements, understandings, pacts, contracts, and other working arrangement currently obtained. These include agreements at every level of organization, of every clique and coalition, and include covert as well as overt agreements.
>
> (1978, pp. 5–6)

The current model is informed by new developments in anthropological theory on culture (Abu-Lughod, 2000; Appuradai, 1996; Clifford, 1988; Clifford and Marcus, 1986; Marcus and Fisher, 1986; Roseberry, 1989; Tomlinson, 1999) and theoretically induced through ethnographic studies of global firms operating in distinct institutional contexts ranging from soft, people-dependent technologies such as theme parks and entertainment (Brannen, 1992; 2004), to hard technologies such as ballbearings (Brannen et al., 1999) and specialty paper (Brannen, 1994), to knowledge-intensive technologies such as pharmaceuticals and semiconductors (Brannen et al., 2009). The model complements our current knowledge of national and organizational culture by suggesting a framework that is at once general in terms of describing how working cultures are "negotiated" in complex cultural contexts as well as specific in incorporating a conceptual base that allows for negotiations that are historically situated and dynamically enacted by individuals in particular organizational contexts.

The model is offered as an alternative to the binary, "billiard ball," version of cultural interaction. The latter suggests that one culture cannot alter the structural integrity or the internal cultural makeup of the other—again, either the billiard balls collide and bounce off of each other, or they roll side by side, co-existing without influencing each other. Rather than understanding cultures as discrete monolithic entities existing alongside without affecting each other, the model of negotiated culture suggests a view of cultural interaction wherein the effects of globalization are such that flows arise in cultures (national, organizational, and even individual cultural identities) from cross-cultural reciprocal action in the various contextual mediums in which they are immersed.

The model presented here takes these fluctuations in the cultural "body" of organizations as negotiated exchanges and describes how culture is thus co-arising in complex cultural contexts. "Negotiate" is used as a verb to encourage us to think of organizational phenomena as individuals actively navigating through specific contextually situated issues in evolving, culturally embedded, organizational settings. As such, the model highlights the constructive and reconstructive nature of culture as individual actors attach meanings to organizational artifacts, processes, and outcomes. Focusing on culture as contextually negotiated content therefore includes examining the cognitions and actions of organizational members, particularly in situations of conflict because it is in such situations that assumptions get raised to the forefront, utilized and critically subjected to the acid test of today's complex cultural realities.

Explanation of the model

The following propositions constitute the theoretical basis of the model.

Proposition 1a: Culture is imperfectly shared.

      1b: Individuals within cultures have "cultures of origins" reflecting their ongoing particular social histories in various cultural contexts (e.g., national, regional, organizational, familial).

      1c: There exists a range of person fit with cultural attributes over three discernable zones: "marginal normal" (MN), "cultural norm(al)" (CN), and "hyper-normal" (HN).

Definition of the three zones:
   Hyper-normal represents outliers within the culture holding more extreme beliefs (HN).
   Cultural norm(al) represents the dominant attitude set (CN).
   Marginally normal represents outliers not so committed to the "normal" beliefs (MN).

Culture is traditionally defined as a shared entity, often depicted in the bounds of a circle as in "the Japanese—circle J" and "the Americans—circle A." The circles are offered as graphical aggregate representations of the cultural norm for individuals within national cultures who represent the cultural norm. We can imagine in Figure 5.1 that culture thus portrayed would be a circle with a diameter roughly plus or minus two standard deviations from the mean of a "normal" curve. However, taking the normal curve analogy further, Figure 5.1 suggests that there is rather a range of person fit with cultural attributes. Put another way, a person within a culture has his/her own "cultural stance" vis-à-vis the cultural norm. National cultures are subjective composites of an individual actor's negotiated cultural stances in regard to the collective norms of their societal group. There are three broad zones characterizing differentiable negotiated stances: "hyper-normal," representing outliers within the culture holding most extreme aspects of the societal norms; "cultural norm(al)," representing the dominant attitude set; and "marginal normal," representing outliers not so attached to the "normal" beliefs. The three zones are not distinct cultural subgroups. Rather, the broken boundaries between the zones indicate that the three zones represent different "attitude sets" along a continuum of values. Importantly, the

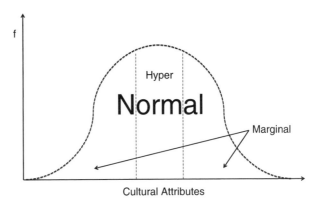

Figure 5.1   Person-fit with cultural norm

boundary of the normal curve itself is a broken line. This is so, in order to depict the dependent co-arising nature of culture as it goes through ongoing fluctuations as a result of recursive cultural interactions. In the context of today's complex globalized world economy, cultures can no longer be dealt with as monolithic entities or cultural isolates.

Proposition 2: Organizational culture may not be representative of national culture.

Organizational culture in today's global firms is enacted by a combination of individuals with diversely embedded cultural profiles often spread out over a variety of national cultural contexts. There is a large range of possible cultural profiles that can accompany people into organizations. It is possible to have an organization that is predominantly made up of people who are "marginal normal" in relation to their originating national cultural group. Some studies have shown that this might naturally be the case among expatriates in subsidiaries of large MNCs where successful expatriates are continually deployed in new locations and thus, having been out of their home country context for so long, they become less and less attached to their home cultural norms (cf. Brannen, 1994). Another organization might be made up of people with a mixture of "negotiated stances" within their national cultural group (hyper-normal, cultural norm(al), and marginal-normal). Yet another might be a tighter cultural group with participants who all have hyper-normal profiles within their national cultural context. Early work on expatriate adjustment showed that first-time expatriates often tended to become more attached to their home country norms (in other words, more "hyper-normal"), initially in response to culture shock and early adjustment difficulties (cf. Arthur and Bennet, 1995; Briody and Chrisman, 1991).

Proposition 3: When individuals from two or more organizations from distinct national cultures come together a "negotiated culture" emerges.

Figure 5.2 is a graphic representation of the national model of negotiated culture/organizational culture interface. As opposed to the "two billiard ball" model of two-cultural interaction, this figure depicts an interchange in which both cultures impact and are acted upon by the other. The diagram also demonstrates the "embeddedness" of the culture. Rather construct offering a view of the multilayered cultural interfaces faced by today's complex cultural organizations. For example, rather than treating nation and culture as cognates, this figure shows that organizational culture is embedded in national culture.

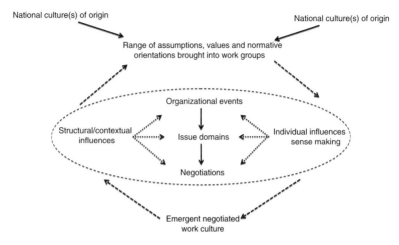

Figure 5.2   Model of negotiated culture

Proposition 4: "Issue cultures" form around key events in the organization's history that affect the proportions of cultural attributes that define and redefine the cultural norm of the new organization.

Proposition 5: Cultural stances of organizational actors may map into "issue cultures" in unexpected ways.

Figure 5.2 is also a graphic representation of Proposition 4, underscoring the notion that different organizational issues will evoke different "cultural stances" on the part of the organizational participants. This figure also posits "cultural negotiation" at the individual issue level and illustrates that different issues will evoke different cultural orientations on the part of organizational participants, so that, for example, a person classified as "culturally normal" as a general cultural description might rather be "hyper-normal" in regard to a specific issue that might become salient in the work environment. This results in the forming of "issues cultures" around key events in the organization's history.

Proposition 6: The evolution of organizational culture occurs at the issue level, where the "cultural norm(al)" is altered, and organizational identities reinterpreted.

Figure 5.2 depicts the above proposition. Feedback loops are shown to illustrate cultural learning at the three levels: national cultural composite, organizational cultural composite, and issues. Whereas culture is a group-level phenomenon, it is enacted at the individual level. Issues trigger cultural negotiations and thus become the catalysts for change.

Further, the negotiated culture that emerges will not necessarily be a blend or hybrid culture. Because many of the issues faced by the individuals in the new, co-created cultural contexts will be related to the cultures outside of the realm of pre-existing culture-of-origin represented, the emergent negotiated culture will not reflect one or the other culture in its entirety. In other words, given culture A and B, the negotiated cultural outcome will be neither A nor B nor AB, but some other outcome, on the analogy of a mutation containing parts of both parents as well as some aspects of its own idiosyncratic making.

Issues that become salient in the course of ongoing interactions across cultural contexts allow for expression of marginal-normal to hyper-normal tendencies of individuals vis-à-vis their cultures of origins. Hence, the domains elevated to the status of an issue (what is termed "issue domains" in Figure 5.2) can be negotiated among individual participants in a number of ways; the working culture that emerges contains the influences of cultures of origins, individual stance-taking, and the particular interplay between and within organizational contexts. Further, individuals might have differentiated cultural stances depending on the cultural attribute in question. For example, a Japanese individual organizational actor might be hyper-normal vis-à-vis the importance of lifetime employment but marginal-normal in regard to having loose boundaries between business and personal life. While the former might be considered a core attribute for some individuals, the latter might be relatively more peripheral to another's cultural makeup. A new cultural context may provide opportunities for individuals to give up certain practices that they only tolerated in their home organization in order to fit into the societal context.

Conclusion

Technological advancement, knowledge-scanning opportunities and competitive pressures to consolidate industries and regions have all contributed to a recent surge in the global integration of organizations (Hitt et al., 2001a, b). Whereas there has been a significant amount of research on the economic motivations and entry modes of such foreign direct investment, cross-border mergers and acquisitions and the like, the social, intraorganizational operational aspects of such complex cultural entities has been inadequately studied (Bhagat et al., 2002). Mindful, effective management requires "new" understandings of the culture construct and concomitant deep contextual understanding. This chapter has outlined the challenge of reconceptualizing the culture construct for today's complex cultural organizations and provided a model of a contextually negotiated content. The ongoing negotiations will decidedly be enacted by individual organizational actors and, in the absence of being bicultural or of mixed cultural identity, managers will need to develop skill sets for deep contextual understanding involving both cognitive and behavioral aspects. These skill sets would include deep cultural sensitivity and contextual acuity, as well as flexible and culturally agile leadership. Cultural sensitivity entails understanding, valuing and mobilizing complex cultural workforces. This encompasses such capabilities as opening to new ideas and practices, loosening boundaries, allowing ideas in from the periphery, and finding creative ways to integrate new ideas at home. Contextual acuity entails leveraging high-context cultural skills to go beyond understanding and adapting to others toward transparency and sharing about our own context. Finally, culturally agile leadership entails recognizing that the truly competitive game is the creation, sharing, and leveraging of new knowledge from around the world. Without bridging skills involving deep knowledge of culture and context, only simple, explicit, codified knowledge can be transferred and shared. The critical caveat is that the most valuable knowledge is complex, tacit, and deeply embedded in each other's cultural context.

References

Abu-Lughod, L. (2000) *Veiled Sentiments: Honor and Poetry in a Bedouin Society*. Berkeley, CA: University of California Press.

Adler, N. J. (1983) "Cross-cultural Management research: The Ostrich and the Trend," *Academy of Management Review*, 8, 226–32.

Alvesson, M. & Sköldberg, K. (2000) *Reflexive Methodology: New Vistas for Qualitative Research*. London, UK: Sage Publications.

Appuradai, A. (1996) *Modernity at Large: Cultural Dimensions of Globalization*. Minneapolis, MN: University of Minnesota Press.

Arthur, W. & Bennet, W. (1995) "The International Assignee: The Relative Importance of Factors Perceived to Contribute to Success," *Personnel Psychology*, 48, 99–114.

Bhagat, R. S., Kedia, B. L., Harveston, P. D., & Triandis, H. C. (2002) "Cultural Variations in the Cross-border Transfer of Organizational Knowledge: An Integrative Framework," *Academy of Management Review*, 27, 204–21.

Bijlsma-Frakema, K. (2005) "Understanding the Trust-control Nexus," *International Sociology*, 20 (3), 259–82.

Boyacigiller, N. & Adler, N. J. (1991) "The Parochial Dinosaur: The Organizational Sciences in a Global Context," *Academy of Management Review*, 16 (2), 1–32.

Brannen, M. Y. (1992) "Bwana Mickey: Constructing Cultural Consumption at Tokyo Disneyland," in J. Tobin (ed.) *Remade in Japan: Consumer Tastes in a Changing Japan*. New Haven, CT: Yale University Press.

Brannen, M. Y. (1994) *Your Next Boss is Japanese: Negotiating Cultural Change at a Western Massachusetts Paper Plant*. Unpublished doctoral dissertation. University of Massachusetts, Amherst.

Brannen, M. Y. (2004) "When Mickey Loses Face: Recontextualization, Semantic Fit, and the Semiotics of Foreignness," *Academy of Management Review*, 29 (4), 593–616.

Brannen, M. Y., Doz, Y., Hill, M., Hunter, M. Osland, A., & Whaley, G. (2009) "FASL (Fujitsu/ AMD Semiconductor Limited Alliance): Collaborating Over Time," INSEAD Case Series, CEDEP, France.

Brannen, M. Y., Doz, Y. & Santos, J. (2007) "Unpacking Absorptive Capacity: Understanding the Nature and Contexts of Knowledge Transfer," Working Paper.

Brannen, M. Y., Liker, J. K., & Fruin, W. M. (1999) "Recontextualization and Factory-to-Factory Knowledge Transfer from Japan to the U.S.: The Case of NSK," in J. K. Liker, W. K. Fruin, & P. S. Adler (eds) *Remade in America: Transplanting and Transforming Japanese Production Systems*. New York, NY: Oxford University Press, 117–54.

Brannen, M. Y. & Peterson, M. F. (2008) "Merging Without Alienating: Interventions Promoting Cross-Cultural Organizational Integration and Their Limitations," *Journal of International Business Studies*, in print.

Brannen, M. Y. & Salk, J. E. (2000) "Partnering Across Borders: Negotiating Organizational Culture in a German-Japanese Joint-Venture," *Human Relations*, 53 (4), 451–87.

Briody, E. & Chrisman, J. B (1991) "Cultural Adaptation and the Overseas Assignment," *Human Organization*, 50, 264–82.

Burrell, G. & Morgan, G. (1979) *Sociological Paradigms and Organizational Analysis: Elements of the Sociology of Corporate Life*. London, UK: Heinemann.

Child, J. (1981) "Culture, Contingency and Capitalism in the Cross-National Study of Organizations," in L. L. Cummings & B. M. Staw (eds), *Research in Organizational Behavior* (Vol. 3). Greenwich, CT: JAI Press, 303–56.

Child, J., Falker, D., & Pitkethy, R. (2001) *The Management of International Acquisitions*. Oxford, UK: Oxford University Press.

Clifford, J. (1988) *The Predicament of Culture: Twentieth-century Ethnography, Literature, and Art*. Cambridge, MA: Harvard University Press.

Clifford, J. & Marcus, G., (1986) (eds) *Writing Culture: The Poetics and Politics of Ethnography*. Berkeley, CA: University of California Press.

Dalton, M. (1959) *Men who manage*. John Wiley and Sons, Ltd.

Datta, D. K. & Puia, G. (1995) "Cross-border Acquisitions: An Examination of the Influence of Relatedness and Cultural Fit on Shareholder Value Creation in US Acquiring Firms," *Management International Review*, 35 (4), 337–59.

Doz, Y., Santos, J., & Williamson, P. (2001) *From Global to Metanational: How Companies Win in the Knowledge Economy*. Boston: Harvard Business School Press.

Dwyer, K. (1982) *Moroccan Dialogues: Anthropology in Question*. Baltimore, MD: Johns Hopkins University Press.

Fang, T. (2003) "A Critique of Hofstede's Fifth National Culture Dimension," *International Journal of Cross Cultural Management*, 3 (3), 347–68.

Fiss, P. C. & Zajac, E. J. (2004) "The Diffusion of Ideas Over Contested Terrain: The (Non)adoption of a Shareholder Value Orientation Among German firms," *Administrative Science Quarterly*, 49, 501–34.

Frost, P. J., Moore, L., Louis, M. R., Lundberg, G., & Martin, J. (1985) *Organizational Culture*. Beverly Hills, CA: Sage Publications.

Gelfand, M. J., Erez, M., & Aycan, Z. (2007) "Cross-Cultural Organizational Behavior," *Annual Review of Psychology*, 58, 479–514.

Geppert, M. & Clark, E. (2003) "Knowledge and Learning in Transnational Ventures: An Actor-centered Approach," *Management Decision*, 41 (5), 433–42.

Goffman, E. (1961) *Encounters: Two Studies in the Sociology of Interaction*. New York, NY: Macmillan Publishing Co.

Gregory, K. (1983) "Native-view Paradigms: Multiple Cultures and Culture Conflicts in Organizations," *Administrative Science Quarterly*, 28, 359–76.

Gupta, A. K. & Govindarajan, V. (2000) "Knowledge Management's Social Dimension: Lessons from Nucor Steel," *MIT Sloan Management Review*, 42 (1), 71–80.

Hitt, M. A., Harrison, J. S., & Ireland, R. D. (2001a) *Mergers and Acquisitions: A Guide to Creating Value for Stakeholders*. New York, NY: Oxford University Press.

Hitt, M. A., Ireland, R. D., Camp, S. M., & Sexton, D. I. (2001b) "Strategic Entrepreneurship: Entrepreneurial Strategies for Creating Wealth," *Strategic Management Journal*, 22, 479–91.

Hofstede, G. (2001) *Culture's Consequences: Comparing Values, Behaviors, Institutions, and Organizations Across Nations*. Thousand Oaks, CA: Sage Publications.

Hughes, E. (1958) *Men and Their Work*. Glencoe, IL: Free Press.

Inkpen, A. C. & Dinur, A. (1998) "Knowledge Management Processes and International Joint Ventures," *Organization Science*, 9 (4), 454–68.

Kanter, R. M. & Corn, B. I. (1994) "Cultural Changes During the Integration Process of Acquisitions: A Comparative Study Between German-Korean Acquisitions," *International Journal of International Relations*, 31 (5), 591–604.

Kostova, T. (1999) "Transnational Transfer of Strategic Organizational Practices: A Contextual Perspective," *Academy of Management Review*, 24 (2), 308–24.

Kostova, T. & Roth, K. (2002) "Adoption of an Organizational Practice by the Subsidiaries of the MNC: Institutional and Relational Effects," *Academy of Management Journal*, 45, 215–33.

Krug, J. A. & Hegarty, W. H. (2001) "Research Notes and Commentaries: Predicting Who Stays and Leaves After an Acquisition: A Study of Top Managers in Multinational Firms," *Strategic Management Journal*, 22, 185–96.

Lane, P. J., Lyles, M. A., & Salk, J. E. (1998) "Relative Absorptive Capacity, Trust, and Interorganizational Learning in International Joint Ventures," in M. Hitt, J. E. Ricart, & R. Nixon (eds) *Managing Strategically in an Interconnected World*. London, UK: John Wiley & Sons, 373–97.

Lee, S. (2003) *Global Acquisitions: Strategic Integration and the Human Factor*. New York, NY: Palgrave Macmillan.

Lowe, A. (2001) "Casemix Accounting Systems and Medical Coding: Organisational Actors Balanced on 'Leaky Black Boxes,'" *Journal of Organizational Change Management*, 14 (1), 79–100.

Marcus, G. E. & Fisher, M. J. (1986) *Anthropology as Cultural Critique*. Chicago, IL: University of Chicago Press.

Markides, C. & Ittner, C. D. (1994) "Shareholder Benefits from Corporate International Diversification: Evidence from US International Acquisitions," *Journal of Business Studies*, 25 (2), 343–60.

Martin, J. & Siehl, C. (1983) "Organizational Culture and Sub-culture: An Uneasy Symbiosis," *Organizational Dynamics*, 12, 52–64.

Mead, M. (1934) Kinship in the Admiralty Islands. New Brunswick, NJ: Transaction Publishers.

Morosini, P., Shane, S., & Singh, S. (1998) "National Cultural Distance and Cross-border Performance," *Journal of International Business Studies*, 29 (1), 137–58.

Ong, A. (1987) *Spirits of Resistance and Capitalist Discipline: Factory Women in Malaysia*. Albany, NY: State University of New York Press.

Pondy, L. R., Frost, P., Morgan, G., & Dandridge, T. (1983) *Organizational Symbolism*. Greenwich, CT: JAI Press

Redding, S. G. (1994) "Comparative Management Theory: Jungle, Zoo or Fossil Bed?," *Organization Studies*, 15 (3), 323–59.

Roberts, K. H. (1970) "On Looking at an Elephant: An Evaluation of Cross-cultural Research Related to Organizations," *Psychological Bulletin*, 74 (5), 327–50.

Romani, L. (2008) *Relating to the Other: Paradigm Interplay for Cross-cultural Management*. Stockholm, Sweden: Elanders.

Roseberry, W. (1989) *Anthropologies and Histories*. New Brunswick, NJ: Rutgers University Press.

Sahlins, M. (1985) *Islands in History*. Chicago, IL: The University of Chicago Press.

Said, E. (1978) *Orientalism*. New York, NY: Pantheon Books.

Salk, J. E. & Brannen, M. Y. (2000) "National Culture, Networks and Individual Influence in a Multinational Management Team," *The Academy of Management Journal*, 43, 191–202.

Salk, J. E. & Shenkar, O. (2001) "Social Identities and Cooperation in an International Joint Venture: An Exploratory Case Study," *Organization Science*, 12, 161–78.

Schein, E. (1985) *Organizational Culture and Leadership*. San Francisco, CA: Jossey-Bass.

Schweiger, D. M. & Lippert, R. L. (2005) "Integration: The Critical Link in M&A Value Creation," in G. Stahl & M. Mendenhall (eds) *Mergers and Acquisitions: Managing Culture and Human Resources*. Palo Alto, CA: Stanford University Press, 17–46.

Shimizu, K., Hitt, M., Vaidyanath, D., & Pisano, V. (2004) "Theoretical Foundations of Cross-border Mergers and Acquisitions: A Review of Current Research and Recommendations for the Future," *Journal of International Management*, 10, 307–53.

Smircich, L. (1983) "Concepts of Culture and Organizational Analysis," *Administrative Science Quarterly*, 28, 339–58.

Stahl, G., Mendenhall, M., Pablo, A., & Javidan, M. (2005) "Sociocultural Integration in Mergers and Acquisitions," in G. K. Stahl & M. E. Mendenhall (eds) *Mergers and Acquisitions: Managing Culture and Human Resources*. Palo Alto, CA: Stanford University Press, 3–16.

Strauss, A. L. (1978) *Social Negotiations: Varieties, Contexts, Processes and Social Order*. San Francisco: Jossey-Bass.

Strauss, A. L. (1982) "Interorganizational Negotiation," *Urban Life*, 11:350–67.

Tayeb, M. H. (2001) "Human Resource Management in Iran," in P. S. Budhwar & Y. Debrah (eds) *Human Resource Management in Developing Countries*. London, UK: Routledge, 121–34.

Thomas, D., Brannen, M. Y., & Garcia, D. (2008) "Bicultural Individuals and Intercultural Effectiveness," Working Paper.

Tomlinson, J. (1999) *Globalization and Culture*. University of Chicago Press.

Turner, B. (1972) *Exploring the Industrial Subculture*. New York, NY: Herder & Herder.

Uhlenbruck, K. (2004) "Developing Acquired Foreign Subsidiaries: The Experience of MNEs in Transition Economies," *Journal of International Business Studies*, 35, 109–23.

Van Maanen, J. & Barley, S. R. (1984) "Occupational Communities: Culture and Control in Organizations," in B. M. Staw & L. L. Cummings (eds) *Research in Organizational Behavior*. Greenwich, CT: JAI Press, 6, 287–365.

Very, P., Lubatkin, M., Calori, R., & Veiga, J. (1996) "Cross-national Assessment of Acculturative Stress in Recent European Mergers," *International Studies of Management and Organization*, 26, 59–88.

Wallace, A. (1970) *Culture and Personality*. New York, NY: Random House.

Weber, Y., Shenkar, O., & Raveh, A. (1996) "National and Corporate Fit in M & A: An Exploratory Study," *Management Science*, 4, 1215–27.

Whyte, W. F. (1948) *Human Relations in the Restaurant Business*. New York, NY: McGraw-Hill.

Wolf, E. (1982) *Europe and the People without History*. Berkeley, CA: University of California Press.

Zellmer-Bruhn, M. E. (2003) "Interruptive Events and Team Knowledge Acquisition," *Management Science*, 49 (4), 514–28.

6
Reflexive Culture's Consequences

Søren Askegaard, Dannie Kjeldgaard, and Eric J. Arnould

Investigations of marketing relations across cultures have traditionally focused on culture as a background variable, a collection of essential character traits, habits, practices, categorizations, and so forth within a given domain that would explain the approach to and degree of acceptance of various marketing practices from abroad. Most often, such discussions are based in a Hofstedean tradition (for a review of the use of particular culture theories in literature and the dominance of Hofstede-based approaches, see Nakata and Izberk-Bilgin this volume). The role of cultural understanding in this perspective aims to predict the problems or potential misunderstandings arising from different cultural backgrounds in a marketing exchange relation or in cross-cultural managerial interactions (see, for example, Douglas and Craig's work in this volume). Moreover, the basic question in the relation between marketing and culture is the standardization–adaptation debate, that is, the degree to which certain established marketing strategies or tactics would be applicable in a different cultural context. The unit of analysis is almost inevitably the nation-state, albeit with occasional references to subcultures, such as different ethnic groups. However, the inherent weaknesses of this approach, focusing on the comparison of cultural similarities and differences between nations, occasionally even turning to measuring the "cultural distances" between them, are becoming more and more evident in today's globalizing environment—hence the need for a different look at relations between culture and marketing.

The culture construct has only been considered seriously within marketing and consumer research for a little over two decades. With the possible exception of certain relatively marginalized consumer research environments, culture has mainly played the role of an externally given antecedent variable that explains similarity and difference among national markets and, hence, provides the foundation for the differentiation or generalization of various marketing activities. In this respect, the culture concept in marketing has always been an essentialist one. Culture, to recycle a popular metaphor used to illustrate the concept to "laypeople" in business schools, is like the water fish swim in; it represents the taken-for-granted physical and ideological environment. One outcome of this essentialism is the way marketers and marketing scholars generally conceive of their relation to culture (in this volume, Brannen provides a paradigmatic discussion of approaches to culture, and Nakata offers a philosophy of science discussion). Here we can identify two major legacies, both originating in the first half of the 1980s. Levitt (1983) argued that though cultural differences exist, they can be overcome and to some extent ignored by marketing strategy, because what he conceives of as non-cultural product attributes, such as low prices and high product quality, always overwhelm differences in cultural tastes and preferences. Hofstede (1983), on the contrary, argued that culture does indeed have consequences that cannot be overlooked by business practitioners and developed a highly influential conceptual apparatus and measurement instrument for breaking down culture into operational dimensions.

The aim of this chapter, in exploring different relations between marketing and culture, is twofold. First, we review the legacies of both Levitt and Hofstede in relation to bringing the concepts of both globalization and culture into marketing literature. This is followed by a deconstruction of some of the assumptions about the nature of globalization and cross-cultural differences that underlie these two positions, in the light of recent globalization theory. The aim is to demonstrate how culture changes as a consequence of globalization processes. Second, because culture from these perspectives is seen as an antecedent and static background variable that determines the scope of variation in marketing and consumption practices, the impact of marketing on culture is normally not taken into consideration in international marketing (Bouchet, 1995). This impact, if addressed at all, mainly appears as an issue in the cases of directly negative or harmful effects of advertisements, for instance, when oriented toward children. In contrast, the aim here is to show how the relations between marketing and culture in conditions of globalization lead to a change in useful ideas about culture itself. This chapter offers some theoretical guidance for understanding the growing importance of marketing for the creation of what we call reflexive culture.

Based on globalization theory, we argue that reflexive culture is an idiom for the expression of new types of potential consumer practice, a cultural response in a time in which national and transnational political-economic entities no longer enjoy the legitimacy and power to socialize through the provision of integrating values with which citizens willingly or unconsciously affiliate (Beck and Sznaider, 2006).

The current accelerated phase of globalization refers to a period with changing and increasingly rapid global flows, in which boundaries across national cultures are dissolving and the landscapes they demarcate are transgressed by evolving real and/or virtual "culturescapes" of technology, media, finance, mixed ethnicities, and ideas (Appadurai, 1990). Cultural encounters proliferate, which has led to an increasing interest in identity-constructive processes in the globalizing world, not least through processes of consumption (Friedman, 1994a). Numerous studies have addressed specific marketing and consumption issues in this multicultural world, and the term "consumptionscapes" has been proposed to foreground the role of consumption as a global flow overlapping those proposed by Appadurai (Ger and Belk, 1996). These and related studies have pushed theoretical debates beyond the discussions of globalization centered on themes of static cultural similarities and differences or strategic choices between standardization or adaptation so prevalent in marketing literature. Consequently, simplistic dichotomous explanations must be eschewed and classificatory systems, such as global–local, Eastern–Western, individualistic–collectivistic, vertical–horizontal, masculine–feminine, and foreign–domestic, must be used with some caution. As Fiske (2002, p. 8) puts it, these binaries are "abstraction[s] that formalize our ideological representation of the antithetical other, a cultural vision of the rest of the world characterized in terms of what we imagine we are not." This clearly has methodological implications for consumer and marketing research in relation to globalization.

Such criticism evidently does not imply the irrelevance of culture—quite the contrary. In this respect, we agree with Hofstede so far as to conclude that culture cannot and should not be ignored. Hence, we start our deconstruction with Levitt's reflections on the irrelevance of cultural differences in a global market economy.

How Levitt was completely wrong . . .

The term "globalization" has become one of the most used and abused buzzwords of the last couple of decades. This has given rise to much public debate and confusion about the causes and nature of, and benefits to and risks from, the globalization of markets. Within the field of marketing, the globalization concept is more sedate, since it was used by one of the discipline's grand old scholars in a seminal article 25 years ago. We are, of course, referring to Theodore Levitt's 1983 *Harvard Business Review* piece, "The Globalization of Markets." This article contains one of the most disputed marketing hypotheses of recent decades. Most of the discussion has centered on the validity of his central idea, namely, that the most successful global business strategy would be a totally standardized approach that ignores what he deemed "superficial" differences in world markets.

Levitt refers to technology as the single most important driving device in the process of the globalization of markets. This can be contrasted with Appadurai's (1990) argument proposing five different "scapes"—ethnoscapes, technoscapes, finanscapes, mediascapes, and ideoscapes—as the structuring forces of globalization. Each of them contributes to diminishing the importance of the traditional geographical landscapes and their distances, proximities, and obstacles as decisive for the global social infrastructures. Even if it can be argued that technological development, or the technoscape, is a precondition for the other scapes, this is by no means self-evident. Such a linear explanation misses the complex interrelatedness of global change processes. For example, global financial markets necessitate and encourage further development of information technology, and technological development is fostered by an ideoscape idealizing 24-hour markets, global arbitrage, market heroism, and so forth.

Although there is evident truth in the argument that technology drives technological commonality in marketing and consumption platforms, and even the demand for participation in the modern consumer world, the argument becomes problematic the moment that Levitt jumps to the conclusion that this desire for modernity as an ideoscape, in Appadurai's terms, leads to demand for *standardized* products. Levitt draws on historian Daniel Boorstin and his concept of the "Republic of Technology" as support for his argument. However, another of Boorstin's (1962) works on "the image" could have been used to illustrate a contrasting feature of globalizing markets. This feature is the spread of commercial hype that constantly nurtures and nourishes itself on symbolic distinction (see Baudrillard, 1970, for an elaboration of this idea). We will return to this argument subsequently.

Levitt's argument pursues the idea that companies can gain competitive advantage by exploiting various economies of scale and thus "decimate competitors that still live in the disabling grip of old assumptions about how the world works" (Levitt, 1983, p. 92). On the one hand, it is true that the globalizing market conditions are instituting new market rules that make it impossible for companies to ignore international market developments, even if they operate only in domestic markets. On the other hand, Ger (1999) has pointed out how through the use of various strategies, local companies may "outlocal" their global competitors and support and/or create domestic consumptionscapes that offer alternatives to the global standard (Ger and Belk, 1996), a twist ignored by Levitt.

The assertion "gone are accustomed differences in national or regional preference" (Levitt 1983, p. 92) is as grossly overstated as the outcry that a global rather than multinational strategy is not a matter of opinion but of necessity. Indeed, it is easy to identify emergent regional consumer preferences, such as the resurgence of artisanal and militantly British cheese culture (see http://www.thecheeseweb.com). The ubiquitous and frequently doggedly managerial discussions about the various degrees of optimal standardization versus adaptation (Wind and Douglas, 1988) in fact may conceal the observation that standardized branding and marketing strategies may say a lot more about marketers' powerful and persistent globalizing ideoscape than about the alleged homogeneity of consumer preferences (Applbaum, 2000; Boyacigillar and Adler, 1991).

The standard globalization argument maintains that brands and products are containers of meanings that are transferred to the consumer when he or she is exposed to these products or brands. But as Miller (1998) so aptly demonstrates, the meaning universe of Coca-Cola, the king of global brands, is subject to local interpretations that do more than slightly alter the meanings of the global brand. Indeed, as the title of Miller's work indicates, Coke is viewed by some local consumers as a local product. In international markets, brand meaning is not absorbed passively but rather in divergent and culturally determined ways. Miller (1998) shows that in Trinidad, the meaning of Coca-Cola is defined by its categorization as a "black" as opposed to a "red" sweet drink (indeed, as the exemplar of that category) and by its associations with non-Asian Trinidadians, with rum and coke, with traditional conceptions of Trinidadian modernity, and with consumer support for a long-standing indigenous bottler. And even the CEO of Coca-Cola has stated that it is a multi-local rather than a global product (Askegaard and Csaba, 2000). Furthermore, that Coca-Cola is "welcomed by everyone" (Levitt, 1983, p. 93) is a sort of monocultural (marketing) myopia, contradicted not merely by the existence of the term "coca-colonization," a term coined to express the fact that Coca-Cola, and the American/Western lifestyle it represents, is *not* welcomed by everyone, but also by the emergence of anti-Coke brands. Doppelganger brands (Thompson et al., 2006) such as

Mecca Cola or Qibla Cola are explicitly positioned as anti-global brands, even if the global diffusion of bottling and distribution technologies and brands as an ideoscape fosters their success.

In general, the anecdotal presence of Western goods and companies is taken as diagnostic of the globalization of preferences. However, Western goods and services may serve a multitude of purposes, be imbued with very different meanings, and reflect different kinds of preferences (e.g., Belk and Zhou, 2004; Eckhardt and Houston, 2002; Friedman, 1994b). For example, the contributors to the collection edited by Watson (1997) show diverse appropriations of McDonald's in several Asian cultures. Consequently, the presence of McDonald's, Sony, Coca-Cola, and other Western brands *in* consumer markets everywhere in no way proves global preferences, as Levitt would have it when he states that "everywhere everything gets more and more like everything else as the world's preference structure is relentlessly homogenized" (1983, p. 93). This claim is a crass and reductionist empiricism.

The major problem with Levitt's argument is, then, that the globalization process is seen as basically demand-driven—perhaps not surprising for the man whose claim to fame is based on pointing out the widespread disease of "marketing myopia." This idea is summed up in the following line: "The commonality of preference leads inescapably to the standardization of products, manufacturing, and the institutions of trade and commerce' (Levitt, 1983, p. 93). Such claims open his argument to critiques from a variety of scholars pointing to Levitt's lack of understanding of the notion of culture and his lack of respect for persistent and resurgent cultural differences in the globalizing world. Many of these criticisms have drawn on Hofstede, either theoretically and/or empirically, in order to demonstrate that culture indeed has consequences. In the following, we attempt to add nuance to this established critique by discussing whether a reference to cross-cultural differences in the Hofstedean perspective might suffer from certain weaknesses, similar to those of Levitt's argument, in that neither side captures the cultural changes brought about by the globalization process or provides appropriate guidance to scholars and managers wrestling with them.

. . . Even when he was right

The standard definition of culture provided by Hofstede in his writings is that culture is "the collective programming of the mind" (e.g., Hofstede, 1980) that can be used to distinguish categories of people. Although Hofstede acknowledges that such categories may reflect different types of cultural differentiations (e.g., regional cultures, organizational cultures, gender cultures), the prime focus of his research has been putatively national cultural differences. Indeed, his whole project sprang from the discovery that an allegedly strong organization culture in a large multinational corporation was unable to override national cultural differences among employees. Hofstede (1983) argues that there are three reasons national culture is crucial for understanding managerial practices. Nationality is important first for its political importance: Nations organize formal and informal institutional and legal systems. Second, nations are important sociologically, as symbols that serve as points of identification for its citizens. Third, and most important for Hofstede, national culture is important psychologically because it is imprinted in our brains through the aforementioned "collective programming," and conditions us to interpret situations and find solutions to problems according to inherited cultural schemes.

Globalization challenges Hofstede's assumption on all three levels. First, institutional and legal arrangements are increasingly subject to international regulation, whether from the IMF, EU, NAFTA, WTO, ICC, or other organizations. Second, the current political scene demonstrates that, in many cases, the monopoly of the nation-state, sanctioned by its membership in the UN and other types of international recognitions in terms of consumer identification, is challenged by regional and local identities, as well as by increased global mobility. Bauman's (1998) "tourists" and "vagabonds"—those who are free and those who are forced to move in the global space—are caught in contemporary identity political systems in which new post-assimilationist ethnic identities (Askegaard et al., 2005) coexist with cosmopolitanism (Thompson and Tambyah, 1999). Furthermore, we witness the dramatic emergence of regional identities and separatist tendencies in "old Europe"—Belgium, Catalonia, Brittany, Scotland, Kosovo, Euskal Herria (Basque country)—all associated with the invention of consumer traditions (Hobsbawm and Ranger, 1983) and a growing interest in searching for local cultural roots and identity systems (Bray, 2006; Rigo and Rahola, 2007; Sahlins, 1993). Third, the search for cultural roots engenders a challenge for Hofstede's psychological argument about the importance of nationality, but in a paradoxical way, because at first glance, it confirms its importance. However, a change from an unconscious "programming of the mind" to a more strategic "choice of cultural profile," as discussed subsequently, makes the use of survey measurement instruments such as Hofstede's much more problematic, because strategically chosen cultural identities invite respondents to answer questions strategically.

The immediate consequences can be summarized in the argument that in a context of increasing cultural interpenetration, migration, and multiculturalism, using the nation as a proxy for culture becomes problematic (Douglas and Craig, 1997). The inability of social theory, broadly defined, to explain transnational phenomena has rendered existing frameworks based on nation-states increasingly problematic (Robinson, 1998). As Robinson (1998, p. 564) argues, "nations are no longer linked externally to a broader system but internally to a singular global social formation." Furthermore, as Beck and Sznaider (2006, p. 6) argue, the decisive point is "that national organization as a structuring principle of societal and political action can no longer serve as the orienting reference point for the social scientific observer." Consequently, scholars from anthropology (Schiller, 2005), political science (Wimmer and Schiller, 2002), sociology (Beck, 2000; Robinson, 1998), and geography (Taylor, 1996) label the use of national framing in research "methodological nationalism" and call for a paradigmatic reorientation to explain transnational phenomena such as migration, global multiculturalism (i.e., multiculturalism that crosses national boundaries; Cohen, 1997; Pieterse, 2007), and cultural hybridity, including hybrid consumer preferences and behaviors (Archer et al., 2007; Çağlar, 2004). Kjeldgaard and colleagues (2006) offer a discussion of the implications of such a paradigm shift for qualitative research in marketing.

It is thus our point that globalization simultaneously challenges the assumption of distinct national differences and the methodological foundation of Hofstede's survey instrument. Obviously, proponents of Hofstede and similar comparative instruments may argue that this criticism fails to acknowledge that cultural changes in the direction of greater cultural similarity will just show up as changes in positions in the different scales, as for example when the level of gross domestic product (GDP) in a country is correlated with the degree of individualism, as measured by Hofstede's (1983) cultural index. Eventually, according to this logic, globalization will lead to decreasing differences in at least some of the indexed value profiles of the different countries. But it will not diminish the value of the index as such. This counterargument, however, builds on the assumption that what is engendered by globalization is, first and foremost, a process of global homogenization in the "programming processes of the minds" but not an alteration of the programming process itself. Cultures changes, but "culture" remains the same. We would like to argue that there is growing evidence that this may not be the case.

Various attempts have been made to home in on the concept of globalization. We sketch the overall development in theories of globalization next, but first must make two points about globalization: (1) Globalization, as we see it, is a process that problematizes the relationship between geographical and social relations (Waters, 1995) and (2) globalization encompasses a wide range of social and cultural spheres (the notion of Appadurai's [1990] "scapes"). The outcomes and manifestations of globalization have been much debated. Some have argued that globalization can be characterized as a universalizing and homogenizing process that creates a new social situation, in which small local cultures erode and become Westernized—in essence, arguing along the same lines as Levitt, though with a distinctly pessimistic outlook about the consequences of such a development (Waters, 1995). Others insist on the autonomy and uniqueness of local cultures that are able to resist the influx of Western culture or at least use it merely as superficial entertainment.

Some have tried to get past this dichotomous debate by considering homogenizing (globalizing) and heterogenizing (localizing) processes as part and parcel of globalization. Such an insight is encompassed in the notion of "glocalization" (Robertson, 1995), which widens the notion of globalization because the local (and localization) is seen as constitutive of globalization rather than contradictory to it. Central to this line of thought is that global flows are not just one-way, center-to-periphery but also periphery-to-center flows (Appadurai, 1990), as in the flow of "authentic" products from the periphery to the center along the channels of distribution established by Fair Trade organizations. Furthermore, local cultures reinterpret the meaning of the imported symbols (as in the case of Coca-Cola evoked previously). Some of the manifestations of glocalization have been conceptualized as instances of "creolization" or "hybridization," which are essentially new cultural forms that emerge as the global is incorporated within the local (Pieterse, 1995). The new cultural forms are seen as mixes of often seemingly incompatible cultural symbols and practices that nevertheless become local in meaning in the conduct of everyday life (e.g., Bray, 2006).

These mixes of the global and the local are at play in James's (1996) study of food discourses in Great Britain. The study provides an illustrative example of the multifaceted nature of the articulation of globalization processes at the local level. James organizes her findings around four discourses—globalism, exoticism (qualified as the "expatriate" discourse by James), creolization, and nostalgia—each of which is constructed around perceptions of local and global, self and other.

As has been argued elsewhere (e.g., Askegaard and Kjeldgaard, 2007), these discourses of the global and the local can be organized around two dimensions: scope and compatibility. Scope basically is a geographical dimension, such as whether the food culture is logically available on a global scale or whether it is logically tied to a specific geographical locality. Compatibility refers to the "fit" that certain food types have with other food cultures, that is, which foods can and cannot be changed, added to, fused, and so on. The decisive difference is the dependence of the food discourses on a preexisting script describing the essentially culturally correct way of preparing and eating a particular kind of food. This script can be in the form of either exotic or foreign *authenticity,* characterized by authentic otherness (e.g., a "real" Italian, Thai, Indian meal). This is the expatriate discourse. Or it can be characterized as the expression of authentic culinary authority, often perceived to be under threat from the invasion of global fast food and foreign, authentic, or creolized cuisines, which must be maintained in purified form (hence, incompatible with other food cultures)—the nostalgic discourse. Using these two dimensions, the discourses can be organized in a two-by-two matrix, as shown in Figure 6.1.

A given cultural manifestation, such as a meal, can be placed within one of these discourses. However, this placement is determined by perceptions about scope and compatibility, rather than some intrinsic attribute of the meal. The discourses emerge as perceptions of what is considered to be local and global in particular contexts. These perceptions,

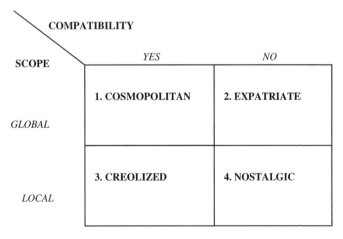

Figure 6.1   A matrix of cultural glocalization discourses

however, are dynamic rather than static, because they are continuously (re)articulated and reconstructed in a negotiation of cultural identity—negotiation intensifies as consumers are increasingly confronted with images of the Other through the globalization process.

So where does Levitt have a point? Levitt's falsity rested in his assumption of a convergence of culture—that is, a convergence of meaning, of content. However, as we discussed previously, in considering homogenizing processes, we cannot ignore the influence of the supply side in shaping globally accessible images of "the good life" and thus generating similarities in consumer desires across cultures (Belk et al., 2003). Nevertheless, there are homogenizing tendencies on the demand side, to stay within the market terminology, which would support Levitt's argument, except on other premises. These premises first and foremost have to do with the globalization of fragmentation and, in a broader context, with the reflexive consumption of culture.

There are consumption objects and practices that are available on a global scale, but this presence does not originate from a one-way flow from center to periphery. Rather, in order to survive as distinct cultural identities, each culture must adopt the logic of the market and commodify its culture so that it is available and present for both direct and mediated touristic consumption (Fırat, 1997). The implication of this is that there is a plethora of consumption objects of diverse cultural origin in the global marketplace, including marketed ethnic enclaves such as Chinatowns, American theme restaurants like Planet Hollywood, Arabian-language satellite channels, Oriental inspiration in fashion themes, and so on. So obviously, Levitt was right insofar as American and Western products are sellable on a worldwide scale—*together with* products from many other parts of the world. Fırat (1997) describes this availability as a "Globalization of Fragmentation," such that what is available in one place is also available in any other place. There is thus a multilayeredness of commercialized elements of cultures existing side by side, a kind of selective cultural mosaic. The simultaneous multilayeredness of commercialized cultural elements enables the consumer to switch between consuming the cosmopolitan and the creolized, the exotic and the nostalgic.

New consumption opportunities pose new existential choices for a major part of the world's population. As noted by Bauman (1998), even vagabonds have access to at least the images of the good life in consumer society. The presence of both global and exotic cultural symbols, alongside local ones in any given locality, expands the resources available—if only as a basis for desire, for daydreaming—for hedonic consumption and identity-play. There is therefore a demand for new sensations and experiences in the market, which enables and brings forth cultural differences in the marketplace. As such, there is in one sense, as Levitt claimed, a *homogenization of demand*, yet this demand is for *differences that fuel social distinctions*, rather than for uniform, standardized products only.

Where do these reflections take us in terms of our juxtaposition of Levitt and Hofstede as proponents of global homogenization and the importance of cultural differences, respectively? Both Levitt's and Hofstede's works have been instrumental in bringing academic attention to globalization and cultural difference within marketing. However, we have to get beyond these "truths" in order to establish a framework for understanding the relationship between marketing and culture in an age of globalization. Levitt was right in pointing out the strong disciplining and structuring dynamics of the market economy in enforcing globalization. Hofstede was right in insisting that culture has consequences, though in a way that the Hofstede cultural index cannot take into consideration.

Levitt's and Hofstede's major fallacy, and that of the marketing field in general, has been to rely on an essentialist understanding of culture; these theories rely on a perception of *closed* cultures. In the following, we will argue that culture is not reducible to an essentialist category that operates like an independent background variable. Rather, it is an organized network of systematic diversity of principles of action and understanding. A culture is reflexively negotiated on a continuous basis, exactly as a result of globalized scaping processes and the increasing multilayeredness of commercialized cultural contents.

Marketing and the notion of cultural reflexivity

In this section, we will argue that marketing further strengthens certain processes of cultural change that potentially may alter fundamentally the way we look at culture from a marketing perspective. We will buttress our arguments by relating them to some of the more recent reflections on culture from the field of cultural theory.

To study the fields of globalization and consumer behavior, as well as how the two influence each other, two approaches appear: (1) providing knowledge about globalization by studying consumer lives, or (2) providing knowledge on consumer lives by studying the processes of globalization. The implication of the first approach would be to study the everyday lives of consumers in order to observe processes of globalization at work—an approach termed "mundane experience of deterritorialization" by Tomlinson (1999, p. 113 ff). The implication of the second, more institutional approach would be to study the structures and institutions that enable and fuel the process of globalization and hence have an influence on the everyday life of consumers. There is little doubt, as we saw in the discussion of Levitt's text and the review of many cultural studies, that more and more products and brands are present on a global or quasi-global scale. However, as we noted in relation to Levitt, this presence is not necessarily or primarily due to a homogenization of preferences but rather to the structures and institutions of global markets.

In other words, the question becomes: Should we analyze changes in consumer culture, indeed, the increased *consumption of culture*, in order to understand the increasing commodification of culture(s) tied to the globalization processes? Or should we investigate the strong institutional force of market institutions, such as advertising and marketing, that enforce commodification and globalization processes? This problem of a phenomenological versus an institutional approach constitutes something akin to Bourdieu's concepts of habitus and practice. For Bourdieu (1979), habitus is a structuring system of consumption significations in which the individual agent is both influenced by and reenacts the overall system. The way this habitus is enacted in everyday life is through systems of practices, which include both what we intentionally choose to do and the tacit normative schemes that compel us to do things in certain ways and not others, and interpret the world according to certain schema and not others (Reckwitz, 2002; Warde, 2005). According to practice theory, then, it makes little sense to distinguish too sharply between the intentional and the norm-driven aspects of our behavior. Reflexive culture, from a practice theory perspective, becomes a reflection of both culture consumed and the role of identity politics in the ideological constitution of the cultural, consuming self.

If we draw together the institutional structuring forces of, say, ethnicity and the market and the actual and intentional consumption patterns of the world's consumers, we see the interplay between the local and the global in this context. We witness the power of *global and homogenizing* structures, which enable particular articulations of local culture, meaning that there is a global system that promotes *difference* at the local level, such as the food system we described previously. This is the point made by Wilk (1996) in his critical discussion of the tendency to regard the global fragmentation of markets and consumer choices as a liberatory movement, providing more freedom for consumer choices.

He suggests the idea of "global structures of common difference" to describe the global institutional framework within which the shaping of consumer choices takes place. Such structures include McDonaldized retailing forms, Disneyfied leisure forms, brands, cosmopolitan cuisine, and many others.

A logical outcome of both these examples of how globalization and marketing processes together structure the living conditions of and identity formation processes for consumers is that this structuration is increasingly reflexive, in particular as it pertains to the concept of culture. That is, culture becomes reflexive. By reflexivity, we mean that individual actors (consumers, marketers) are *aware* of dynamic social structures; engage in constant *self-monitoring* of action (consumers' choices, marketers strategic use of culture); and attempt to engage in *correction of individual action*, all of which in turn affect social structures (Giddens, 1991). A reflexive culture is hence one in which marketers and consumers are aware of cultures and cultural symbolism, and monitor and modify their actions accordingly (marketing strategies, or consumers' strategies of identity with regard to social differentiation), which consequently feeds into the dynamic change process of culture and globalization. In such a cultural context, discourses of cultural membership and difference become a mode of being. Consumption, as Douglas and Isherwood (1979) pointed out long ago, substantiates otherwise rather fluid, discursive cultural categories. This leads to a new situation for cross-cultural studies. For culturally sensitive marketing scholars, culture usually appears as the independent variable through which variations in behavior could and should be explained. But when culture becomes reflexive, it becomes in itself part of what should be explained.

Let us elaborate a little on this curious corollary of globalization, the apparent explosion of both claims to ethnicity and expressions of subculture through consumption. Many of the world's most brutal conflicts are waged in terms of culture, from the Turkic-speaking Uighurs in China to the Kurds in Turkey, Iran, and Iraq, the Maya in Guatemala and Mexico, and so on. Transnational ethnic dress enjoys renewed popularity among African-Americans in the United States. Wearing the Islamic veil becomes a politicized act. Ethnic cuisine, such as "Mexican" and even the creolized "Tex-Mex" version is hot transnationally. Ethnic arts and experiences commercialized to appeal to cosmopolitan tastes figure in treasured touristic excursions to New Guinea, the Pacific, Latin America, Africa, and the American Southwest. Culture itself is marketed across ethnic boundaries, as in the attempts to appropriate Native American spirituality by some New Agers or to popularize Islamic sacred music (Shannon, 2003). And commercially reinvented, culturally or subculturally affiliated holidays that enliven the calendar, such as Halloween, Carnival, or Cinqo de Mayo, are marketed across borders. This consciousness of the consumption of culture is due not least to the constant confrontation with "other" cultures, whether through immigration, global businesses and expatriate positions, tourism, or mass media.

In these eıxamples, commodified culture becomes part of a global structuring framework used to mark new sources of differentiation between consumers and people (Bouchet, 1995). However, one is inclined to ask, with Fırat (1995, p. 120), whether

> a culture so marketized [is] true to its original identity? Is a culture that ensures its livelihood through commodifying its qualities preserving what it originally was, or is it preserving something different from the original although resembling it in some respects?

These questions reveal the problematic issue of the authenticity of a culture that depends on a script of authenticity for its own persistence. This issue is evident in another study (Wilk, 1999) in which as part of a search for national cultural identity, Belizeans construct a "true" Belizean food culture. Wilk shows that Belizeans see this "authentic" food culture as an element in the global scheme of what constitutes a national culture; thus, they enter into an intense articulation of the local within a global structure. Other examples emerge in the domain of popular music (Bilby, 1999; Marlin-Curiel, 2001).

This is what we define as cultural reflexivity: a simulation, where cultural tradition increasingly exists mainly as a reflexive and conscious practical realization of some idea of culture. Culture, then, could be said to increasingly take the shape of hype, a simulation of a possibly imaginary or purified version of that particular culture. The problem boils down to the essentialism and the uncertainty about what constitutes the essentials of a culture. A similar problem of what we could call divergent or fragmented essentialism haunts Douglas and Craig's (1997) otherwise elaborate attempt to search for a new unit of analysis in cross-cultural consumer research.

Given the weaknesses recognized in the essentialist cultural position, researchers sometimes take recourse in the idea of hybridity (e.g., Pieterse, 1995). Hybridity alludes to the idea that any culture must be seen as an amalgamation of various inputs from other cultures locally adopted and changed to form a new constellation. But to indicate that present cultures are hybrid in the sense that they have all adopted cultural forms, consumption patterns, ideas, media, and technology from other cultures does not solve the problem. The idea of hybridity is itself too dependent on essentialism, because the hybrid puzzle, albeit implicitly, is made up of "pure" cultural traits brought from a "pure" origin somewhere (see Geertz, 1973). Wouldn't the reference to hybrid cultures as an ever more valid portrayal of postmodern mosaics of original and authentic elements spin into an infinite regress, where it becomes hybridity all the way down? The essential and "authentic" culture, slippery as an eel, perpetually slides out of our hands until it is lost in the mysterious depths of the Bermuda Triangle in the Sargasso Sea.

Not only is the notion of hybrid cultures subject to the same essentialist problem as the culture construct, as employed in marketing theory in general. The process of cultural reflexivity also robs hybridization of its seeming naturalness. As Thompson and Troester (2002) demonstrate, hybridity may in itself become an ideology expressed in various kinds of New Age holisms. "The best of different worlds" discourse in Thompson and Troester's analysis of natural health consumption or, indeed, the dissolution of differences in what Hannerz (1996) has called a "global ecumene" (e.g., religious movements of the type "there-is-only-one-God, -we-just-call-him[sic!]-different-names") provide examples of reflexive cultural hybridity.

A more fruitful approach to the understanding of culture than hybridization would be to understand culture and cultural difference as globalizing aspects of modernity (Hannerz, 1996), a "universalization of the particular" (Robertson, 1995), or a globalization of the idea of the concept of culture. Culture in such a perspective itself becomes a "global structure of common differences." With self-consciousness about culture (Cayla and Eckhardt, 2008; Davila, 2001), people are trying not to become just like us but more like themselves (Sahlins, 1993) and hence fuelling further cultural reflexivity.

The process of cultural reflexivity necessitates a new vernacular for talking about culture, the relations between culture and consumption, and the relations between culture and marketing. It does not necessarily mean that all traits we would call "cultural" in standard language use become reflexive or that tacit knowledge no longer exists in society. But in contexts in which culture is considered as a project rather than as a set of given, existential conditions, arguably some of the connections that are most typical and descriptive for cultural self-consciousness, it becomes obvious how culture not only determines consumption but also how consumption is applied as a determinant of culture. And it becomes evident that culture not only provides the framework for unfolding marketing activities but that marketing increasingly constitutes the framework for how culture unfolds as in commercialized and marketer-constructed holidays and celebration and market-place orchestration of ethnicity (Bouchet, 1995).

Given the proposed inversion of culture, from an independent variable to a malleable set of institutional elements and a marketable set of symbols, it becomes apparent that in spite of homogenization processes due to globalization, culture does not lose relevance. This point is where Levitt was completely wrong even as he was right. At the same time, culture's consequences can no longer be defined in the universalistic and essentializing terms that are the foundation of Hofstede's project. As we have seen, what seems to differentiate cultures can often conceal profound similarities. The existence of transnational cultural communities, such as environmentalists or investment bankers, testifies to how global ideoscapes and local (e.g., French; British) contexts interact to generate cultural formats ("environmentalism" and "investment banking") that are glocal in the profoundest sense: always tied to global imagery of environmental issues or finance capital, and always lived and experienced in a local political and commercial setting. The global is incorporated into the local according to its standard practices, and, so far, Hofstede might have been helpful for understanding the encounter of environmentalism or investment banking with high power distance versus low power distance contexts. But the reflexivity of the local members of the global community of environmentalists or investment bankers leads to a relativization of the local, understood through the lens of the global, and the global, understood through the lens of the local. Henceforth, French or British culture is no longer what it used to be, and its universalistic and essentializing measurements start to conceal more than they reveal.

Conclusion

The approaches to culture adopted within marketing are, perhaps not unsurprisingly, deeply embedded in the tendencies of Western modernism of "transforming difference into essence" (Friedman, 1995, p. 80). This tendency explains the allure of Appadurai's (1990) scapes in terms of describing sets of globalizing practices without falling into the trap of "culturalizing" these practices. The ethnoscapes, technoscapes, finanscapes, mediascapes, and ideoscapes remind us that culture is practiced and constituted out of practice (Bourdieu, 1979; Friedman, 1995).

And they remind us about the role of marketing as one of the most important commercial global systems of practice that has "a propensity to produce the kinds of identity spaces that we refer to as 'modernities'" (Friedman, 1995, p. 88). Ethnicity, culture, subculture, hybridization, and creolization are all examples of such modernities, constructed and constituted in part by marketing practices, basically essentializing themselves either in material culture or in more ephemeral ideas of cultural essence. Most often, though, as demonstrated by the example of Belizean food culture (Wilk, 1999), we deal not with one or the other but with both. Marketed goods in this light become material manifestations of the "cultural ideoscape." But this should not lead us to confuse essentializations with essence. Marketing scholars have hitherto tended to neglect the complexities at stake in the production of culture. In light of our arguments, comparative analysis is no longer the most obvious goal for research activities, but rather a starting point. Culture, rather than an explanatory framework of essential traits, becomes a paradigm based on which the praxis and practices of marketers and consumers become meaningful to researchers. Culture is not an object of study but a necessary approach for obtaining insights into the ongoing constitution of human societies.

Strategies for understanding ethnically or geographically located consumer culture should move away from modernist efforts to describe (presumably) temporally or spatially stable cultural identities or even lifestyles fixed within the boundaries of nation-states. Instead, we should move toward a strategy more appropriate to the emergent globalized situation, one focused on analyzing strategies and processes whereby meaningful, but inherently malleable and unmanageable, consumer identities are created, legitimated, contested, and resisted. In some cases, it may appear meaningful to classify these processes as creolization, hybridization, or even domestication when goods are recontextualized by consumers and institutions. But this classification must be done with great caution, because in itself it requires an authoritative performance, by which temporary adherence to a limited set of cultural conventions is effected.

If culture is no longer what it used to be, one possible solution in terms of methodology is to have recourse to the seemingly stable unit of analysis, the individual. Within consumer culture theory (Arnould and Thompson, 2005), this recourse may be witnessed by the proliferation of phenomenological approaches to consumer behavior, such as in *Journal of Consumer Research*, the leading journal in the field. As interesting as they are, such studies provide a very microcultural perspective on consumption patterns and generally lack a broader cultural framework for the understanding and structuration of these issues. Hence, we note the continued importance of balancing approaches that focus on consumers' phenomenological worlds of self-construction and identity formation with a more institutionally based approach that enables us to understand those processes in marketing, organization, finance, politics, and economics, which provide the plethora of consumption opportunities or, in other words, shape the universe in which consumer choices can unfold.

References

Appadurai, A. (1990) "Disjuncture and Difference in the Global Cultural Economy," *Theory, Culture and Society*, 7, 295–310.

Applbaum, K. (2000) "Crossing Borders: Globalization as Myth and Charter in American Transnational Consumer Marketing," *American Ethnologist*, 27 (2), 257–82.

Archer, K., Bosman, M. M., Amen, M. M., & Schmidt, E. (2007) "Hegemony/Counter-Hegemony: Imagining a New, Post-Nation-State Cartography of Culture in an Age of Globalization," *Globalizations*, 4 (March), 115–36.

Arnould, E. J. & Thompson, C. J. (2005) "Consumer Culture Theory: Twenty Years of Research," *Journal of Consumer Research*, 31 (March), 780–90.

Askegaard, S., Arnould, E. J., & Kjeldgaard, D. (2005) "Post-Assimilationist Ethnic Consumer Research: Qualifications and Extensions," *Journal of Consumer Research*, 32 (June), 160–70.

Askegaard, S. & Csaba, F. (2000) "The Good, the Bad and the Jolly: Taste, Image and Symbolic Resistance to the Coca-Colonization of Denmark," in S. Brown & A. Patterson (eds), *Imagining Marketing*. London, UK: Routledge, 124–40.

Askegaard, S. & Kjeldgaard, D. (2007) "Here, There and Everywhere: Place Branding and Gastronomical Glocalization in a Macromarketing Perspective," *Journal of Macromarketing*, 27 (June), 138–47.

Baudrillard, J. (1970) *La Société de Consommation*. Paris, France: Gallimard.

Bauman, Z. (1998) *Globalization: The Human Consequences*. Cambridge, UK: Polity Press.

Beck, U. (2000) "The Cosmopolitan Perspective: Sociology of the Second Age of Modernity," *The British Journal of Sociology*, 51 (1), 79–105.

Beck, U. & Sznaider, N. (2006) "Unpacking Cosmopolitanism for the Social Sciences: A Research Agenda," *British Journal of Sociology*, 57 (1), 1–23.

Belk, R. W., Ger, G., & Askegaard, S. (2003) "The Fire of Desire: A Multi-Sited Inquiry into Consumer Passion," *Journal of Consumer Research*, 30 (December), 311–25.

Belk, R. W. & Zhou, N. (2004) "Chinese Consumer Readings of Global and Local Advertising Appeals," *Journal of Advertising*, 33 (4), 63–76.

Bilby, K. (1999) "'Roots Explosion': Indigenization and Cosmopolitanism in Contemporary Surinamese Popular Music," *Ethnomusicology*, 43 (2), 256–97.

Boorstin, D. (1962) *The Image*. Harmondsworth, UK: Penguin.

Bouchet, D. (1995) "Marketing and the Redefinition of Ethnicity," in J. A. Costa & G. Bamossy (eds) *Marketing in a Multicultural World*. Thousand Oaks, CA: Sage, 68–104.

Bourdieu, P. (1979) *La distinction. Critique sociale de jugement*. Paris, France: Editions de Minuit.

Boyacigiller, N. & Adler, N. J. (1991) "The Parochial Dinosaur: Organizational Science in a Global Context," *Academy of Management Review*, 16 (2), 262–90.

Bray, Z. (2006) "Basque Militant Youths in France: New Experiences of Ethnonational Identity in the European Context," *Nationalism & Ethnic Politics*, 12 (Autumn/Winter), 533–53.

Çağlar, A. (2004) "Mediascapes, Advertisement Industries and Cosmopolitan Transformations: German Turks in Germany," *New German Critique*, 92 (Spring/ Summer), 39–61.

Cayla, J. & Eckhardt, G. M. (2008) "Asian Brands and the Shaping of a Transnational Imagined Community," *Journal of Consumer Research*, 35(2), 216–30.

Cohen, R. (1997) *Global Diasporas: An Introduction*. Seattle: University of Washington Press.

Davila, A. (2001) *The Marketing and Making of a People*. Berkeley, CA: University of California Press.

Douglas, M. & Isherwood, B. (1979) *The World of Goods*. New York, NY: Basic Books.

Douglas, S. P. & Craig, C. S. (1997) "The Changing Dynamic of Consumer Behavior: Implications for Cross-Cultural Research," *International Journal of Research in Marketing*, 14, 379–95.

Eckhardt, G. M. & Houston, M. J. (2001) "Cultural Paradoxes Reflected in Brand Meaning: McDonald's in Shanghai, China," *Journal of International Marketing*, 10 (2), 68–82.

Fırat, A. F. (1995) "Consumer Culture or Culture Consumed?," in J. A. Costa & G. Bamossy (eds) *Marketing in a Multicultural World*. Thousand Oaks, CA: Sage, 105–25.

Fırat, A. F. (1997) "Globalization of Fragmentation–A Framework for Understanding Contemporary Global Markets," *Journal of International Marketing*, 5 (2), 77–86.

Fiske, A. P. (2002) "Using Individualism and Collectivism to Compare Cultures–A Critique of the Validity and Measurements of the Constructs: Comment on Oyserman et al. (2002)," *Psychological Bulletin*, 128 (1), 78–88.

Friedman, J. (1994) *Cultural Identity and Global Process*. London, UK: Sage.

Friedman, J. (1994b) "The Political Economy of Elegance: An African Cult of Beauty," in Friedman, J. (ed.), *Consumption and Identity*. London, UK: Harwood, 167–88.

Friedman, J. (1995) "Global System, Globalization and the Parameters of Modernity," in M. Featherstone, S. Lash, & R. Robertson, (eds), *Global Modernities*. London, UK: Sage, 69–90.

Friedman, J. (1997) "Global Crises, the Struggle for Cultural Identity and Intellectual Porkbarrelling: Cosmopolitans versus Locals, Ethnics and Nationals in an Era of De-hegemonisation," in P. Werbner & T. Modood (eds), *Debating Cultural Hybridity. Multicultural Identities and the Politics of Racism*. London, UK: Zed Books, 70–89.

Geertz, C. (1973) *The Interpretation of Cultures*, New York, NY: Basic Books.

Ger, G. (1999) "Outlocaling the Global Competition," *California Management Review*, 41 (4), 64–83.

Ger, G. & Belk, R. W. (1996) "I'd Like to Buy the World a Coke: Consumption-scapes of the 'Less Affluent World,'" *Journal of Consumer Policy*, 19 (3), 1–34.

Giddens, A. (1991) Modernity and Self Identity: Self and Society in the Late Modern Age. Stanford, CA: Stanford University Press.

Hannerz, U. (1996) *Transnational Connections*. London, UK: Routledge.

Hobsbawm, E. & Ranger, T. (eds) (1983) *The Invention of Tradition*. Cambridge, UK: Cambridge University Press.

Hofstede, G. (1980) Culture's Consequences: International Differences in Work-Related Values. Beverly Hills/London: Sage.

Hofstede, G. (1983) "The Cultural Relativity of Organizational Practices and Theories," *Journal of International Business Studies*, 14 (Fall), 75–89.

James, A. (1996) "Cooking the Books: Global or Local Identities in Contemporary British Food Cultures," in D. Howes (ed.) *Cross-Cultural Consumption*. London, UK: Routledge, 77–92.

Kjeldgaard, D., Csaba, F., & Ger, G. (1996) "Grasping the Global: Multi-sited Ethnographic Market Studies," in Russell W. Belk (ed.) *Handbook of Qualitative Research Methods in Marketing*. Northampton, UK: Edward Elgar Press, 521–33.

Levitt, T. (1983) "The Globalization of Markets," *Harvard Business Review*, (May–June), 92–102.

Marlin-Curiel, S. (2001) "Rave New World: Trance-Mission, Trance-Nationalism, and Trance-Scendence in the 'New' South Africa," *TDR: The Drama Review*, 45 (3), 149–68.

Miller, D. (1998) "Coca-Cola, a Black, Sweet Drink from Trinidad," in E. Miller (ed.), *Why Some Things Matter*. Chicago, IL: Chicago University Press, 169–87.

Pieterse, J. N. (1995) "Globalization as Hybridization," in M. Featherstone, S. Lash, & R. Robertson (eds), *Global Modernities*. London, UK: Sage, 45–68.

Pieterse, J. N. (2007) "Global Multiculture, Flexible Acculturation," *Globalizations*, 4 (1), 65–79.

Reckwitz, A. (2002) "Towards a Theory of Social Practices: A Development in Culturalist Theorizing," *European Journal of Social Theory*, 5 (2), 243–63.

Rigo, E. & Rahola, F. (2007) "Regions, Minorities and European Integration," *Romanian Journal of Political Science*, 7 (Spring), 72–99.

Robertson, R. (1995) "Glocalization: Time-Space and Homogeneity-Heterogeneity," in M. Featherstone, S. Lash, & R. Robertson (eds) *Global Modernities*. London, UK: Sage, 25–44.

Robinson, W. I. (1998) "Beyond Nation-State Paradigms: Globalization, Sociology, and the Challenge of Transnational Studies," *Sociological Forum*, 13 (4), 561–95.

Sahlins, M. I. (1993) "Goodbye to Tristes Tropes: Ethnography in the Context of Modern World History," *Journal of Modern History*, 65, 1–25.

Schiller, N. G. (2005) "Transnational Social Fields and Imperialism," *Anthropological Theory*, 5 (December), 439–61.

Shannon, J. H. (2003) "Sultans of Spin: Syrian Sacred Music on the World Stage," *American Anthropologist*, 105 (2), 266–77.

Taylor, P. J. (1996) "Embedded Statism and the Social Sciences: Opening Up to new Spaces," *Environment and Planning*, 28, 1917–28.

Thompson, C. J., Rindfleisch, A., & Arsel, Z. (2006) "Emotional Branding and the Strategic Value of the Doppelgänger Brand Image," *Journal of Marketing*, 70 (January), 50–64.

Thompson, C. J. & Tambyah, S. (1999) "Trying to be Cosmopolitan," *Journal of Consumer Research*, 26 (3), 214–41.

Thompson, C. J. & Troester, M. (2002) "Consumer Values Systems in the Age of Postmodern Fragmentation: The Case of Natural Health Microculture," *Journal of Consumer Research*, 28 (March), 550–71.

Tomlinson, J. (1999) *Globalization and Culture*. London, UK: Polity Press.

Warde, A. (2005) "Consumption and Theories of Practice," *Journal of Consumer Culture*, 5 (2), 131–53.

Waters, M. (1995) *Globalization*. London, UK: Routledge.

Watson, J. L. (ed.) (1997) *Golden Arches East: McDonalds in East Asia*. San Francisco, CA: Stanford University Press.

Wilk, R. (1996) "Learning to be Local in Belize: Global Systems of Common Difference," in D. Miller (ed.) *Worlds Apart: Modernity Through the Prism of the Local*. London, UK: Routledge, 110–33.

Wilk, R. (1999) "'Real Belizean Food': Building Local Identity in the Transnational Caribbean," *American Anthropologist*, 101 (2), 244–55.

Wimmer, A. & Schiller, N. G. (2002) "Methodological Nationalism and Beyond: Nation-State Builiding, Migration, and the Social Sciences," *Global Networks: A Journal of Transnational Affairs*, 2 (4), 301–34.

Wind, Y. & Douglas, S. P. (1988) "The Myth of Globalization," *Columbia Journal of World Business*, 12 (Winter), 19–31.

Part IV   Extensions of and Advances in Culture Frameworks

7
Impact of Context on Cross-Cultural Research

Susan P. Douglas and C. Samuel Craig

Introduction

Culture has been studied extensively in diverse disciplines, each focusing on different elements and employing different research paradigms. Anthropology and sociolinguistics have focused on cultural content, examining, for example, a culture's artifacts, rites and rituals, and modes of communication. Cross-cultural psychology, developmental psychology, social psychology, and comparative sociology have paid greater attention to examining the influence of variables such as dominant value orientations, personality or social structure on cognitions, attitudes, modes of personal interaction, and behavior patterns. Each of these approaches provides a perspective on culture, focusing on a particular aspect and its impact on attitudes and behavior. However, the different perspectives largely ignore the impact of the contextual setting in which cultural phenomena take place.

Typically, the country is viewed as the appropriate unit of analysis in studying cultures. Inferences are made about the impact of culture based on observed differences in value orientations, sociocultural norms, cognitive processes, or other phenomena between two or more countries (Clark, 1990; Georgas and Berry, 1995; Sivakumar and Nakata, 2001). Consequently, there is a mistaken tendency to equate "culture" with nation or "ethnic group" and to use the concept of the nation-state in both defining samples and interpreting results. This has been termed, by Georgas and Berry (1995), "the onomastic fallacy," in which the name of a country is used to identify the culture and serves as a surrogate for a range of variables that may account for observed similarities and differences between cultures. Often interpretations are after the fact, based on the choice of a cultural antecedent that "pops" into the author's mind (Berry, 1992).

Similarly, in marketing, a variety of different approaches to the study of culture have been adopted, typically grounded in the research tradition of a parent discipline, such as anthropology, cognitive psychology, developmental psychology, linguistics, or sociology. Each incorporates its own implicit or explicit conceptualization of culture. Again, the country or subcultural group is used as the unit of analysis (i.e., the basis for the sampling frame or factor in an experimental design), and inferences are made about culture based on implicit or explicit comparisons of the phenomena studied between countries or subgroupings. As in other social sciences, the impact of contextual factors associated with that sampling frame is typically ignored. Yet, these powerful forces are responsible for shaping the observed outcomes. Figure 7.1 shows the overall relationship between context and culture. Each culture (and subculture) exists within a context, and the context helps shape the culture. Different aspects of context may influence the nature of a culture. In comparative studies, this can introduce a confounding effect, in that observed differences between consumer values and attitudes or consumption may be the result of context rather than culture.

The purpose of this chapter is to suggest the importance of examining the role of contextual factors when conducting cross-cultural research and to suggest various methodological techniques that can be used to take these factors into account. First, the various research traditions in cross-cultural consumer research are examined together with the implicit or explicit conceptualization of culture. Second, the importance of contextual factors in influencing cultural phenomena is then examined. Third, some alternative approaches for examining the

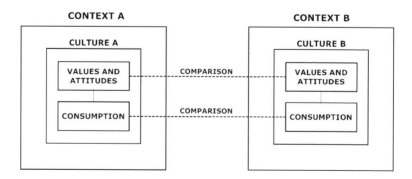

Figure 7.1   The context of culture

impact of contextual factors on culture and consumption are discussed. Finally, increased attention to the impact of contextual variables in cross-cultural research is advocated, which it is believed will lead to improved understanding of cultural influences on consumer behavior. It is important to note that although these issues are discussed here in relation to cross-cultural consumer research, they are also relevant to cross-cultural management studies and apply broadly to any research that examines the impact of culture across different contexts.

Culture in marketing

Culture is a complex, amorphous, and ambiguous concept. As indicated previously, it has been studied from a variety of perspectives that stress different aspects. Depending on the research tradition and paradigm, the perspective on culture differs, as well as, and more importantly, the specific aspects studied. This diversity is compounded by the use of a variety of research methodologies, including observational studies, participant/observer studies, experimental and developmental studies, and survey research. As a result, there is no one overarching perspective that enables the integration or even comparison of the findings of these various literatures into a unified whole.

Studies of the role of culture and consumer behavior have typically either explored the cultural embeddedness and meaning of consumption objects and behavior or examined the influence of culture on consumer attitudes and behavior patterns. In the latter case, culture has been conceived in terms of the value orientations that characterize a given society and govern its modes of interaction or behavior, the characteristic lifestyles, and the behavior patterns of specific national, linguistic, or ethnic groupings. In some instances, this view of culture has been explicitly operationalized, whereas in others, it is implicit in the choice of the sampling unit. At least five major threads, each incorporating different conceptualizations of culture, can be identified. These differ essentially in terms of whether they focus on the content of culture or the unit of cultural analysis and in the extent to which cultural phenomena are the central focus of research or rather are viewed as influences on the phenomena studied. More critically, in each of these approaches, culture is necessarily studied within a context that helps shape it.

Content of culture

Culture as Artifact

Each culture has its own vision of the world and set of culturally constituted meanings that provide understandings and rules for its members, and may often seem unintelligible to others. Within this stream, McCracken's (1986) work provides a framework for understanding the cultural meaning of consumer goods and consumption patterns, and identifies cultural categories of time, space, nature, and person as the fundamental coordinates of meaning that organize the phenomenal world. Brands serve as cultural markers, reinforcing status boundaries and helping to denote social identities (Arnould and Thompson, 2005). The cultural meaning embodied in brands, as well as other status objects, may however vary, depending on the affluence and social aspirations of a culture's members (Belk, 1988; Belk and Ger, 1999).

Rituals associated with consumption behavior or specific consumption occasions provide insights into the way in which consumer goods are embedded in and form an integral part of the cultural fabric of society (Arnould, 1989; Belk et al., 1989). For example, rituals and behavior associated with gift-giving are an important element in promoting social ties and bonding between individuals in a culture (Joy, 2001). Equally, rites of passage such as marriage and death can result in conspicuous consumption associated with the search for new social identities (Bonsu and Belk, 2003). Studies of favorite objectives in developing countries also underscore differences in preference formation from one culture to another and the importance of understanding the cultural factors underlying diffusion patterns within each society (Wallendorf and Arnould, 1988).

Although these studies provide a rich understanding of the content of culture, there is little information on how the specific context shapes the content. While context is viewed as an integral part of culture, and cultural phenomena are interpreted in relation to a context, the challenge is to disentangle one from the other. As a result, the integration of findings relating to specific sites into a broader understanding of contextual versus cultural influences on consumption, across multiple sites, is somewhat problematic. Ultimately, much depends on how sites are selected and the extent to which contextual factors vary.

Culture as Communication

Closely related to this view of culture as content is research that examines the meaning and implications of language as an interpretation of culture. While both streams examine similar stimuli, the focus is different. Content studies examine the role and meaning of an object as it is used by consumers—for example, favorite objects of specific cultural groups such as the Hausa of Africa (Arnould, 1989). Communication studies, on the other hand, examine the use of objects and language as conveyors of culture, such as the use of ideographic writing systems in brand recall (Schmitt et al., 1994).

Language has many facets that relate to the meaning of consumer products. Linguistic structure plays an important role in the formation of cognitive processes such as perception, and hence judgment and choice (Schmitt and Zhang, 1998) and the encoding and recall of information (Tavassoli, 1999). The use of a minority subculture's language in advertising (Zhang and Schmitt, 2004) has also been found to impact consumer response. Language is shown to be an important thread of culture, not only in communication within a culture but also in categorizing cultural content and in retaining information relating to that culture.

Culture as Value Orientation

In marketing, several approaches have been adopted to examine the impact of a society's cultural value orientation on consumer behavior. Principal among these is the individualism–collectivism dimension (Hofstede, 1980, 2001; Triandis, 1995). Schwartz's (1992) framework of motivational values, derived from Rokeach's (1973) Value Survey, has also been used, though not as extensively. In the case of individualism–collectivism, countries typically are selected as exemplars of either individualist or collectivist societies, and the cognitive processes or behavior patterns of respondents in two or more countries are compared (Sivakumar and Nakata, 2001). A key objective is to determine whether cognitive processes and constructs, typically identified in an individualist society such as the United States, can be generalized to collectivist societies such as Hong Kong, Taiwan, or Japan.

In marketing, cultural orientation has been studied primarily in relation to marketing communications and cognitive processes. Differences have been found between individualist and collectivist societies in relation to the influence of consensus information on product evaluation (Aaker and Maheswaran, 1997), emotional appeals in advertising (Aaker and Williams, 1998) and the accessibility or diagnosticity of persuasion appeals (Aaker, 2000). These studies suggest the existence of major differences in the salience of appeals between individualist and collectivist societies (i.e., importance of the individual relative to the group).

More recently, attention has been drawn to the horizontal (valuing equality) or vertical (emphasizing hierarchy) nature of cultures and cultural orientations (Shavitt et al., 2006). This is analogous to Hofstede's (2001) measure of power distance and has been found to influence factors such as personal values, for example the importance placed on achievement, display of success, gaining influence and egalitarian reward systems, as well as impression management, for example emphasizing sociability, benevolence versus self-competence and self-direction, and advertising appeals (Shavitt et al., 2007).

While cultural value orientations tap a central dimension of cultural variation and provide a highly parsimonious approach to studying culture, they constitute broad societal constructs that do not reflect more nuanced or process-oriented aspects of society or the importance of contextual variables in influencing behavior and cognition (Miller, 2002; Oysermann et al., 2002). In particular, they ignore differences between individuals in the extent to which they subscribe to the dominant societal cultural orientation (Triandis and Gelfand, 1998), as well as the extent to which cultural influences may be activated in a given situation (Briley et al., 2000).

Unit of cultural analysis

Culture as Country

A large body of research has either explicitly or implicitly viewed culture as synonymous with country and hence equates cultural boundaries with political entities (Clark, 1990; Nakata and Sivakumar, 1996; Sivakumar and Nakata, 2001). In these studies, as noted by Georgas and Berry (1995), country is used as the geographic unit or domain to define the boundaries of analysis. The country becomes the spatial unit in relation to which samples are drawn, surveys or experiments designed, and inferences made about similarities and differences. As a political and organizational entity, the country provides a practical and convenient unit for data collection. Most secondary and industry data are available on a country-by-country basis. Countries also provide distinctive linguistic entities and typically have official language(s). In addition, since countries are customarily used as the unit of analysis, findings can be related to and interpreted in the light of previous research.

Early comparative studies (Green and Langeard, 1975) *implicitly* equated "culture" with country without any explicit operationalization of cultural variables or influences. Without a clear articulation of culture, the interpretation of these findings is problematic. For example, differences and similarities observed between countries are attributed to "culture" and interpreted in the light of national stereotypes or knowledge about a country or "culture." Results are thus idiosyncratic to the specific countries being compared, and generalizability to other countries or cultures is problematic.

In addition, nations are not necessarily comparable entities with regard to aspects such as the nature of their linguistic and cultural heritage. Particularly problematic is the situation in which countries appear to be appropriate entities, for example, in terms of individualism and collectivism, but are not comparable with regard to other aspects, such as the level of economic development, form of government, dominant religion, colonial heritage, etc. Many international marketing studies examine attitudes such as nationalism, ethnocentrism, and animosity within the context of large industrialized countries with large internal markets (Klein et al., 1998). The findings may not be readily generalizable to small, open societies, which have high levels of external trade and communication (Nijssen and Douglas, 2004).

Culture as Subculture

Subcultures, such as ethnic, sociodemographic, or other groupings, exist within countries and often have their own distinctive interests, consumption, and purchasing behavior patterns. Mexican Americans (Peñaloza, 1994) and Indian immigrants to the United States (Mehta and Belk, 1991), for example, have interests in specific product attributes, brands, or product categories and use different distribution outlets. The context for each subculture is the dominant culture that surrounds it, as well as the micro-context (e.g., neighborhood, living conditions, urban vs rural) in which they live.

In Canada, differences have been identified among different linguistic groupings. Francophones, for example, tend to be more introspective, emotional, and humanistic and less materialistic than Anglophones (Heon, 1999). Anglophones were also found to be less innovative, fashion conscious, and to rely less on opinion leadership, while demonstrating greater price consciousness and brand loyalty (Hui et al., 1993). Differences in search behavior for gifts between Anglophones and Francophones have also been identified (Laroche et al., 2000). Here, the geographic context is similar, but other factors such as national cultural origin and income level differ.

In some cases, similarities have been found in similar demographic groupings in different countries, which suggests a certain degree of independence between the context and shared values. For example, the attitudes and behavior of groups such as teenagers, young adults, and environmentally concerned consumers in different regions or countries throughout the world show strong similarities (Kjeldgaard and Askegaard, 2006). Equally, consumers with a global as opposed to local or hybrid consumption orientation and greater responsiveness to global brand positioning have been identified in cities in several countries (Alden et al., 2006). However, much of this research has focused on upscale consumers and young adults in urban areas, interjecting a bias toward similarity as well as reflecting their exposure to trends and lifestyles in other countries through television, the Internet, e-mail, social networking, etc.

In general, therefore, the impact of culture on consumer behavior has been studied in different ways, focusing on different facets of culture or types of cultural influence. In some instances, culture has been viewed as embedded in consumption behavior, in the meaning of goods consumed, or the setting in which consumption takes place. In others, the effect of cultural influences, such as value orientations on consumer attitudes or behavior, is examined. In general, however, the geographic unit of analysis—and hence the population base for the sampling frame in survey research or the criteria for selecting subjects in an experimental design—is either a country/nationality or alternatively a subgrouping within a country. Consequently, inferences made about culture may reflect the confounding effects of macro- or micro-level contextual factors, such as societal affluence, climate, religion, or population density.

Examining contextual effects on culture and consumption

Culture's context

While culture is often a key variable impacting consumer attitudes and behavior, it is important to recognize that culture's influence does not occur in a vacuum. Numerous other variables (both macro- and micro-environmental) coexist with and impact culture and hence may affect consumer behavior, both directly and indirectly. Culture may be viewed as the causal factor, but underlying contextual variables such as the affluence of a society or cultural grouping, level of education, degree of urbanization, the topographical or climatic context, or even the political system may be at least partially responsible for the observed differences or confound the impact of cultural influences. The context is particularly crucial when cross-cultural comparisons are being made, as not only do the cultures potentially differ but the contexts invariably do. Failure to take such contextual factors into consideration in cross-cultural research can result in mistaken inferences. Even if contextual effects are subtle, they still may alter observations and relationships.

A wide variety of different contextual factors may be identified that potentially influence values and consumption behavior. These include macro-environmental variables such as income, economic growth, population, education, health, religion, and climate, and micro-environmental variables such as family, local educational or government institutions, social organizations, population density, and other geographic characteristics. Equally, media and distribution infrastructure may help to form consumer attitudes and purchase behavior habits. All of these provide a backdrop or context in which cultural influences play out and may directly or indirectly influence consumer values and behavior.

Berry's eco-cultural or eco-social model (Berry, 1975, 1976, 2001; Georgas and Berry, 1995) provides a framework for examining the role of contextual factors in influencing behavior. Human diversity, both cultural and psychological, is viewed as a set of collective and individual adaptations to contextual factors and, more specifically, to the ecological and sociopolitical system. Ecological and sociopolitical influences are not seen as deterministic, but rather as following a pattern of mutual adaptation in which changes in one part follow changes in other parts through a dual process of acculturation and adaptation. On the one hand, human organisms interact with and adapt to their physical environment in order to satisfy their needs. On the other hand, cultural change occurs through sociopolitical institutions, such as education and employment, which alter extant cultural patterns.

A recent study (Georgas et al., 2004) applying the ecological framework (Berry, 1976, 1995, 2001) to account for differences in psychological characteristics and, in particular, psychological values across countries and geographic zones identifies six principal contextual dimensions: ecology, economy, education, mass media, population, and religion. These are considered critical in understanding the variation in psychological variables. Following this view, such contextual factors may also be expected to impact consumer values, attitudes, and behavior patterns. In particular, three distinct categories of contextual variables relevant to behavior as consumers can be identified: the ecological context, the level of societal affluence (i.e., wealth of a society), and the religious context.

Ecological Context

Ecology, measured in terms of factors such as monthly levels of precipitation, temperature, or climatic zone, has been found to influence both values and consumption patterns (Georgas et al., 2004; Parker and Tavasolli, 2000). Georgas and colleagues (2004), for example, find ecological factors have an important impact on psychological variables such as involvement, power distance, and individualism. Similarly, Parker and Tavassoli (2000) find that climate has an important influence on the consumption of pharmacological products such as alcohol, cocoa, coffee, tea, and tobacco.

According to Parker and Tavassoli (2000), the physio-economic environment encompasses both *abiotic* factors, such as climate, terrain, navigable waterways, and access to oceans and rivers, as well as *biotic* factors, such as the nature of vegetation and animal life and availability of arable land, water, minerals, and resources to produce food and build lodgings. Such factors result in differences in homeothermic consumption, including dress, caloric intake, and energy and architectural design, as well as nonhomeothermic consumption, such as food, medicine, leisure, art, and entertainment. Climate and terrain are viewed as shaping social processes and economic activity, and as particularly important factors in influencing the location of centers of cultural growth.

Climate, for example, is an important factor influencing food and clothing needs as well as housing. Clearly, individuals living in cold climates need warm clothing such as furs, wool, and leather, influencing modes of dress. Conversely, warmer climates require lighter clothing and the use of fabrics such as cotton and silk. In addition, other important cultural artifacts relate to housing needs. Again, the nature of buildings is influenced by climate and local vegetation. In Scandinavian countries, where forests are abundant, housing is typically made of wood. In countries where clay is more widely available, houses are more likely to be built of bricks. Climate also has an important impact on temperament. Since most humans tend to respond to light and warmth, people living in warmer climates and those where the hours of light remain the same throughout the year are more likely to be happy, cheerful and to respond and communicate with enthusiasm. Levels of suicide also have been found to be higher among those who live with little light for long periods of the year.

Climate and terrain influence what crops will grow in a given location, as well as what natural plants and other vegetation exist and whether cattle, sheep, and goats can be herded or fish caught as sources of food. Differences in food consumption patterns are a central element of cultural behavior and influence other factors, such as health, energy, and sporting activity. In hotter climates, people eat less food that requires higher levels of energy to digest, such as meat. People in colder climates engage in higher consumption of alcoholic beverages (Parker, 1997).

This approach emphasizes the role of ecological factors in shaping culture but ignores the role of sociopolitical and economic factors, such as wealth, education, employment, and governmental and social institutions, in fostering and filtering adaptation to the physical environment. However, it highlights key and often-neglected physio-economic variables and illustrates the importance of considering the role of the physical/ecological context in which individuals live in shaping cultural patterning.

Societal Affluence

The affluence of society is another powerful factor impacting culture and mediating its role on consumer behavior. Levels of gross domestic product (GDP) per capita, for example, have been found to be correlated with national value orientations and, in particular, with Hofstede's measures of individualism and collectivism (Hofstede, 2001). Highly developed countries are more likely to have high levels of individualism and value individualistic values, such as personal achievement and ambition. These are often important motivational factors driving the engine of economic growth and entrepreneurship. Furthermore, in poor countries, people depend on support from in-groups, such as families or local communities, but as wealth increases, individuals gain access to resources that enable them to make their own personal choices and spend according to their own individual interests.

The affluence of a society also influences the nature of its material possessions. Most treasured possessions and status symbols depend on the affluence of a culture and hence what an individual can afford to purchase. While in developed countries, the possession of an expensive model of car may be an important status symbol, in western Africa, the possession of a bicycle or a radio may confer similar status. Similarly, in developing markets, the possession of brands that are perceived as symbols of a Western lifestyle, such as adidas, Nike, and Levi's, is highly valued, as are brands that reflect the local culture (Belk, 1988).

The level of education in a country, measured, for example, in terms of factors such as levels of illiteracy, education, or expenditures on R&D, also impacts culturally embedded consumption behavior. Professionals and individuals with high levels of education are, for example, more likely to buy products such as books and certain types of entertainment products, such as opera, classical music, or classical ballet, as well as to travel to other countries to explore different cultures, than those with lower levels of education (Katz-Gerro, 1999). They also are more likely to be ecologically concerned and purchase in environmentally friendly stores, such as The Body Shop or Whole Foods Markets, and be more concerned with fitness and health, exercise regularly, and belong to gyms and health spas (Lee and Holden, 1999). In addition, they are more likely to be aware of and open to ideas and information from other cultures and be willing to try unfamiliar products from other countries, even if these are relatively expensive, such as exotic foods like frogs' legs or truffles (Nijssen and Douglas, 2008).

Social, economic, and political institutions also play an important role in forming and perpetuating cultural patterns and behavior. In some societies, there are social hierarchies, such as the social class structure typical of certain Western European countries or the caste system in India (Berry, 2006). Membership in a given social class, often defined by a combination of occupation, wealth, and birth, implies a certain social status. Each social class is bound by a system of social norms and obligations, and social interaction occurs predominantly within members of the same group, resulting in pressures for social conformity and similar consumption patterns (Berry, 2006).

Since wealth and possessions are key factors defining membership in a given social class, the distribution of wealth is often closely linked to the degree of social stratification and hence variation in consumption patterns within society. Many Latin American countries, with highly skewed income distributions, are also marked by high variation in consumption patterns and price sensitivity. Stratified societies also vary in terms of the extent to which individuals are tightly enmeshed in the social structure or rather are free to develop their own lifestyles and patterns of social interaction (e.g., Western Europe vs India). Conversely, in egalitarian societies, such as the Scandinavian countries, Japan, or Iceland, there is substantial social homogeneity and minimal variation in consumption patterns and behavior.

Former communist societies such as in Eastern Europe and Russia are also characterized by relatively egalitarian consumption patterns, although in Eastern Europe, privatization of the economy is resulting in the emergence of a middle class who are adopting Western consumer values and behavior patterns and look to the Western consumption society as its model. For example, Central European women's concern about their appearance and hence use of and involvement in cosmetics and branded products has been evolving as these countries transition from socialism to capitalism (Coulter et al., 2003). At the same time, in Russia, the emergence of business moguls in the energy and commodity sectors has resulted in the creation of a class of wealthy nouveaux riches, which engages in conspicuous consumption.

Religious Context

Religion is another factor with a strong influence on cultural values and consumption patterns. Some religions, such as Judaism, Islam, and Hinduism, have very clearly prescribed rules for consumption behavior, particularly with regard to food and alcohol, which in some cases also extends to dress, particularly for women. Strong religious beliefs typically are also associated with conservative, traditional values (Spika et al., 1985) with regard to social conformity and social issues such as feminism, divorce, and sexuality. These in turn may have either a direct or an indirect effect on behavior by consumers and, in particular, on their responses to certain types of advertising appeals or product positioning strategies.

The religious environment of a nation has been found to influence individual religious beliefs and the extent to which religious beliefs are passed from one generation to another (Kelley and de Graaf, 1997). Individuals living in religious nations are more likely to acquire ortho-dox beliefs than are those living in secular nations. In relatively secular nations, family religiosity influences the strength of children's religious belief, whereas in religious nations, family religiosity has less effect than does the national context. In the latter case, contacts with friends outside the family and with other peer groups, teachers in school, or colleagues at work may all become important influences on their lives. These influences reflect the national religious context and play a key role in shaping religious beliefs and values.

In essence, therefore, ecological, social, and religious contextual fac-tors play key roles in the formation and perpetuation of cultural values and behavior, as well as directly impacting consumer attitudes and behavior. Interactions within the family unit and with friends, teach-ers, or colleagues at work, as well as with members of other social and religious organizations to which an individual belongs, mediate the impact of macro-environmental forces. In some cases, these interactions may reinforce the impact of contextual variables on behavior, whereas in other cases, they may mediate the influence on values, attitudes, and behavior and act as barriers to change, at both societal and individual levels. Contextual factors are thus important elements influencing con-sumer attitudes and behavior. Even where their influence is subtle and indirect, they need to be taken into account when studying cultural influences on consumer behavior.

Accounting for the influence of context

Theory and prior empirical research may suggest that a particular macro-level contextual variable, such as wealth or religion, may have some influence on the dependent variables. However, because the impact of context has received relatively little attention, it is more likely that the researcher will need to make the assessment independently. In some cases, qualitative research, including focus groups, personal interviews, or living in a particular culture, can provide useful insights about the role of context (for more information about conducting multicountry qualitative research, see Craig and Douglas, 2005). Once there is an indication that context may have an effect on culture and the dependent variable(s), the next step is to incorporate context into the research design, the analysis, and the interpretation of the results. Accounting for the effect of context can be accomplished in a variety of ways. First, context may be examined directly as a factor in an experimental design. The effect of context can also be examined through the use of country-level covariates in an analysis of variance or country-level control variables in multiple regression. A third approach is analysis that compares the pattern of relationships within countries or between locations or consumer groupings within countries, rather than comparing the level of variables. Finally, hierarchical linear regression can combine both individual and country-level variables in order to assess the effect of context on culture and consumption.

Comparing contexts between countries

Experimental Design

If the unit of analysis is the country, countries should be selected either because they are exemplars of certain cultural characteristics, such as individualistic or collectivist societies, or alternatively because they differ on some contextual variable, such as wealth, level of economic development, climate, or religion, that is expected to impact the cultural or consumption phenomena studied. For example, Sivakumar and Nakata (2001) suggest a procedure for calculating preferred country samples using Hofstede's national culture values in four scenarios, two of which control for the effect of non-focal variables, other than national value orientations.

Subjects can also be selected from different locations (contexts) within countries, for example, cities or villages. Here the different contexts (locations) become a factor in the experimental design and analysis is first done within country and between contexts within countries. If there are significant within-country effects (i.e., between contexts), the similarity of the within-country context needs to be examined across countries, and the interpretation of the results should be tempered accordingly. If there are no significant differences within countries, then the analysis can be continued at the country level and the impact of macro-environmental contextual variables examined. This allows assessment of whether similarities are observed in countries at similar levels of development, with similar ecological contexts, in similar geographic locations, or with similar linguistic groupings.

Use of Covariates or Control Variables

If there is reason to believe that a particular macro-level contextual variable influences the level of the dependent variable, then this variable can be used as a covariate or control variable in the analysis. If the covariate is not significant, then greater confidence can be placed in the results. If a covariate is significant and the main effect is not, then it is reasonable to conclude that the contextual variable is primarily responsible for observed differences. If multiple regression is used, macro-environmental contextual variables can also be included as control variables (though in this case, it may be preferable to use hierarchical regression, as discussed subsequently). It may also be desirable to include an interaction term if there is theory or reason to suggest that a contextual variable interacts with a particular independent variable. This also implies that a large sample of countries will be needed so that statistical tests that are sensitive to sample size can be used effectively.

Pattern Versus Level

Most cross-cultural research examines whether the observed levels, typically the mean values, of variables differ between two or more countries. If contextual variables influence the level of a variable, this may result in a mistaken inference about cultural differences that simply reflect systematic variation in context. Generation of a correlation matrix of all dependent variables, independent variables, and contextual variables provides an overview of the pattern of relationships and an indication of the role of context. Examination of the pattern of relationships between independent and dependent variables within each country provides an indication of the similarity or differences in these associations across countries (see Van de Vijver and Leung, 1997). The mean values of the dependent and independent variables may be different, but if the correlation coefficients are the same, then a similar association between the variables holds across countries. This may be particularly important to examine when attention is focused on understanding the underlying mechanisms or factors associated with consumption behavior, rather than comparing the strength of a relationship between dependent and independent attitudinal or behavioral variables.

Hierarchical Linear Modeling

The importance of incorporating contextual effects directly into the analysis has been underscored by Blalock (1984), who argued that analytic models should incorporate both individual-level and macro-level variables. Discussion of this issue was extended in a subsequent review by DiPrete and Forristal (1994), who also reviewed appropriate methods for multilevel analysis. This discussion has, however, largely been confined to sociological literature.

A technique that is particularly appropriate for examining multilevel contextual effects is hierarchical linear modeling, which allows both individual-level and country-level variables to be included in the same analysis. Furthermore, it can deal with the problems of dependency, random effects, hierarchical nesting, and cross-level interactions (Hox and

Kreft, 1994). It can also handle unequal sample sizes as well as different time periods for repeated measures. Craig and colleagues (2006) used a random parameters hierarchical linear regression to estimate the success of U.S. films in eight foreign countries. The model incorporated film-level data (US box office revenue, genre) and country-level data (McDonald's per capita, cultural distance from the United States) while controlling for differences in per capita GDP.

Assessing the impact of context within country

The preceding section dealt primarily with contextual effects in cross-cultural research, where results between two or more countries are compared. It is also possible to examine the effect of context in single or multicountry research by examining different strata or groups, either within a country or across countries. Alternatively, either countries or groups within or across countries can be examined over time to determine how a changing context impacts values, artifacts, and communication.

Between-Strata Within-Country Analysis

The impact of context can be assessed within countries. When members of a given culture have immigrated to another country or macro-culture and settled in different areas in the country, each area presents a different context and may exert influence on how the subculture evolves (Douglas and Craig, 1997). At the same time, each immigrant group may create and develop its own context—for example, setting up retail stores or community groups and activities that cater to its specific needs. The impact of this micro-context and other factors associated with a particular location, as well as the macro-country context common to all subgroups, can be examined and compared across locations. The local contextual variables, such as population density, wealth, and housing size, and group-specific variables such as the number of local ethnic retail stores, ethnic schools, or community associations can be obtained from observation or census data and used to determine whether there are differences attributable to such factors. In situations with insufficient observations to conduct a statistical analysis, qualitative analysis can be used to ascertain whether context is at least in part responsible for differences in consumption patterns and behavior, such as product or store choice, between different locations.

Longitudinal Analysis

Analyses can be conducted over time within a country, across subcultures, or between countries (Nakata and Huang, 2005). There should be some expectation that the context has changed, based on factors such as economic growth, migration, political context, etc. Ideally, this should have changed at different rates between the locations compared, so that there should be varying effects of change in the macro-context. An added complexity that makes it difficult to make inferences is that in addition to the context, many other factors are changing over time. Also, with enhanced mass communication and Internet access across countries and cultures, it is increasingly difficult, if not impossible, to isolate the effects due to cultural factors from those due to other factors, such as technological or economic progress.

Conclusion

The complexity of cultural influences, the range of different contexts in which cultural influences are examined, and the numerous and diverse ways in which both culture and context are changing (Craig and Douglas, 2006) suggest the need to adopt a broader perspective that goes beyond the traditional approach of focusing on national culture and using the country as the unit of analysis. Irrespective of how culture is defined and the ways in which cultural influences on consumer behavior are examined, the influence of the cultural context at both the macro (i.e., country) and micro (i.e., community) level needs to be acknowledged and incorporated into the research design. In addition, analytical techniques should be employed to enable the researcher to assess the impact of contextual influences. This explicit consideration of the influence of the cultural context on consumer behavior will lead to a more complete understanding of culture, as well as greater confidence in the attribution of observed differences to culture.

References

Aaker, J. L. (2000) "Accessibility or Diagnosticity? Disentangling the Influence of Culture on Persuasion Processes and Attitudes," *Journal of Consumer Research*, 24, 340–57.

Aaker, J. L. & Maheswaran, M. (1997) "The Effect of Cultural Orientation on Persuasion," *Journal of Consumer Research*, 24, 315–28.

Aaker, J. L. & Williams, P. (1998) "Empathy Versus Pride: The Influence of Emotional Appeals across Cultures," *Journal of Consumer Research*, 25, 24–261.

Alden, D. L., Steenkamp, J.-B., & Batra, R. (2006) "Consumer Attitudes Towards Marketplace Globalization: Structure, Antecedents and Consequences," *International Journal of Research in Marketing*, 23 (3), 227–39.

Arnould, E. J. (1989) "Toward a Broadened Theory of Preference Formation and the Diffusion of Innovations: Cases from Zinder Province Niger Republic," *Journal of Consumer Research*, 16 (2), 239–67.

Arnould, E. J. & Thompson, C. J. (2005) "Consumer Culture Theory (CCT): Twenty Years of Research," *Journal of Consumer Research*, 31 (4), 868–82.

Belk, R. W. (1988) "Third World Consumer Culture," in E. Kumcu and A. F. Firat (eds) *Marketing and Development: Toward Broader Dimensions*. Greenwich, CT: JAI Press.

Belk, R. W. & Ger, G. (1999) "Accounting for Materialism in Four Cultures," *Journal of Material Culture*, 4 (2), 183–204.

Belk, R. W., Wallendorf, M., & Sherry Jr., J. F. (1989) "The Sacred and Profane in Consumer Behavior: Theodicy on the Odyssey," *Journal of Consumer Research*, 16 (1), 1–35.

Berry, J. W. (1975) "An Ecological Approach to Cross-Cultural Psychology," *Nederlands Tijdschrift voor de Psycholgie*, 30, 51–84.

Berry, J. W. (1976) *Human Ecology and Cognitive Style: Comparative Studies in Cultural and Psychological Adaptation*. Beverly Hills, CA: Sage.

Berry, J. W. (1992) "The Cross-Cultural study of Values: The Jack Horner Strategy and Alternative Approaches," paper presented at symposium, Antecedents and Consequences of Value Priorities: Cross-Cultural Perspectives, XXV International Congress of Psychology, Brussels, Belgium.

Berry, J. W. (2001) "Contextual Studies of Cognitive Adaptation," in J. M. Collis and S. Messick (eds) *Intelligence and Personality: Bridging the Gap in Theory and Measurement*. Mahwah, NJ: Lawrence Erlbaum Associates.

Berry, J. W. (2006) "Contexts of Acculturation," in D. L. Sam and J. W. Berry (eds) *The Cambridge Handbook of Acculturation Psychology*. Cambridge, UK: Cambridge University Press.

Blalock, H. M., Jr. (1984) "Contextual Effects Models: Theoretical and Methodological Issues," *Annual Review of Sociology*, 10, 353–72.

Bonsu, S. K. & Belk, R. W. (2003) "Do Not Go Cheaply into that Good Night: Death-Ritual Consumption in Asante, Ghana," *Journal of Consumer Research*, 30 (1), 41–55.

Briley, D. A., Morris, M. W., & Simonson, I. (2000) "Reasons as Carriers of Culture: Dynamic vs. Dispositional Models of Cultural Influences on Decision Making," *Journal of Consumer Research*, 27, 157–78.

Clark, T. (1990) "International Marketing and National Character: A Review and Proposal for an Integrative Theory," *Journal of Marketing*, 54 (October), 66–79.

Coulter, R., Price, L., & Feick, L. (2003) "Rethinking the Origins of Involvement and Brand Commitment: Insights from Postsocialist Central Europe," *Journal of Consumer Research*, 30 (2), 151–69.

Craig, C. S. & Douglas, S. P. (2005) *International Marketing Research*, 3rd edition. London, UK: John Wiley & Sons.

Craig, C. S. & Douglas, S. P. (2006) "Beyond National Culture: Implications of Cultural Dynamics for Consumer Research," *International Marketing Review*, 23, 322–42.

Craig, C. S., Greene W. H., & Douglas, S. P. (2006) "Culture Matters: Consumer Acceptance of US Films in Foreign Markets," *Journal of International Marketing*, 13 (4), 80–103.

DiPrete, T. A. & Forristal J. D. (1994) "Multi-Level Models: Methods and Substance," *Annual Review of Sociology*, 20, 331–57.

Douglas, S. P. & Craig, C. S. (1997) "The Changing Dynamic of Consumer Behavior: Implications for Cross-Cultural Research," *International Journal of Research in Marketing*, 14, 379–95.

Georgas, J. & Berry, J. W. (1995) "An Ecocultural Taxonomy for Cross-Cultural Psychology," *Cross-Cultural Research*, 29 (2), 121–57.

Georgas, J., van de Vijver, F. J. R., & Berry, J. W. (2004) "The Ecological Framework, Ecosocial Indices, and Psychological Variables in Cross-Cultural Research," *Journal of Cross-Cultural Psychology*, 35, 74–96.

Green, R. E. & Langeard, E. (1975) "A Cross-National Comparison of Consumer Habits and Innovator Characteristics," *Journal of Marketing*, 39 (July), 34–41.

Heon, E. (1990) "Excess Means Success in Quebec Market," *Marketing*, August 6.

Hofstede, G. (1980) *Culture's Consequences: International Differences in Work-Related Values Comparing*. Beverley Hills, CA: Sage.

Hofstede, G. (2001) *Culture's Consequences: Comparing Values, Behaviors, Institutions and Organizations Across Cultures*. Thousand Oaks, CA: Sage.

Hox, J. J. & Kreft, I. G. (1994) "Multilevel Analysis Methods," *Sociological Methods and Research*, 22, 283–99.

Hui, M., Joy, A., Kim, C., & Laroche, M. (1993) "Equivalence of Lifestyle Dimensions across Four Major Subcultures in Canada," *Journal of International Consumer Marketing*, 5, 15–35.

Joy, A. (2001) "Gift-Giving in Hong Kong and the Continuum of Social Ties," *Journal of Consumer Research*, 28 (2), 239–56.

Katz-Gerro, T. (1999) "Cultural Consumption and Social Stratification: Leisure Activities, Musical Tastes, and Social Location," *Sociological Perspectives*, 42 (4), 627–46.

Kelley, J. & de Graaf, Dirk N. (1997) "National Context, Parental Socialization and Religious Belief: Results from 15 Nations," *American Sociological Review*, 62 (4), 639–59.

Kjeldgaard, D. & Askegaard, S. (2006) "The Glocalization of Youth Culture: The Global Youth Segment as Structures of Common Difference," *Journal of Consumer Research*, 33 (2), 231–47.

Klein, J. G., Ettenson, R., & Morris, M. (1998) "The Animosity Model of Foreign Product Purchase: An Empirical Test in the People's Republic of China," *Journal of Marketing*, 62 (January), 89–100.

Laroche, M., Saad, G., Kim, C., & Brown, E. (2000) "A Cross-Cultural Study of In-Store Information Search Strategies for a Christmas Gift," *Journal of Business Research*, 49, 113–26.

Lee, J. A. & Holden, S. J. S. (1999) "Understanding the Determinants of Environmentally Conscious Behavior," *Psychology & Marketing*, 16 (5), 373–92.

McCracken, G. (1986) "Culture and Consumption: A Theoretical Account of the Structure and Movement of the Cultural Meaning of Consumer Goods," *Journal of Consumer Research*, 13, 71–84.

Mehta, R. & Belk, R. W. (1991) "Artifacts, Identity and Transition: Favorite Possessions of Indians and Indian Immigrants to the United States," *Journal of Consumer Research*, 17 (4), 398–411.

Miller, J. (2002) "Bringing Culture to Basic Psychological Theory–Beyond Individualism and Collectivism Comment on Oysermann et al.," *Psychological Bulletin*, 128, 97–109.

Nakata, C. & Huang, Y. (2005) "Progress and Promise: The Last Decade of International Marketing Research," *Journal of Business Research*, 58 (5), 611–18.

Nakata, C. & Sivakumar, K. (1996), "National Culture and New Product Development: An Integrative Review," *Journal of Marketing*, 60 (January), 61–72.

Nijssen, E. J. & Douglas, S. P. (2004) "Examining the Animosity Model in a Country with a High Level of Foreign Trade," *International Journal of Research in Marketing*, 21, 23–38.

Nijssen, E. J. & Douglas, S. P. (2008) "Consumer World-mindedness, Social-mindedness and Store Image," *Journal of International Marketing*, 16 (3), 84–107.

Oysermann, D., Coon, H., & Kemmelmeier, M. (2002) "Rethinking Individualism and Collectivism: Evaluation of Theoretical Assumptions and Meta-Analyses," *Psychological Bulletin*, 128 (1), 3–72.

Parker, P. M. (1997) *National Cultures of the World: A Statistical Reference*. Westport, CT: Greenwood Press.

Parker, P. M. & Tavassoli, N. T. (2000) "Homeostasis and Consumer Behavior Across Cultures," *International Journal of Research in Marketing*, 17 (1), 33–53.

Peñaloza, L. (1994) *"Atravesando Fronteras*/Border Crossings: A Critical Ethnographic Exploration of the Consumer Acculturation of Mexican Immigrants," *Journal of Consumer Research*, 21 (1), 32–54.

Rokeach, M. (1973), *The Nature of Human Values*. New York: John Wiley & Sons.

Schmitt, B. H., Pan, Y., & Tavassoli, N. T. (1994) "Language and Consumer Memory: The Impact of Linguistic Differences between Chinese and English," *Journal of Consumer Research*, 21 (3), 419–31.

Schmitt, B. H. & Zhang, S. (1998) "Language, Structure and Categorization: A Study of Classifiers in Consumer Cognition, Judgment and Choice," *Journal of Consumer Research*, 25 (2), 108–22.

Schwartz, S. H. (1992) "Universals in the Content and Structure of Values: Theoretical Advances Empirical Tests in 20 Countries," in M. Zinna, (ed.) *Advances in Experimental Social Psychology*, Vol. 25. Orlando, FL: Academic Press, 1–65.

Shavitt, S., Lalwani, A. K., Zhang, J., & Torelli, C. J. (2006) "The Horizontal/ Vertical Distinction in Cross-Cultural Research," *Journal of Consumer Psychology*, 16 (4), 325–56.

Shavitt, S., Lee, A., & Johnson, T. P. (2007) "Cross-Cultural Consumer Psychology," in C. Haugtveldt, P. Herr, & F. Kardes (eds), *Handbook of Consumer Psychology*. Mahwah, NJ: Lawrence Erlbaum Associates.

Sivakumar, K. & Nakata, C. (2001) "The Stampede Toward Hofstede's Framework: Avoiding the Sample Design Pit in Cross-Cultural Research," *Journal of International Business*, 32 (3), 555–74.

Spika, B., Hood, R., & Gorsuch, R. (1985) *The Psychology of Religion: An Empirical Approach*. Englewood Cliffs, NJ: Prentice Hall.

Tavassoli, N. (1999) "Temporal and Associative Memory in Chinese and English," *Journal of Consumer Research*, 26 (September), 170–81.

Triandis, H. (1995) *Individualism and Collectivism*. Bolder, CO: Westview Press.

Triandis, H. & Gelfand, M. (1998) "Converging Measurements of Horizontal and Vertical Individualism and Collectivism," *Journal of Personality and Social Psychology*, 78, 118–28.

Van de Vijver, F. & Leung K. (1997) *Methods and Data Analysis for Cross-Cultural Research*. Thousand Oaks, CA: Sage.

Wallendorf, M. & Arnould, E. K. (1988) "My Favorite Things: A Cross-Cultural Inquiry into Object Attachment, Possession and Social Linkage," *Journal of Consumer Research*, 14 (4), 531–47.

Zhang, S. & Schmitt, B. H. (2004) "Activating Sound and Meaning: The Role of Language Proficiency in Bilingual Consumer Environments," *Journal of Consumer Research*, 31 (1), 220–8.

8
Conceptualizing Culture as Communication in Management and Marketing Research

*Wendi L. Adair, Nancy R. Buchan, and Xiao-Ping Chen**

> Culture is communication and communication is culture.
>
> Hall, 1959, p. 169

Decades of management and marketing researchers are grateful to Geert Hofstede for bringing an empirical approach to studying culture in the workplace. Since Hofstede's (1980) original publication of the cultural values of IBM employees in 40 nations, hundreds of researchers have used the Hofstedean framework to understand culture's influence on managerial, consumer, and organizational behavior. This includes conceptualizing culture as a nation-level construct capturing a set of shared values and measuring culture empirically through self-reports of value statements. For managers and marketers, this approach has proven fruitful. When our goals are to explain and predict the behavior of employees, managers, and consumers in an increasingly global workplace, we agree that there is utility in measuring culture empirically at the individual level, in describing and categorizing individuals from different nationalities when shared values are apparent (though some authors in this volume might question the value of such an approach), and in empirically testing the relationship between cultural values and organizational outcomes. At the same time, we believe that it is time to move beyond the empirical study of cultural values to address other facets of culture that have the power to predict marketing and management behaviors.

Despite our tendency to focus on culture as values, many definitions of culture go beyond this conceptualization. For example, Parsons and Shils (1951) note that culture includes an organized set of rules or standards to which an individual is committed. D'Andrade (1984) sees

146

culture as not only shared meaning but also as symbolic discourse. And Herskovits (1955) defines culture even more broadly as the human-made part of the environment. However, in management and marketing, researchers have not taken advantage of many of these alternative conceptualizations of culture.

To help understand our perspective on where Hofstede began and where we propose to go from here, we turn to Triandis's (1994, p. 6) definition of culture as "unstated assumptions, standard operating procedures, ways of doing things that have been internalized to such an extent that people do not argue about them." Within the field of cross-cultural management, the study of culture has largely been focused on what anthropologists refer to as "culture as an ideational system" (Gudykunst and Ting-Toomey, 1988, p. 29). That is, we have focused, à la Hofstede, on the study of the cognitive aspects of a culture (the unstated assumptions); its values, beliefs, and norms; and the development of empirical tools to measure them. Since Hofstede first measured individualism–collectivism in 1980, there have been many theoretical advances (Triandis, 1995), including the introduction of a vertical–horizontal subdimension (e.g., Chen and Li, 2005; Triandis and Gelfand, 1998) and the vast literature on the independent–interdependent self-concept (e.g., Markus and Kitayama, 1991). There have also been empirical advances in the measurement of individualism–collectivism, such as subsequent individualism–collectivism scales (Singelis, 1994), Schwartz's (1994) scales for tradition and achievement, and House's scales for institutional and in-group collectivism (House et al., 2004).

What has received significantly less attention from cross-cultural management scholars is the study of the standard operating procedures and internalized ways of doing things that is also included in Triandis's definition. There has been relatively little management research into culture as an adaptive system, that is, an examination of culture that links groups of people and their adapted behavioral patterns to the ecological setting in which they live (Gudykunst and Ting-Toomey, 1988). It is in this vein that we turn to anthropologist Edward Hall's conceptualization of culture as a way to move cross-cultural research beyond Hofstede.

In his seminal book, *The Silent Language* (Hall, 1959) and in numerous publications that followed, anthropologist Edward Hall proposed that cultures could be differentiated on the basis of the relationship between communication in that culture and the interactants' reliance on the context in which it is presented. Hall noted that individuals within certain cultures—those he labeled as high context—rely on indirect communication and contextual information, such as the distance between interactants or the nature of the relationship between them, to convey meaning, stating that, "Without context, the (linguistic) code is incomplete since it encompasses only part of the message" (Hall, 1976, p. 86). In contrast, Hall proposed that individuals in low-context cultures rely more on direct communication and explicit words to convey meaning. Unlike Hofstede's, Hall's research methodology was not based on quantitative analyses of survey responses but instead on anthropological observations. These observations led him to propose that populations in Eastern societies, for example, Japan and China, tend to be more high context culturally, and populations in Western societies, for example, the United States and Germany, tend to be more low context. Essentially, Hall suggested that people are embedded within a social context and that culture can be captured in the different ways people communicate—specifically, in the extent to which they rely on cues within their context to convey meaning. Clearly, this conceptualization of culture as an adaptive system goes beyond value models such as Hofstede's that focus on culture as an ideation system.

Hall's theories regarding culture have been shown to have external validity by numerous practitioners, consultants, and diplomats and by academics writing for practitioner audiences. For example, the theory of high- and low-context cultures is a foundation for books and training seminars regarding cross-cultural management and communication (e.g., Gesteland, 1999; Harris and Moran, 1991; Lewis, 2006; Trompenaars and Hampden-Turner, 1997) and negotiations across cultures (Cohen, 1991). Hall's theory of direct and indirect communication was discussed by Brett, Behfar and Kern (2006) in *Harvard Business Review*, and his theory regarding reliance on the context of time was addressed by Bluedorn, Felker, and Lane (1992) in the *Academy of Management Executive*. We also note that Hall himself often consults for government and businesses, that he frequently uses organizational examples in his books, and that his 1960 *Harvard Business Review* article, "The Silent Language in Overseas Business," remains a staple in many cross-cultural business classes. Thus, there seems to be wide acceptance among practitioners of international management and marketing that Hall's ideas regarding culture ring true.

It is interesting, then, given the new conceptualization of culture that Hall presents and the apparent external validity of Hall's theories, that the attention given to Hall in academic literature has been extremely limited. In this chapter, we propose a thorough examination of Hall's conceptualization of culture—both by comprehensively examining the theory and by reviewing how Hall's theory has been treated within management and marketing literature—with the goal of offering new ways to operationalize culture and model its effect on behavior in and between organizations.

In the next section, we review and synthesize Hall's work on culture as communication, breaking down his comprehensive theory into four key components. We then discuss how Hall's general theory and these four components have been presented within prominent journals in the management and marketing disciplines. Our review of the academic literature demonstrates that research regarding high- and low-context theory has been sparse and shallow at best. The full scope of Hall's conceptualization of communication as culture has not been examined by management and marketing researchers. Furthermore, our review demonstrates that we have little understanding of the antecedents of the four components of Hall's theory and their organizational consequences. Finally, our summary reveals that measurement of high- and low-context cultures falls prey to the same weaknesses that many see in Hofstedean research; measurement is virtually always done by aggregate categorization of countries as high or low context, not on an individual level.

Based on this understanding of where we stand in the management and marketing literature with respect to Hall, we conclude this chapter by discussing how we can advance our full understanding of Hall's theory of culture as communication within cross-cultural research. We note some of the limitations of Hall's work and suggest how they might be overcome, and we propose avenues to extend Hall's model of culture to understand the antecedents and consequences of high- and low-context communication fully in an organizational setting.

Culture as communication in management and marketing literature

Upon a thorough reading of Hall's many works on culture (1959, 1966, 1976, 1983; Hall and Hall, 1987, 1990), it quickly becomes apparent that his conceptualization of culture as communication is deep and multi-faceted. Hall notes that communication occurs through many channels in the interaction context (e.g., tone of voice, space between interactants, status of interactants), and that one way to understand culture is to examine the different ways that people attend to and rely on these many contextual factors when communicating and interacting with others. Hall describes cultures as falling somewhere along a low–high context continuum that is bounded by low reliance on these contextual factors to convey meaning at one end and high reliance on context on the other. In other words, in low-context cultures, people do not use many different channels to communicate but instead communicate directly with unambiguous words. In contrast, in high-context cultures, people use many different channels and sources of information to convey meaning; communication occurs within a complex and rich interaction context.

Hall's (1959) general model of culture is quite complex, composed of nine distinct primary message systems. However, we believe the fundamental elements of Hall's conceptualization of culture as communication can be distilled into four key (non-orthogonal) components. The first component, communication style, relates to Hall's ideas about the degree to which messages are conveyed directly or indirectly and the extent to which people rely on explicit or implicit meaning. The second component, relationship context, captures Hall's ideas about the degree to which people attend to the nature and strength of relationships and to which relationships influence their communication and interaction patterns. The third component, time context, a dimension Hall termed monochronic–polychronic, captures the way people attend to time and let time influence their communication and social interaction. Finally, the fourth component, space context, relates to the degree to which people use and attend to space, for example physical or auditory, in social interaction.

According to our conceptualization, low–high context is not just about how we say or do not say things but also refers to how we use different kinds of information in our environment when we communicate and interact with others. Clearly such aspects of culture are relevant to the workplace, and Hall (1960) himself introduced many organizational applications. For example, in a description of the German workplace, Hall and Hall (1990, p. 64) note, "directness will govern human relations" (communication style), "formality and politeness, including proper respect for social and business status, will pervade daily business life" (relationship context), and "privacy and personal space will be safe from intrusion" (space context). Furthermore, Hall describes the differences in time context in Ethiopian organizations: "The time required for a decision is directly proportional to its importance. This is so much the case that low level bureaucrats there have a way of trying to elevate the prestige of their work by taking a long time to make up their minds" (Hall, 1960, p. 88).

Despite Hall's own application of his theory to business, a review of articles mentioning Hall that have appeared in prominent journals within management and marketing demonstrates that researchers in these fields have not embraced Hall's work in theory development or empirical research (see Tables 8.1–8.5). In the remainder of this section, we will first review research articles in management and marketing that have referenced Hall in a broad, general sense. Then we will briefly discuss each of the four components of low–high context and review how they have been addressed by management and marketing researchers. In the final discussion section of this chapter, we will suggest how researchers can improve the understanding and application of Hall's theory in both theoretical and empirical research.

References to Hall's theory in general

In Table 8.1, we include articles that mention Hall's theory in general, without reference to a particular facet of low–high context. We found only eight such articles appearing since 1990. We see a call for deeper examination of the role of context within organizational research (Boyacigiller and Adler, 1991) and a call to be aware of the influence of context on the methodologies we use in international business research (Mueller, 1991); both articles highlight the need for a deeper understanding of Hall's theory. Most of the articles that mention Hall do so only briefly to justify an untested proposition or as an ex-post explanation of findings, without a deeper examination of specifically which component of Hall might be influential in the research or exactly why. For example, Takada and Jain (1991) and Helsen, Jedidi, and DeSarbo (1993) hypothesize that the rate of new product adoption will be faster in high-context cultures than in low-context cultures without explaining the operant mechanism; what is it about high-context cultures that would lead them to this hypothesis, and why? Similarly, in the models proposed by Shaw (1990) and Weiss (1993), it is not clear whether the propositions are motivated by differences in communication style or by the differing levels of attention paid to nature of the relationship between the interactants (relationship context). As a result, across all these articles, theory development is lacking.

Finally, the literature in Table 8.1 highlights a weakness in operationalization and measurement that is demonstrated repeatedly in research applying Hall's theories. Those studies that did have testable hypotheses assigned countries into categories of high or low context without any confirmatory measurement. Can Hennart and Zeng (2002), for example, be certain that their populations in Japan and the

Table 8.1   Articles addressing Hall in general

Author	Journal, Year	A priori hypothesis/proposition or post-hoc analysis/interpretation of findings	Cultural group(s) studied	Method and measurement
Boyacigiller and Adler	*Academy of Management Review*, 1991	Proposition • "The low-context orientation of the United States (and also England) may explain the minimal emphasis organizational theory historically has placed on such contextual factors as history, social setting, culture, and government. Organizational science has become trapped, that is, trapped within geographical, cultural, temporal, and conceptual parochialism." (p. 276)		• Propositional paper concerning the content of organizational research
Helsen, Jedidi, and DeSarbo	*Journal of Marketing*, 1993	Post hoc analysis: • Analyzed relationship among low-, medium-, high-context countries and diffusion patterns (no relationship found). • Follows up on Takada and Jain, 1991 who suggested the rate of adoption is higher in high-context cultures.	Austria, Belgium, Denmark, Finland, France, Japan, Netherlands, Norway, Sweden, Switzerland, UK, US.	• Latent class analysis of diffusion patterns • Country-level categorization
Hennart and Zeng	*Journal of International Business Studies*, 2002	Hypothesis • Parents of international joint ventures do not have a common silent language, which will affect longevity.	Japan, US	• Proportional hazard model • Country-level categorization
Kim, Pan, and Park	*Psychology and Marketing*, 1998	Post hoc interpretation of findings • Chinese and Korean subjects exhibit high-context tendencies and American subjects exhibit low-context tendencies	China, Korea, US	• 16-item low-/ high- context scale • Items mainly value-based

Author	Journal	Findings/Propositions	Countries	Contributions
Mueller	*Journal of International Business Studies*, 1991	Post hoc interpretation of findings • "were this study to be replicated, an effort would be made to employ several translators for each language. There is a potential for the loss of information in the translation process. This potential is particularly strong in the case of the Japanese sample, as Japan is considered a high context culture." (p. 30)	US, Germany, Japan	• Content analysis of advertisements
Shaw	*Academy of Management Review*, 1990	Proposition • Individuals from high-context cultures are more likely to engage in controlled information processing than persons from low-context cultures		• Proposes a cultural model of cognitive processing
Takada and Jain	*Journal of Marketing*, 1991	Hypothesis: • The rate of adoption is faster in high-context cultures than in low-context cultures (supported)	Japan, South Korea, Taiwan	• Bass new product growth model • Country-level categorization
Weiss	*Organization Science*, 1993	Proposition • Low-context negotiators do not understand rejection statements made by high-context negotiators		• Proposes model of cross-cultural negotiations

United States differ with respect to high- and low-context communication, and indeed, differ in their "silent language" (an assumption in their hypothesis) without first measuring that this is so? Of all the articles listed in Tables 8.1–8.5, Kim, Pan, and Park's (1998) is the only example that includes a measurement of high and low context. However, the 16 items used in their scale are mainly value-based (similar to those found in the scales of Hofstede) rather than measuring communication and interaction styles and behaviors. Therefore, possible antecedents of communication behaviors are confounded with the behaviors themselves.

Communication style: Direct–indirect and explicit–implicit messages

The component of Hall's low–high context theory with which most people are familiar captures the degree to which people are direct or indirect when communicating. Hall (1976) notes that in low-context cultures people tend to say directly in unambiguous words the message they want their interlocutor to hear. Thus, meaning is explicit; it is not hidden in subtle nonverbal cues or obscure metaphors. In contrast, in high-context cultures, people rely on internal and external context as channels to convey information. Internal context refers to information carried by the individual, for example in the non-verbal cues or previous experience one brings to a social interaction. External context refers to information contained in the environment, for example in the subtle information that can be conveyed by one's choice of location for a meeting. Interestingly, in high-context communications, it is not only the sender who will encode an indirect or implicit meaning, but it is expected that the receiver will search for and decode the intended implicit meaning as well. Hall (1976) makes clear the distinction between low- versus high-context communications and the demands placed upon both parties to the communication with the following description:

> People raised in high-context systems expect more of others than do the participants in low-context systems. When talking about something they have on their minds, a high-context individual will expect his [or her] interlocutor to know what's bothering him [or her], so that he [or she] doesn't have to be specific. The result is that he [or she] will talk around and around the point, in effect putting all the pieces in place except the crucial one. Placing it properly—this keystone—is the role of his [or her] interlocutor.
>
> (p. 113)

It has been proposed that the directness–indirectness of low–high context communication also relates to how people in different cultures make arguments. The styles of persuasion characteristic of low-context cultures in the West are primarily direct and include Aristotelian argument (Johnstone, 1989; Walker, 1990), appeals to fact and objective proof (Walker, 1990), logic-based argument (Harris and Moran, 1991), and rational argument (Glenn et al., 1977). The styles of persuasion characteristic of high-context cultures in the East are more indirect and include appeals to ideology and general principles (Glenn et al., 1977; Pye, 1982; Walker, 1990), spiral reasoning (Ting-Toomey, 1988), and appeals to emotion (Glenn et al., 1977; Johnstone, 1989).

Of the four components of Hall's theory of culture as communication, it is the direct–indirect communication style that has been studied most extensively by academic researchers, particularly in the field of communication (Gudykunst, 1983; Holtgraves, 1997; Ting-Toomey, 1985, 1999). In the fields of management and marketing, direct–indirect communication as a cultural dimension has been addressed primarily in the negotiation, advertising, and feedback literature. In Table 8.2 we briefly summarize the management and marketing literature employing the construct of direct–indirect communication styles.

One area of research that has relied on Hall's low–high context theory to predict differences in direct and indirect communication is negotiation and conflict. For example, Adair and colleagues (Adair et al., 2001, 2007; Adair and Brett, 2005) have grounded their predictions in Hall's theory and found that low-context negotiators are more likely to state their preferences directly in words, whereas high-context negotiators are more likely to reveal their preference structure indirectly by making multiple offers. These authors also use low–high context to explain negotiators' use of rational versus affective persuasive strategies and negotiators' interaction patterns, for example reciprocity and other behavioral sequences (Adair, 2003; Adair and Brett, 2005; Adair et al., 2004).

Researchers investigating the provision of feedback across cultures have also employed Hall's theories. Sully de Luque and Sommer (2000) present a model in which organizations in what they termed "holistic cultures" ("specific-oriented cultures") were proposed to provide feedback more (less) through context using indirect, implicit (specific, explicit) messages. Rao and Hashimoto's (1996) examination of Canadian and Japanese organizations demonstrates that Japanese managers used more influence and reason with their Canadian subordinates than with their Japanese ones. Bailey and colleagues (1997) show that respondents from the United States will seek more direct, individualized feedback than will respondents in Japan, but not those in China.

Table 8.2 Articles addressing Hall's theory of communication style

Author	Journal, Year	A priori hypothesis/proposition or post-hoc analysis/interpretation of findings	Cultural group(s) studied	Method & measurement
Adair	*International Journal of Conflict Management*, 2003	Hypotheses: • Low- and high-context negotiators will reciprocate behaviors that are culturally normative to them (supported)	Germany, US, Israel, Sweden, Russia, Japan, Hong Kong, Thailand	• Negotiation simulation • Country-level categorization
Adair and Brett	*Organization Science*, 2005	Hypotheses: • Low- and high-context dyads will differ in the kind of behavioral sequences they exhibit owing to the indirect and flexible nature of high-context communication (supported)	Germany, US, Israel, Sweden, Russia, Japan, Hong Kong, Thailand	• Negotiation simulation • Country-level categorization
Adair et al.	*Negotiation Journal*, 2004	Hypotheses: • High context dyads will use more affective persuasion and low context dyads will use more rational persuasion (partially supported).	France, Russia, Japan, Hong Kong, Brazil, US	• Negotiation simulation • Country-level categorization
Adair, Okumura, and Brett	*Journal of Applied Psychology*, 2001	Hypothesis: • Low-context US negotiators will explicitly state preferences and priorities more often, and high-context Japanese negotiators will use offers more often to express preferences (supported)	US, Japan	• Negotiation simulation • Country-level categorization

Author(s)	Journal, Year	Hypotheses/Findings	Countries	Method
Adair, Weingart, and Brett	*Journal of Applied Psychology*, 2007	Hypotheses: • Multiple hypotheses to show offers are a source of information for Japanese negotiators but act as anchors for US negotiators (supported)	US, Japan	• Negotiation simulation • Country-level categorization
Al-Olayan and Karande	*Journal of Advertising*, 2000	Hypothesis: • Arabic magazine ads contain fewer information cues and less price information than US magazine ads (supported)	United States and the Arab world (12 Middle Eastern and 10 African countries)	• Content analysis of advertisements • Country-level categorization
An	*International Journal of Advertising*, 1992	Hypothesis: • Multinational brands' local Web ads are likely to use symbolic visuals for high-context nations and literal visuals for low-context nations (supported)	US, UK, Germany, Japan, China, Korea	• Content analysis of Web advertising • Country-level categorization
Bailey, Chen, and Dou	*Journal of International Business Studies*, 1997	Hypothesis: • US respondents will take more initiative to seek individual performance feedback than respondents from Japan or China (partially supported, in Japan but not in China)	China, Japan, US	• Questionnaire • Country-level categorization
Biswas, Olsen, and Carlet	*Journal of Advertising*, 1992	Hypothesis: • French ads use more emotional appeals than American ads; American ads contain more informational cues than French ads (supported)	France, US	• Content analysis of advertisements • Country-level categorization

(Continued)

Table 8.2 (Continued)

Author	Journal, Year	A priori hypothesis/proposition or post-hoc analysis/interpretation of findings	Cultural group(s) studied	Method & measurement
Choi, Lee, and Kim	*Journal of Advertising,* 2005	Proposition: • As cultural icons, celebrity endorsers can be used effectively in high-context cultures as an implicit means of conveying messages to consumers (supported)	South Korea, US	• Content analysis of commercials • Country-level categorization
George, Jones, and Gonzalez	*Journal of International Business Studies,* 1998	Proposition: • Low-context direct style and high-context indirect style can lead to negative affect in cross-cultural encounters		• Propose model of affect in cross-cultural negotiations
Lin	*Journal of Advertising Research,* 1993	Post hoc interpretation of findings • In high-context cultures, comparative or logic- based appeals are not desired, and familiar symbols or icons more effectively convey product image; in low-context cultures reliance is on rhetoric and logic (supported)	Japan, US	• Content analysis of commercials • Country-level categorization
Mueller	*Journal of International Business Studies,* 1991	Exploratory study: • Examined link between high-low context and use of soft sell, hard sell, and advertising based on product merit	Japan, US	• Content analysis of commercials • Country-level categorization

Author	Source	Findings / Proposition	Sample	Method
Rao and Hashimoto	*Journal of International Business Studies*, 1996	Hypothesis: • Japanese managers use more total influence and reason with their Canadian subordinates than with their Japanese subordinates (supported)	Canada, Japan	• Survey • Country-level categorization
Rao and Schmidt	*Journal of International Business Studies*, 1998	Post hoc discussion: • Negotiators may be adapting to their Far Eastern and Eastern European counterparts by adopting a soft and indirect, high-context style	Examination of US cross-national business alliances in 41 countries	• Questionnaire • Country-level categorization
Sully de Luque and Sommer	*The Academy of Management Review*, 2000	Proposition: • Organizations in holistic cultures will convey feedback more through context using indirect and implicit messages; organizations in specific-oriented cultures will convey feedback more through information exchanged by direct messages		• Cultural model of the feedback-seeking process
Ting-Toomey	*International and Intercultural Communication Annual*, 1985	Proposition: • Attitudes toward conflict will be direct and confrontational in low-context cultures, and indirect and nonconfrontational in high-context cultures		• Model of conflict and culture

(Continued)

Table 8.2 (Continued)

Author	Journal, Year	A priori hypothesis/proposition or post-hoc analysis/interpretation of findings	Cultural group(s) studied	Method & measurement
Tse, Francis, and Walls	*Journal of International Business Studies*, 1994	Hypothesis: • High and low context used to support hypothesis that individualism–collectivism influences reactions to conflict. Specifically, collectivists will have more negative reactions to conflict (supported)	Canada, China	• Experimental–negotiation scenarios • Country-level categorization
Zhou, Zhou, and Xue	*Journal of Advertising*, 2005	Hypotheses: • US ads use more direct, visual product comparisons than Japanese ads (supported); US ads visually identify brand names earlier than Chinese ads (supported); pacing is faster in US ads (supported)	China, US	• Content analysis of advertisements • Country-level categorization

Researchers in advertising have clearly capitalized on low–high context theory to explain differences in advertising content across cultures. This literature demonstrates that advertising in high-context cultures is likely to include fewer informational cues and less price information (Al-Olayan and Karande, 2000), more symbolic visuals relative to literal visuals (An, 1992), more emotional appeals (Biswas et al., 1992), more use of celebrity endorsers, cultural icons, and symbols relative to rhetorical and logical appeals (Choi et al., 2005; Lin, 1993), and less use of directly comparative visuals (Zhou et al., 2005) compared with advertisements in low-context cultures.

This body of research employing Hall's theory on communication style has clearly expanded our understanding of the organizational consequences of direct–indirect communication. Yet to highlight the research in just one area—feedback—a number of theoretically important questions are unanswered. For example, are Canadian managers (Rao and Hashimoto, 1996), who are probably lower context than Japanese ones, as adept at altering their communication style to the local context as are Japanese managers, who, because of their high-context nature, are attuned to adapting communication to a given context? Or why in the study by Bailey and colleagues (1997) do respondents from China and Japan, countries both aggregately categorized as high-context cultures, act differently in seeking feedback?

Furthermore, it is interesting that despite the plethora of studies that have been conducted on direct–indirect communication style, we have little understanding of the antecedents of this component of low–high context cultures. It is important to note that, as shown in the research of Tse and colleagues (1994) and Drake (1995), low–high context is sometimes even treated synonymously with individualism and collectivism, further confusing behavior with values—which, as we discuss in the conclusion, are likely antecedents of behavior. Finally, we observe that though the research cited here was conducted in numerous countries, measurement of low–high context was consistently done by aggregate country categorization, a weakness that leaves open the opportunity for explanations other than differences in propensities toward direct–indirect communication styles.

Contextual information I: The language of interpersonal relationships

According to Hall (1960), one of the channels through which information is conveyed in communication is the relationship between the interlocutors. In some cultures, things like status or relationship history convey important information that is used to guide social interaction. Hall notes that it is particularly in high-context cultures that people attend to and draw meaning from the relationship context between the two parties. For example, in his 1960 *Harvard Business Review* article, "The Silent Language of Overseas Business," Hall stresses the importance of understanding the "language of friendship":

> As a general rule in foreign countries friendships are not formed as quickly as in the United States but go much deeper, last longer, and involve real obligations. . . . Friends and family around the world represent a sort of social insurance that would be difficult to find in the United States.
>
> (p. 91)

It is not surprising then that research by Gudykunst (1983) demonstrates that members from high-context cultures are more cautious in interactions with strangers, rely more on cues about strangers' backgrounds, such as status, and ask more questions about strangers' backgrounds, such as their network of colleagues, than do members of low-context cultures. This is because the relationship context influences the manner and context of communication.

The relationship context also influences the degree to which face-saving measures will be employed in communication and the extent to which communication is in service of relationship promotion rather than conveyance of information. For example, Ting-Toomey (1999) notes that concern for face in low-context cultures is primarily for self-preservation, whereas in high-context cultures, people are more likely to engage in both self- and other-face maintenance. She also characterizes the different communication styles as person-oriented (i.e., low context) versus status-oriented (i.e., high context).

Hall discussed the importance of managers' understanding the role of relationships in different cultures. For example, he suggests that in low-context cultures, a written contract defines a relationship and one's ability to end or promote it; however, in high-context cultures, the relationship itself determines how business is conducted. Thus, he recommends that to succeed, managers from low-context cultures conducting business in high-context cultures need to learn the language of relationships.

Marketer John Graham, with colleagues from both management and marketing, has conducted virtually all of the academic research employing Hall's theory regarding relationship context (see Table 8.3). One set of articles demonstrates the relatively greater importance of relationships in high-context cultures. Money, Gilly, and Graham (1998) show the emphasis on the strength of network ties and extensive social interaction in business networks in Japan compared with the United States, and Money and Graham (1999) demonstrate among sales force employees that valence for pay influences Americans' job performance but not Japanese and that the overall job satisfaction of Japanese was most influenced by value congruence. Graham, Mintu, and Rodgers's (1994) negotiation simulation in 10 countries shows that in high-context cultures, personal relations are more important for negotiation satisfaction, and status relations are more important for negotiation profits. Another set of articles by Graham and colleagues demonstrates that relationship context impacts negotiation behavior and outcomes in high-context cultures. For example, in Japan, relationship context dictates that buyers typically have more power and therefore earn more than sellers (Campbell et al., 1988; Graham et al., 1988). But in high-context China, when the relationship context changes owing to a strong seller's market, Adler, Brahm, and Graham (1992) find that buyers did not earn more than sellers.

Graham's research has advanced our understanding of how Hall's theory of relationship context is concretely manifested, particularly in business negotiations, and highlights the importance of relationship networks and status within high-context cultures. However, our understanding of the antecedents of these behaviors related to relationship context remains clouded. For example, Money and Graham (1999, p. 198) describe their results as "consistent with Hofstede's (1991) characterization of the United States as a highly individualistic culture and Japan as a collectivistic culture . . . and Hall and Hall's (1987) description of the United States as a low-context culture and Japan as a high-context culture." Once again, the theories of Hall and Hofstede are simultaneously used as explanations, leaving little understanding of how the two theories are truly related.

Finally, the advertising article by Biswas and colleagues (1992) demonstrates again the weaknesses regarding the measurement of low/high context. The authors show that sex appeals are used more in French advertisements than in American ones, and suggest that this is because high-context French people have closer interpersonal relationships than do low-context Americans. Because of the aggregate country categorization of high- and low-context cultures, however, rather than the individual level measurement of communication and relationship context, we cannot be certain as to the mechanism of causality.

Table 8.3　Articles addressing Hall's theory of relationship context

Author	Journal, year	A priori hypothesis/proposition or post-hoc analysis/interpretation of findings	Cultural group(s) studied	Method & measurement
Adler, Brahm, and Graham	*Strategic Management Journal*, 1992	Hypothesis: • Chinese buyers will achieve higher profits than sellers (not supported)	China, US	• Negotiation simulation • Country-level categorization
Biswas, Olsen, and Carlet	*Journal of Advertising*, 1992	Hypothesis: • Sexual appeals are used more frequently in French ads than in American ads because of closer interpersonal relationships in France (supported)	France, US	• Content analysis of advertisements • Country-level categorization
Campbell, Graham, Jolibert, and Meissner	*Journal of Marketing*, 1988	Post hoc interpretation: • Buyers earn more than sellers in high-context, but not medium- or low-context cultures (supported)	France, Germany, UK, US	• Negotiation simulation • Country-level categorization
Graham, Kim, Lin, and Robinson	*Journal of Consumer Research*, 1988	Hypothesis: • Buyers earn more than sellers in high-context, but not medium- or low-context cultures (partially supported)	China, Japan, Korea, US	• Negotiation simulation • Country-level categorization
Graham, Mintu, and Rodgers	*Management Science*, 1994	Hypothesis: • Relative to low-context cultures, in high-context cultures, personal relations are more important for negotiation satisfaction, and status relations are more important for negotiation profits (supported)	US, Canada, Mexico, UK, France, Germany, USSR, Taiwan, China, Korea	• Negotiation simulation • Country-level categorization

Money and Graham	*Journal of International Business Studies*, 1999	Japan, US	Multiple hypotheses • Summary of findings: Education and valence for pay influenced the Americans' performance, but not the Japanese. Pay level was tied to individual performance for the Americans, but not for the Japanese. For the Japanese, overall job satisfaction was influenced by value congruence	• Causal model • Country-level categorization
Money, Gilly, and Graham	*Journal of Marketing*, 1998	Japan, US	Hypothesis: • Long business relationships that are characterized by high levels of trust and extensive social interaction with business contacts are manifested in higher levels of word-of-mouth activity among Japanese firms (supported) • Strength of ties is higher in the referral networks of Japanese buying companies than it is in American companies, both in the United States and Japan (supported)	• Qualitative, interview • Country-level categorization

Contextual information II: The language of time

A third aspect of low–high context is how people draw on the context of time when relating to others. Hall (1960, p. 17) characterized cultures according to their perspective on time, and stated that the "importance of this basic dichotomy cannot be overemphasized." At one end of the dichotomy, he described polychronic cultures in which people have a fluid and flexible view of time. In such cultures, time is in the background. People handle interruptions and simultaneous processing seamlessly, and relationships and meetings are not constricted by schedules and clock time. Hall suggests that Arab, African, Latin American, Asian, and Mediterranean societies are examples of polychronic cultures (Hall and Hall, 1987). At the other end of the dichotomy, Hall described monochronic cultures in which time is fixed and measurable. It speaks loud and clear, and thus people are highly attentive to clock time. Because of this attention to clock time, people in monochronic cultures tend to process information and arrange tasks sequentially. Their day is oriented around schedules and deadlines, and disruptions are not only annoying but also disorienting. Not surprisingly, examples of monochronic cultures include the United States, Germany, and Switzerland (Hall and Hall, 1987). This distinction between the strict, objective, monochronic view of time and the more fluid, contextual, polychronic view of time is part of the context-free and context-rich forms of relating in low- versus high-context cultures, respectively. This is because in polychronic cultures, time is not just about the clock; it is also relational (Ting-Toomey, 1999).

Hall's study of time launched the field of chronemics, which is defined as the study of temporal communication, including the way people organize and react to time in contexts such as negotiation (Macduff, 2006). A number of studies have reinforced the notion that perceptions of time are culturally bound (e.g., Jones, 1988; Levine, 1988; Trompenaars and Hampden-Turner, 1997, who refer to this dichotomy as sequential versus synchronic). The use of scheduling—and indeed of clock time—has been linked to the Industrial Revolution in the West, and with increasing globalization, technology makes the use of clock time pervasive in markets around the world (Goudsblom, 2001). Yet Trompenaars and Hampden-Turner (1997) suggest that even with these developments, non-industrial, polychronic perceptions of time are firmly ingrained and are likely to remain in many parts of the world.

Hall discussed the implications of the monochronic and polychronic views of time for international business managers. The time context component seems to be one that raises the most intense emotions because adherence to time, or the adjustment of it in lieu of relationship concerns, often implies respect. For the monochronic individual, being forced to wait 40 minutes for a meeting that had been scheduled far ahead of time is often taken as a show of disrespect. And it seems inconceivable—and likely rude—that during the business meeting their polychronic partner would allow constant interruptions—by phone calls, messages, even other people (Gesteland, 1999; Hall, 1960; Hall and Hall, 1990).

Research addressing Hall's theory of time is presented in Table 8.4. Organizational researcher Richard Brislin has explored Hall's theory of time as it relates to international business and proposed ten different time components that international managers should consider (Brislin and Kim, 2003; Brislin and Lo, 2006). Other researchers have proposed bringing the study of time into research on organizational culture and strategic planning (Bluedorn et al., 1999; Schnieder, 1989). There has been little on the empirical side, however, particularly with respect to national culture. Much of this research has focused on developing scales to capture organizational time values, for example the Polychronic Value Scale (Bluedorn et al., 1999) or the Polychronic Attitude Index (Kaufman et al., 1991). We found only two quantitative studies investigating organizational consequences of Hall's time context. Cunha and Cunha (2004) study the conflict that polychronic Southern European managers experienced when they were pressured to adopt a Northern, monochronic model of time management. Manrai and Manrai (1995) measure perceptions of time devoted to work versus social endeavors in low- and high-context cultures.

Virtually all the research cited here suggests the importance of understanding monochronic and polychronic cultures. With few exceptions, however, what is needed is further examination and a deeper understanding of how different views of time influence business practice, performance, management, strategy, and negotiation and of the factors that prompt such differing time-related behaviors.

Contextual information III: The language of space

Hall suggests that space too—or proxemics—is an important communication channel. Most obvious is the level of the physical boundary; one can state territory, or "communicate power," by maintaining (or infringing on another's) "invisible bubble of space" or by choosing a corner office on a top floor (Hall and Hall, 1990). Also, cultural studies of haptics, or the use of touch in social interaction, are related to the language of space. Similarly, Ting-Toomey (1999) characterizes cultures

Table 8.4 Articles addressing Hall's theory of time context

Author	Journal, Year	A priori hypothesis/proposition or post-hoc analysis/interpretation of findings	Cultural group(s) studied	Method & measurement
Armagan, Ferreira, Bonner, and Okhuysen	*Research on Managing Groups and Teams*, 2006	Proposition • Managers from Turkey and Portugal will do more multi-tasking, spend more time, and build more relationships during negotiation than managers from the United States		• Propose model of time and culture in negotiation
Bluedorn and Denhardt	*Journal of Management*, 1988	Proposition • Monochronic American managers experience stress when they visit polychronic cultures		• Review of time in organizational literature
Bluedorn, Kalliath, Strube, and Martin	*Journal of Managerial Psychology*, 1999	Proposition • Polychronicity should be studied as a dimension of organizational culture		• Develop inventory of polychronic values
Brislin and Kim	*Applied Psychology: An International Review*, 2003	Proposition • Culture affects time in international business interactions		• Propose 10 time concepts in international business

Cunha and Cunha	*Journal of Managerial Psychology*, 2004	Proposition • International managers in Portugal must find synthesis between Northern time and Latin time		• Semiotic analysis • Interviews
Kaufman, Lane, and Lindquist	*Journal of Consumer Research*, 1991	Implications • Polychronicity can be used to study culture and consumer behavior		• Develop polychronic attitude index
Manrai and Manrai	*Journal of Business Research*, 1995	Hypotheses • In high-context cultures, people perceive more time is devoted to work, and in low-context cultures it is perceived more time is devoted to social/leisure activities (supported)	International student sample	• Causal model • Country-level categorization
Schneider	*Organization Studies*, 1989	Proposition • Strategic planning in low-context cultures will be more urgent and pressured than in high-context cultures		• Propose model of culture and strategy formulation

as high or low contact, though she does not relate this directly to the low–high context distinction.

Hall (1960) relates the importance of understanding space as a form of communication for the cross-cultural manager. He tells the American businessperson:

> In the Middle East and Latin America, the [US] businessman [or woman] is likely to feel left out in time and overcrowded in space. People get too close to him [or her], lay their hands on him [or her], and generally crowd his [or her] physical being. In Scandinavia and Germany, he [or she] feels more at home, but at the same time the people are a little cold and distant. It is space itself that conveys this feeling.
>
> (p. 90)

Less obvious than personal distance is when space communication works at the level of the other senses, because "Few people realize that space is perceived by all the senses, not by vision alone. Auditory space is perceived by the ears, thermal space by the skin, kinesthetic space by the muscles, and olfactory space by the nose" (Hall and Hall, 1990, p. 11). Thus, factors such as the use of silence or interruption, emotion, and body language come into play. How people define and interpret these different forms of space in communication and social interaction provides another piece of contextual information that differentiates the low- and high-context cultures.

For example, silence is interpreted by low-context people as an uncomfortable void and a space to be filled with more conversation. In high-context cultures, however, silence is not an empty space but a communicative act; the empty auditory space communicates meaning (Gudykunst and Matsumoto, 1996). Thus, Graham (1985) finds that Japanese negotiators used silence more than either US or Brazilian negotiators. Graham (1985) also finds that Brazilian negotiators engaged in more facial gazing, interruptions, and touching, all examples of using space to communicate, than did US or Japanese negotiators, though he does not explicitly mention Hall or low–high context theory in that study.

Emotion and body language are also important space elements that have implications for social interaction in international marketing and management. As discussed by Cohen (1991, p. 33), "people are justifiably receptive to hidden meanings, always on the alert for subtle hints known from experience to be potentially present in the tone of conversation and the accompanying facial expressions and gestures (body language) of their interlocutors." However, in high-context cultures, people are more likely to be attuned to auditory and physical cues than in low-context cultures.

Despite the clear relevance of space for international business communication, both within and between organizations, there has been very little research on this dimension of low–high context (Table 8.5). The only article that specifically mentions Hall as a theoretical motivation is George, Jones, and Gonzales (1998); they propose in their model of affect in cross-cultural negotiations that individuals from high-context cultures use more touching during communication, which can be uncomfortable for low-context negotiators.

It is important to note that this work raises an issue that ultimately is a key limitation of Hall's theory. The term "high context" as applied by Hall includes people from Latin America, Asia, the Middle East, and Africa. The hypothesis of George and colleagues would seem to be true in Latin American cultures, for example. But clearly, the prediction would not apply to less affective but also high-context cultures such as Japan or China. We will discuss this limitation at more length in the conclusion. More generally, this limitation and the overall lack of understanding of the space context suggests that it is imperative that we gain a greater understanding of how communication and space context influence business behavior and performance and the antecedents of an interactant's attention to and use of space.

Discussion: Conceptualizing culture as communication

In 1959, Edward Hall proposed a novel theory of culture, one that examined culture as an adaptive system—linking groups of people and their adapted behavioral patterns to the ecological setting in which they live (Gudykunst and Ting-Toomey, 1988). Specifically, he suggested that culture is captured in communication and that communication is based upon the context in which it is presented. This view of culture is radically different from the dominant cultural paradigm within management and marketing, that of Geert Hofstede (1980), who, two decades after Hall, presented an ideation system of culture based upon values and beliefs. Based on our synthesis of Hall's theory and review of it as employed in the management and marketing literature, we draw several conclusions and propose a number of ways to move cross-cultural research beyond Hofstede. Essentially, we want to reach back into Hall's theory to move cross-cultural business research into the future.

Table 8.5   Articles addressing Hall's theory of space context

Author	Journal, Year	A priori hypothesis/proposition or post-hoc analysis/interpretation of findings	Cultural group(s) studied	Method & measurement
George, Jones, and Gonzalez	*Journal of International Business Studies,* 1998	Proposition • Individuals from high-context cultures use more touching during communication, which can be uncomfortable for low- context negotiators		• Propose model of affect in cross-cultural negotiations

First, low–high context communication is not simply about conversational directness and indirectness but also about what kind of context people attend to and how people rely upon cues within that context to convey meaning. Specifically, we propose that Hall's conceptualization of culture as communication consists of four core components: communication style, and the contexts of interpersonal relationships, time, and space. While several researchers have referred to Hall's general theory in passing, the management and marketing community has not incorporated the full depth and breadth of Hall's theory in its theoretical and empirical endeavors. The component of direct–indirect communication has received considerable examination from an array of researchers, but the components of relationship, time, and space context remain relatively unexplored. We suggest that perhaps it is better to think of Hall's contribution not merely as a single low–high context dimension but as something akin to a "cultural syndrome" (Triandis, 1995) that reflects multiple dimensions of communication and social interaction style. By understanding how people in different cultures use multiple channels and rely on information from multiple contexts to communicate, we can better understand the different patterns of social interaction that take place in organizations.

Second, we have little understanding of the antecedents of communication and interaction behaviors and patterns and only an embryonic understanding of the organizational consequences. Some scholars have suggested individualism/collectivism as an antecedent to direct/indirect communication (Gibson, 1997; Holtgraves, 1997) or facework (Ting-Toomey, 2005). But clearly, as noted by Gibson (1997), there are additional psychological antecedents that explain the communication style and behaviors captured by low–high context. Also, many of the scholars who have explored low–high context behaviors in the workplace have focused first on individualism–collectivism, rather than Hall's low–high context, as the explanatory framework. We propose that what is needed is a framework that will clearly specify antecedents for each of the four components of Hall's theory as well as the consequences. It is our belief that within this framework, Hofstedean values will likely be viewed as explanatory variables for Hallsian communication behaviors. Just as Ajzen and Fishbein (1980) propose that attitudes precede behaviors, we suggest that the specific values inherent in individualism–collectivism (I/C) may lead to specific high- and low-context behaviors. Clarifying which I/C values prompt which low–high context behaviors will not only provide us with a stronger theoretical framework of culture as communication but also help dispel the notion that the theories of Hofstede and Hall are perfectly correlated or some-how synonymous. In addition, we suggest that values other than I/C will be needed to explain certain high–low context behaviors. For exam-ple, values related to high and low power distance should be influential in prompting behaviors related to status in relationships.

Third, our review of the literature very clearly points out the need for a tool to measure, at the individual level, Hall's four components of culture as communication. Without such a measurement scale, researchers who employ Hall will be susceptible to the same criticisms levied at researchers of Hofstedean values who aggregately categorized nations as individualist or collectivist. And important, theoretical advancements—such as the framework suggested—can be made only if measurement is done at the individual level, allowing researchers to pinpoint or eliminate alternative explanations for high- or low-context behavior. For example, a clearly specified framework will allow research-ers to identify more precisely the value antecedents of high- or low-context communication and its influence on misunderstanding and conflict between work team members (based on a measure of commu-nication style), planning behavior (based on a measure of time context), and the role of relationships, status, or social norms in the workplace (based on measures of the contexts of relationship and space).

Now that we have an understanding of the state of knowledge sur-rounding Hall's low–high context theory in management and mar-keting, we suggest that we can embrace Hall and at the same time recognize and build on existing limitations in the theory. Specifically, we note that the theory does not adequately predict communica-tion in all high-context cultures. For example, on the one hand Latin American cultures are low context, because they are very direct and expressive when relating to others. On the other hand, these cultures are high context because they have a strong relational focus and a fluid and long-term view of time. So how would Hall characterize these cul-tures? Do they fall on the midpoint between low and high context on Hall's dichotomous continuum? Or is there yet another dimension we need to consider to account for styles of relating in these cultures?

Management consultant Richard Lewis recognized this distinct style of relating in Latin and Mediterranean cultures, and he proposed a tripartite model of culture in his book *When Cultures Collide* (2006). Rather than a continuum, he proposed a triangle with three points that represent three distinct types of cultures. One point of the triangle is represented by purely low-context cultures, which Lewis calls "linear active." Another point represents Latin and Mediterranean cultures, which Lewis describes as "lively, loquacious peoples who do many things at once" and calls "multiactive" (Lewis, 2006, pp. xviii–ix). At the third point are high-context Eastern cultures, which Lewis (2006) calls reactive. While some cultures are extreme linear-active (the United States), multiactive (Brazil), or reactive (Japan), other cultures fall somewhere between the extremes or even in the middle of the triangle. It is important to note that Lewis's categorization is based on his many years of qualitative observations and quantitative assessments of managerial communication styles around the world. But after taking a step back and examining what might be the theoretical underpinnings of Lewis's categorization scheme, we find that his categorization of cultural communication styles is best construed as an extension of Hall's low/high context theory.

So what does this mean for management and marketing research? We propose that scholars should embrace and extend Hall, considering how we can use his theory to develop models that account for the different cultural styles of relating within and between organizations around the globe. To this end, the suggestions just provided will allow us to overcome the current limitations in Hall's theory and to develop research that more accurately captures what Lewis suggests is the external reality of high- and low-context behaviors.

We propose the development of frameworks that do not simply identify antecedents and consequences of high- versus low-context behaviors but rather will specify the causal relationships for each separate component in Hall's conceptualization. Furthermore, the measurement of each of the four components will allow us to present a continuous variable for each component, rather than a dichotomous one. For example, an individual would not simply be classified as high or low context but rather as relatively more direct and explicit in communicating, relatively less attuned to the relationship context, and so forth. Thus, high and low context need no longer be viewed as a single, dichotomous construct but rather as four continuous constructs. The suggested framework and measurement will facilitate the examination and identification of respondents who may be relatively more high context in some aspects of their communication and relatively lower context in other aspects. Essentially, we could identify not only two cultural types as Hall proposed, or even three cultural types as are suggested by Lewis, but rather a multiplicity of cultural types, some that may have yet to be explored. We will then truly be able to move cross-cultural research beyond Hofstede by comprehensively examining the specific antecedents and organizational consequences of multiple types of communication and interaction patterns across individuals and societies, thus deepening our understanding of culture as communication.

Note

* All authors contributed equally to this chapter and order of authorship was determined alphabetically.

References

Adair, W. (2003) "Integrative Sequences and Negotiation Outcome in Same- and Mixed-Culture Negotiation," *International Journal of Conflict Management*, 14, 273–96.

Adair, W. L., & Brett, J. M. (2005) "The Negotiation Dance: Time, Culture, and Behavioral Sequences in Negotiation," *Organizational Science*, 16, 33–5.

Adair, W. L., Brett, J. M., Lempereur, A., Okumura, T., Shikhirev, P., Tinsley, C., & Lytle, A. (2004) "Culture and Negotiation Strategy," *Negotiation Journal*, 20, 87–111.

Adair, W. L., Okumura, T. & Brett, J. M. (2001) "Negotiation Behavior when Cultures Collide: The U.S. and Japan," *Journal of Applied Psychology*, 86, 371–85.

Adair, W. L., Weingart, L. R., & Brett, J. M. (2007) "The Timing and Function of Offers in US and Japanese Negotiation," *Journal of Applied Psychology*, 92, 1056–68.

Adler, N. J., Brahm, R., & Graham, J. L. (1992) "Strategy Implementation: A Comparison of Face-to-Face Negotiations in the People's Republic of China and the United States," *Strategic Management Journal*, 13, 449–66.

Ajzen, I., & Fishbein, M. (1980), *Understanding Attitudes and Predicting Social Behavior*. Englewood Cliffs, NJ: Prentice Hall.

Al-Olayan, F. S., & Karande, K. (2000) "A Content Analysis of Magazine Advertisements from the United States and the Arab World," *Journal of Advertising*, 29, 69–83.

An, D. (1992) "Advertising Visuals in Global Brands' Local Websites: A Six-Country Comparison," *International Journal of Advertising*, 26, 303–32.

Armagan, S., Ferrera, M. P., Bonner, B. L., & Okhuysen, G. A. (2006) "Temporality in Negotiations: A Cultural Perspective," in Y. R. Chen (ed.) *Research on Managing Groups and Teams: National Culture and Groups*, Vol. 9. San Diego, CA: Elsevier, 115–45.

Bailey, J. R., Chen, C. C., & Dou, S. (1997) "Conceptions of Self and Performance-Related Feedback in the US, Japan and China," *Journal of International Business Studies*, 28, 605–25.

Biswas, A., Olsen, J.E., & Carlet, V. (1992) "A Comparison of Print Advertisements from the United States and France," *Journal of Advertising*, 21, 73–81.

Bluedorn, A. C., & Denhardt, R. B. (1988) "Time and Organizations," *Journal of Management*, 14, 299–320.

Bluedorn, A. C., Felker, K., & Lane, P.M. (1992) "How Many Things Do You Like To Do at Once? An Introduction to Monochronic and Polychronic Time," *Academy of Management Executive*, 6, 17–27.

Bluedorn, A. C., Kalliath, T. J., Strube, M. J., & Martin, G. D. (1999) "Polychronicity and the Inventory of Polychromic Values (IPV). The Development of an Instrument to Measure a Fundamental Dimension of Organizational Culture," *Journal of Managerial Psychology*, 3, 205–30.

Boyacigiller, N. A., & Adler, N. J. (1991) "Parochial Dinosaur: Organizational Science in a Global Context," *Academy of Management Review*, 16, 262–90.

Brett, J., Behfar, K., & Kern, M. (2006)"Managing Multicultural Teams," *Harvard Business Review* (November), 84–91.

Brislin, W. R. & Kim, E. S. (2003) "Cultural Diversity in People's Understanding and Use of Time," *Applied Psychology: An International Review*, 52, 363–82.

Brislin, W. R. & Lo, K. D. (2006) "Culture, Personality, and People's Uses of Time: Key Interrelationships," in J. C. Thomas, D. L. Segal, & M. Hersen (eds) *Comprehensive Handbook of Personality and Psychopathology, Vol. 1: Personality and Everyday Functioning*. Englewood Cliffs, NJ: John Wiley & Sons, 44–61.

Campbell, C. N., Graham, J. L., Jolibert, A., & Meissner, H. G. (1988) "Marketing Negotiations in France Germany, The United Kingdom and the United States," *Journal of Marketing*, 52, 49–63.

Chen, X. P., & Li, S. (2005) "Cross-National Differences in Cooperative Decision Making in Mixed-Motive Business Contexts: The Mediating and Moderating Effects of Vertical and Horizontal Individualism," *Journal of International Business Studies*, 36, 622–36.

Choi, S. M., Lee, W., & Kim, H. (2005) "A Cross-Cultural Comparison of Celebrity Endorsement in Advertising," *Journal of Advertising*, 43, 85–98.

Cohen, R. (1991) *Negotiating Across Cultures: Communication Obstacles in International Diplomacy.* Washington, DC: United States Institute of Peace Press.

Cunha, M. P. E., & Cunha, R. C. E. (2004) "Changing a Cultural Grammar?: The Pressure towards the Adoption of 'Northern Time' by Southern European Managers," *Journal of Managerial Psychology*, 19 (Special Issue: Timescapes in Management: Creative Inquiries and Critical Examinations), 795–808.

D'Andrade, R. G. (1984) "Cultural Meaning Systems," in R. A. Shweder & R. LeVine (eds), *Culture Theory: Essays on Mind, Self, and Emotion.* Cambridge, UK: Cambridge University Press, 88–119.

Drake, L. E. (1995) "Negotiation Styles in Intercultural Communication," *International Journal of Conflict Management*, 6, 72–90.

George, J. M., Jones, G. R., & Gonzalez, J. A. (1998) "The Role of Affect in Cross-Cultural Negotiations," *Journal of International Business Studies*, 29, 749–72.

Gesteland, R. R. (1999) *Cross-Cultural Business Behavior: Marketing, Negotiating and Managing across Cultures.* Copenhagen, Denmark: Copenhagen Business School Press.

Gibson, C. B. (1997) "Do You Hear What I Hear: A Framework for Reconciling Intercultural Communication Difficulties Arising from Cognitive Styles and Cultural Values," in P. C. Earley & M. Erez (eds) *New Perspectives on International Industrial/Organizational Psychology.* San Francisco, CA: New Lexington Press, 335–62.

Glenn, E. S., Witmeyer, D., & Stevenson, K. A. (1977) "Cultural Styles of Persuasion," *International Journal of Intercultural Relations*, 1, 52–66.

Goudsblom, J. (2001) "The Work and the Clock: On the Genesis of a Global Time Regime," in W. van Schendal & H. S. Nordholt (eds), *Time Matters: Global and Local Time in Asian Societies.* Amsterdam, Netherlands: VU Press.

Graham, J. L. (1985) "The Influence of Culture on the Process of Business Negotiations: An Exploratory Study," *Journal of International Business Studies*, 16, 81–96.

Graham, J. L., Kim, D. K., Lin, C., & Robinson, M. (1988) "Buyer-Seller Negotiations Around the Pacific Rim: Differences in Fundamental Exchange Processes," *Journal of Consumer Research*, 15, 48–55.

Graham, J. L., Mintu, A. T., & Rodgers, W. (1994) "Explorations of Negotiation Behaviors in Ten Foreign Cultures Using a Model Developed in the United States," *Management Science*, 40, 72–95.

Gudykunst, W. B. (1983) "Uncertainty Reduction and Predictability of Behavior in Low- and High-Context Cultures," *Communication Quarterly*, 31, 49–55.

Gudykunst, W. B., & Matsumoto, Y. (1996) "Cultural Variability in Communication in Personal Relationships," in W. B. Gudykunst, S. Ting-Toomey, & T. Nishida, (eds), *Communication in Personal Relationships Across Cultures*. Thousand Oaks, CA: Sage.

Gudykunst, W. B. & Ting-Toomey, S. (1988) *Culture and Interpersonal Communication*. Newbury Park, CA: Sage Publications.

Hall, E. T. (1959) *The Silent Language*. New York, NY: Random House.

Hall, E. T. (1960) "The Silent Language in Overseas Business," *Harvard Business Review*, 38, 87–96.

Hall, E.T. (1966) *The Hidden Dimension*. New York, NY: Doubleday.

Hall, E. T. (1976) *Beyond Culture*. New York, NY: Random House.

Hall, E. T. (1983) *The Dance of Life: The Other Dimension of Time*. Garden City, NY: Anchor Press/Doubleday.

Hall, E. T. & Hall, M. R. (1987) *Hidden Differences: Doing Business with the Japanese*. New York, NY: Anchor Press/Doubleday.

Hall, E. T. & Hall, M. R. (1990) *Understanding Cultural Differences: Germans, French, and Americans*. Yarmouth, ME: Intercultural Press.

Harris, P. R. & Moran, R. T. (1991) *Managing Cultural Differences*. Houston, TX: Gulf Publishing.

Helsen, K., Jedidi, K., & DeSarbo, W. S. (1993) "A New Approach to Country Segmentation Utilizing Multinational Diffusion Patterns," *Journal of Marketing*, 57, 60–71.

Hennart, J., & Zeng, M. (2002) "Cross-Cultural Differences and Joint Venture Longevity," *Journal of International Business Studies*, 33, 699–716.

Herskovits, M. J. (1955) *Cultural Anthropology*. Oxford, England: Knopf.

Hofstede, G. (1980) *Culture's Consequences: International Differences in Work-Related Values*. Newbury Park, CA: Sage.

Holtgraves, T. (1997) "Styles of Language Use: Individual and Cultural Variability in Conversational Indirectness," *Journal of Personality and Social Psychology*, 73, 624–37.

House, R. J., Hanges, P. J., Javidan, M., Dorfman, P. W., & Gupta, V. (2004) *Culture, Leadership, and Organizations: The GLOBE Study of 62 Societies*. Newbury Park, CA: Sage.

Johnstone, B. (1989) "Linguistic Strategies and Cultural Styles for Persuasive Discourse," in S. Ting-Toomey & F. Korzenny (eds) *Language, Communication, and Culture*. Newbury Park, CA: Sage, 139–56.

Jones, J. (1988) "Cultural Differences in Temporal Patterns," in J. McGrath (ed.) *The Social Psychology of Time*. Newbury Park, CA: Sage.

Kaufman, C. F., Lane, P. M., & Lindquist, J. D. (1991) "Exploring More than 24 Hours a Day: Preliminary Investigation of Polychromic Time Use," *Journal of Consumer Research*, 18, 392–401.

Kim, D., Pan, Y. & Park, H. S. (1998) "High- Versus Low-Context Culture: A Comparison of Chinese, Korean and American Cultures," *Psychology and Marketing*, 15 (6), 507–21.

Levine, R. (1988) "The Pace of Life across Cultures," in J. McGrath (ed), *The Social Psychology of Time*. Newbury Park, CA: Sage, 39–59.

Lewis, R. D. (2006), *When Cultures Collide: Managing Successfully Across Cultures*, 3rd edn. London, UK: Nicholas Brealey Publishing.

Lin, C. A. (1993) "Cultural Differences in Message Strategies: A Comparison Between American and Japanese TV Commercials," *Journal of Advertising Research*, (July/August), 40–8.

Macduff, I. (2006) "Your Pace or Mine? Culture, Time and Negotiation," *Negotiation Journal*, 22, 31–45.

Manrai, L. A., & Manrai, A. K. (1995) "Effects of Cultural-Context, Gender, and Acculturation on Perceptions of Work Versus Social/Leisure Time Usage," *Journal of Business Research*, 32, 115–28.

Markus, H. R. & Kitayama, S. (1991) "Culture and the Self: Implications for Cognition, Emotion, and Motivation," in R. F. Baumeister (ed.) *The Self in Social Psychology: Key Readings in Social Psychology*. Philadelphia, PA: Psychology Press/Taylor & Francis, 339–71.

Money, B. R., Gilly, M. C., & Graham, J. L. (1998) "Explorations of National Culture and Word-of-Mouth Referral Behavior in the Purchase of Industrial Services in the United States and Japan," *Journal of Marketing*, 62, 76–88.

Money, R. B. & Graham, J. L. (1999) "Salesperson Performance, Pay and Job Satisfaction: Tests of a Model Using Data Collected in the United States and Japan," *Journal of International Business Studies*, 30, 149–72.

Mueller, B. (1991) "An Analysis of Information Content in Standardized vs. Specialized Multinational Advertisement," *Journal of International Business Studies*, 22, 23–39.

Parsons, T. & Shils, E. A. (1951) *Toward a General Theory of Action*. Cambridge, MA: Harvard University Press.

Pina, M., Cunha, E., & Cunha, C. E. (2004) "Changing a Cultural Grammar? The Pressure towards the Adoption of 'Northern Time' by Southern European Managers," *Journal of Managerial Psychology*, 19, 795–808.

Pye, L.W. (1982) *Chinese Commercial Negotiating Style*. Cambridge, MA: Oelgeschlager, Gunn & Hain.

Rao, A. & Hashimoto, K. (1996) "Intercultural Influence: A Study of Japanese Expatriate Managers in Canada," *Journal of International Business Studies*, 27, 443–67.

Rao, A. & Schmidt, S. M. (1998) "A Behavioral Perspective on Negotiating International Alliances," *Journal of International Business Studies*, 29, 665–90.

Roth, M. S. (1992) "Depth Versus Breadth Strategies for Global Brand Image Management," *Journal of Advertising*, 21, 23–36.

Schneider, S. C. (1989) "Strategy Formulation: The Impact of National Culture," *Organization Studies*, 10, 149–68.

Schwartz, S. H. (1994) "Beyond Individualism/Collectivism: New Cultural Dimensions of Values," in H. C. Triandis, U. Kim, & G. Yoon (eds) *Individualism and Collectivism*. London, UK: Sage Publications.

Shaw, J. B. (1990) "A Cognitive Categorization Model for the Study of Intercultural Management," *Academy of Management Review*, 15, 626–45.

Singelis, T. M. (1994) "The Measurement of Independent and Interdependent Self-Construals," *Personality and Social Psychology Bulletin*, 20, 580–91.

Sully de Luque, M. F. & Sommer, S. M. (2000) "The Impact of Culture on Feedback-Seeking Behavior: An Integrated Model of Propositions," *Academy of Management Review*, 25, 829–49.

Takada, H. & Jain, D. (1991) "Cross-National Analysis of Diffusion of Consumer Durable Goods in Pacific Rim Countries," *Journal of Marketing*, 55, 48–55.

Ting-Toomey, S. (1985) "Toward a Theory of Conflict and Culture," in B. W. Gudykunst, P. L. Stewart, & S. Ting-Toomey (eds) *International and Intercultural Communication Annual: Communication, Culture, and Organizational Processes*, Vol. 9. Thousand Oaks, CA: Sage Publications, 71–86.

Ting-Toomey, S. (1988) "Intercultural Conflict Styles: A Face Negotiation Theory," in Y. Y. Kim & W. B. Gudykunst (eds) *Theories in Intercultural Communication*. Thousand Oaks, CA: Sage Publications, 213–34.

Ting-Toomey, S. (1999) *Communicating across Cultures*. New York, NY: The Guilford Press.

Ting-Toomey, S. (2005) "The Matrix of Face: An Updated Face Negotiation Theory," in W. B. Gudykunst (ed.) *Theorizing about Intercultural Communication*. Thousand Oaks, CA: Sage Publications, 71–92.

Triandis, H. C. (1994) *Culture and Social Behavior*. New York, NY: McGraw-Hill.

Triandis, H. C. (1995) *Individualism and Collectivism*. Boulder, CO: Westview Press.

Triandis, H. C. & Gelfand, M. J. (1998) "Converging Measurement of Horizontal and Vertical Individualism and Collectivism," *Journal of Personality and Social Psychology*, 74, 118–28.

Trompenaars, F. & Hampden-Turner, C. (1997) *Riding the Waves of Culture: Understanding Diversity in Global Business*, 2nd edn. New York, NY: McGraw-Hill.

Tse, D. K., Francis, J., & Walls, J. (1994) "Cultural Differences in Conducting Intra- and Inter-Cultural Negotiations: A Sino-Canadian Comparison," *Journal of International Business Studies*, 25, 537–55.

Walker, G. B. (1990) "Cultural Orientation of Argument in International Disputes: Negotiating the Law of the Sea," in F. Korzenny & S. Ting-Toomey (eds) *Communicating for Peace: Diplomacy and Negotiation*. Newbury Park, CA: Sage, 96–117.

Weiss, S. E. (1993) "Analysis of Complex Negotiations in International Business: The RBC Perspective," *Organization Science*, 4, 269–300.

Zhou, S., Zhou, P., & Xue, F. (2005) "Visual Differences in U.S. and Chinese Television Commercials," *Journal of Advertising*, 34, 111–19.

9
Cultural Influence on Consumer Motivations: A Dynamic View

Donnel A. Briley

Cultural dimensions: Background

An understanding of the differences in the norms and values that predominate across societies can provide important theoretical and practical insights to those interested in the international environment. Recognizing this opportunity, researchers have identified various dichotomous value dimensions by administering extensive survey questionnaires to respondents from several different countries, then analyzing the responses to isolate those value characteristics that presumably differentiate one society from another. Hofstede (1980) completed seminal work in this research domain, prompting similar large-scale efforts, including the Cross Cultural Connection's study of 22 countries (Bond, 1987), the GLOBE study of 62 countries (House et al., 2004), and Shalom Schwartz's study of 38 countries (Schwartz, 1994, 1999).

As psychologists and sociologists have endeavored to mine dimensions describing societal differences in core values, business and other researchers have drawn on this work to explain and predict behaviors. Indeed, this approach has been the dominant paradigm used for cultural analyses in marketing and other social sciences. In marketing, an array of values dimensions have been used to yield insights regarding differences across consumers in a variety of processes, including perceptions of prices (Watchravesringkan and Yurchisin, 2007), responses to advertising themes (Han and Shavitt, 1994) and quality signals (Dawar and Parker, 1994), decision-making styles (Leo et al., 2005), tipping decisions (Lynn et al., 1993), and innovativeness (Steenkamp et al., 1999).

Advantages and limitations: An illustration

Research in the persuasion domain illustrates the potential of the cultural dimensions pioneered by Hofstede, as well as some limitations. As an example, persuasion researchers have examined how responses to various types of advertising appeals are affected by differences across cultures in the tendencies to view people as independent beings versus members of a larger collective. Constructs that reflect this dimension include individualism–collectivism (e.g., Hofstede, 1980, 1991; Triandis, 1995) and independence–interdependence (Markus and Kitayama, 1991). Consumers from countries that view the individual as interconnected with the larger group (collectivistic, interdependent) evaluate more positively advertisements that tout the popularity of the target brand (Aaker and Maheswaran, 1997), appeal to consumers' desires to assimilate others (Aaker and Schmitt, 2001), focus on family cohesion and harmony (Han and Shavitt, 1994), and emphasize conformity rather than uniqueness (Kim and Markus, 1999).

Thus, this single dimension has stimulated quite a bit of research examining the advertising domain and has yielded important insights. An important benefit of this research approach is that it is quite parsimonious. Cultural differences in a particular behavior can be ascribed to specific, measurable mediating constructs. And once an association is established between a particular value dimension and some behavior of interest, the predominant behavior in any given society can be inferred based on its score on that dimension. For marketing practitioners, this sort of analysis can inform international segmentation and targeting efforts.

However, some important limitations of this approach should be acknowledged. First, the individualism–collectivism dimension, like many others that purportedly distinguish cultures, is imprecise because it encompasses a broad range of more specific concepts. In Ho and Chiu's (1994) analysis of the individualism–collectivism dimension, they identify 18 independent components that could compose a more general construct. Some of the facets they identify include uniqueness versus uniformity, self-reliance versus conformity, and economic independence versus interdependence. Empirical analyses have also revealed the multidimensional nature of individualism–collectivism. In Briley and Wyer's (2001) factor analysis of a popular measure of this construct (Triandis, 1995), they find five independent factors rather than the expected bipolar form. The multifaceted nature of individualism–collectivism impedes the interpretation of findings in studies in which this construct is used. In particular, with various underlying facets included in construct measures, it is not clear which of these components drive significant results, and whether one or some amalgam of these is involved.

Second, the extent to which an individual embraces a particular value can change. Researchers who propose the use of value constructs to predict behaviors implicitly—and sometimes explicitly—assume that societies are relatively static and independent of each other. For this assumption to be valid, countries must have stable membership (i.e., populations are minimally mobile), and interactions should not be sufficiently frequent or extensive to prompt rethinking of accepted ideas and principles. Several factors tied to globalization may present challenges to these assumptions. In today's global village, societies and the values that underlie them are increasingly interconnected and potentially dynamic, rather than coherent and stable (Hermans and Kempen, 1998). Rather than being bounded, independent units, cultures are increasingly becoming interrelated systems (Chapter 6 in this volume). Our societies are more connected now than ever, and this trend seems likely to continue.

But in addition to the broad, society-based shifts in values that occur over years or even months, individuals can undergo changes in values from one moment to the next. For example, people have been shown to shift the values they report depending on the reference group they consider at the time their values are elicited (Heine et al., 2002) and after being exposed to icons that remind them of their cultural identity (Briley and Wyer, 2001). In the present chapter, I present a model of cultural influence that attempts to address these limitations—the broad, unwieldy nature of value dimensions and the shifting nature of people's endorsement of these values. This "dynamic view" builds on existing value dimension work, shifting the focus away from these dimensions and toward the forces that bring cultural influence into play. Similar to the conceptual approach taken by Adair, Buchan, and Chen in this volume, the dynamic view draws its inspiration from cognitive psychology principles.

A dynamic view of cultural influence

The view of culture that underlies the bipolar dimensions mentioned previously conceptualizes cultural knowledge in terms of very general constructs that are assumed to apply to all aspects of life. Culture's influence on judgment and behavior, according to this view, is constant and unwavering. This perspective aligns with personality psychology, suggesting that socio-cultural training leaves people from different cultural groups with different "personalities." Rather than conceptualizing culture in terms of broad, domain-general values, I attempt to understand cultural influence from a dynamic perspective, rooted in social cognition theory (Wyer and Srull, 1989; see also Hong et al., 2000).

According to this view, cultural influence arises due to a loose network of domain-specific knowledge structures (Bruner, 1990; D'Andrade, 1984), rather than due to an integrated, general worldview or value orientation. Some of the types of knowledge structures included in this network are norms, schemas, implicit theories, goals, and motives. Furthermore, a person can possess knowledge constructs that conflict with those that are a part of the cultural knowledge network, and this conflicting knowledge can guide behaviors sometimes. Thus, though cultural knowledge might be applied frequently in day-to-day situations, because it has become chronically accessible, it is not relied upon continuously. (For discussions of the determinants and effects of chronically accessible concepts and knowledge, see Bargh et al., 1986, 1988; Higgins, 1996.)

This perspective on cultural influence can offer some useful insights. Whereas prior work often characterized culture as possessing a "have or do not have" quality, the approach taken here allows for a more nuanced understanding of culture-driven behavior. I draw on the emerging view that cultural influence can be better understood by examining its influence on cognitions (for a review, see Morris et al., 2001). This approach captures the often-shifting attitudes and behaviors of multiethnic people (Benet-Martínez et al., 2002; Lau-Gesk, 2003) and the important influence of situational forces on all people (Hassin et al., 2004; Hong et al., 2000).

The focus on situational forces that flows from this conceptualization aligns with the notion that preferences are "constructed" at the time that judgments or decisions arise and that the context in which the construction occurs helps shape these preferences (for reviews, see Lichtenstein and Slovic, 2006; Loewenstein, 2007). Whereas classic economic utility theory suggests that people's consumption selections are determined only by the fit between their own urges and the features of available alternatives, developments from the behavioral decision theory stream show the importance of the decision context. This research demonstrates that people determine their preferences "on the fly," utilizing information and inputs drawn from the situation at hand.

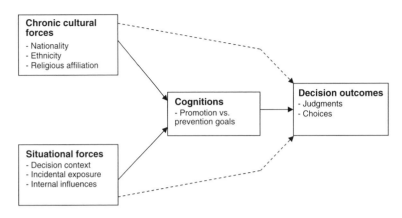

Figure 9.1 Dynamic view of cultural influence
Source: Adapted from Briley and Aaker (2006b)

People typically have an array of knowledge that is relevant to any given judgment or decision they face, and aspects of this knowledge can be in conflict, pulling toward different outcomes. The assessment or choice that emerges will depend on which knowledge is most prominent in informing it. A dynamic view of cultural influence addresses the question of when consumers' judgments and behaviors will be guided by cultural knowledge and when they will not, as suggested by Figure 9.1. In the absence of situational influences, the particular subset of behavior-relevant cognitions (e.g., goals and motives) activated and applied is determined largely by culture-related factors that have led these cognitions to become chronically accessible. However, features of the situational context in which the judgment or decision is made, or other recent experiences, can also influence the accessibility of these cognitions. The effects of knowledge activated by these situational factors could either add to or diminish the effects of chronically accessible cognitions on behavior (Hong et al., 2000; Oishi et al., 2000). In the present chapter, I apply this model to understand the effects of situational forces on consumers' goals and motives.

Culture and goals

According to regulatory focus theory (Higgins, 1997, 1998), people can pursue desired end-states using either promotion-focused or prevention-focused strategies. Promotion-focused strategies offer means through which a person can move toward a goal and thus are *approach oriented*, whereas prevention-focused strategies are *avoidance oriented*, offering means through which a person can avoid missing a goal. Suppose that a person has the goal of performing well at work. With a promotion-focused strategy, the person would endeavor to undertake activities and efforts that help her reach this end-state (e.g., arriving on time for work). Conversely, with a prevention-focused strategy, the person would endeavor to avoid activities and actions that hinder success (e.g., trying not to argue with colleagues). Regulatory focus theory suggests that promotion-focused strategies are characterized by greater eagerness and are more likely to be used in the pursuit of goals that relate to advancement and accomplishment. In contrast, prevention-focused strategies are characterized by greater vigilance and are more likely to be used in the pursuit of goals that are related to security and protection.

Importantly, the tendency to rely on one or the other of these strategies is influenced by a person's cultural background, because each individual's self-definition drives the type of goal pursuit strategy on which he or she tends to rely (Gardner, Gabriel and Lee, 1999). Self-definition describes a person's relation to others and has broad implications for cognitions, emotion, and behavior (Markus and Kitayama, 1991). Western societies engender the belief that the self is a unique, independent whole; East Asian societies engender the belief that the self is interdependent and thus defined by close relationships.

These alternative ways of construing the self are associated with distinct psychological goals. The primary goal of the independent self is to distinguish oneself from others in a positive manner; the emphasis is on achievement and autonomy. In contrast, the primary goal of the interdependent self is to maintain harmony with others in the social setting; the emphasis is on fulfilling social roles and maintaining connections with others (Heine and Lehman, 1999). Promotion goals help advance the independent self's need to distinguish itself from others in a positive manner, whereas prevention goals support the interdependent self's need to maintain good relationships and harmony with others (Kitayama et al., 2004; for a review, see Markus and Kitayama, 2004). As a result of these distinct motivational tendencies, cultures in which the independent self is fostered tend to be guided by promotion goals and strategies, and cultures in which the interdependent self is fostered tend to be guided by prevention goals and strategies (Lee et al., 2000).

Although a person's cultural background helps determine the regulatory strategy on which he or she relies when making decisions, transitory situational factors can alter these patterns by influencing which knowledge is influential. First, aspects of the particular decision situation can shift preferences between promotion-focus and prevention-focus strategies. Second, incidental events to which people are exposed prior to decision situations can have effects as well. Third, a person's motivational focus can depend on factors related to the way in which the decision maker approaches and processes the decision problem. These factors are discussed next.

When does culture matter?: Consumers' shifting goals

Decision context

Pursuit of regulatory fit

Interestingly, though culture can have a chronic influence on self-construal leanings, the two views of the self coexist within every person and can each guide decisions at different points in time. The relative strength of these two competing self-definitions depends on the particular situation a person faces. Therefore, features of the context that frame decisions can alter these construals and, consequently, shift the type of goal focus embraced. Studies by Aaker and Lee (2001) demonstrated this phenomenon in an advertising context.

In two of their studies, participants imagined themselves as the protagonists in an advertising scenario about the finals of a tennis tournament. The scenario referred to the protagonist as either an individual or a member of a team and was worded in a way that emphasized either the desirability of winning or the undesirability of losing. Later, some participants recalled aspects of the scenarios they had read, whereas others estimated their liking for the tennis racquet that ostensibly was being advertised. When participants had been induced to think of themselves as individuals, they recalled relatively more aspects of the story and evaluated the product more favorably when the story emphasized winning—a promotion-focused orientation. When participants had been stimulated to think of themselves as members of a team, however, they retained more information and made more favorable product evaluations when the story focused on the possibility of losing—a prevention-focused orientation.

Importantly, this pattern emerged in a study that included both American and Chinese participants. Thus, both cultural groups readily shifted their self-construals to match the scenarios with which they were presented and, as a consequence, shifted their preference for goal types.

Biculturals and language

Rather than having a single cultural identity, many consumers in today's increasingly global environment are biculturals, who have internalized two distinct sets of socio-cultural practices. These individuals often respond to the social demands of their respective cultural environments, switching between these cultural "frames." A cultural frame provides the "rules" that are associated with a particular cultural setting. So, in order to interpret their surroundings and determine appropriate actions, biculturals engage in frame switching as they move from one cultural context to another. For example, bicultural Hispanic Americans tend to exhibit prototypically Western patterns of speech and behavior to a greater extent when associating with European Americans than with members of their own ethnic group (Padilla, 1994).

Many biculturals speak and understand the languages associated with their bicultural identities, and distinct sets of behavioral tendencies often become associated with these languages (Phinney, 1996). If languages and frames are indeed connected in the minds of bilingual individuals, then exposure to a particular language might bring to the fore the related cultural frame, along with a set of prototypical decision strategies that fit with the group with which they interact. Research by Briley and his colleagues (2005) suggests that this is the case. According to their studies, bicultural individuals seek to fit in with their social environs and use language as an indicator of the identity of the audience that will observe their behaviors. This account emphasizes the deliberate, active role that biculturals take in interpreting social situations they encounter and determining appropriate actions for each (cf. Chiu and Hong, 2005).

Briley and his colleagues also examine the extent to which the language environment that bilingual individuals experience when making decisions affects the underlying regulatory strategies they use. In particular, their studies focus on choice situations in which the decision maker can apply a prevention strategy by seeking to avoid negative outcomes. People can minimize their potential losses when making a choice by selecting a "compromise" alternative (Simonson, 1989) or deferring the selection (Dhar, 1996, 1997). In situations that allow the decision maker to compromise, the person confronts a choice between a product with a very favorable value along one attribute dimension and a very unfavorable value along a second dimension, and a product with moderate values along both dimensions—a compromise. When both attribute dimensions are similar in importance, the compromise is sometimes particularly attractive to individuals who seek to avoid the feeling of a large loss on any dimension (Kahneman et al., 1991). Similarly, decision makers can stave off the experience of regret by deferring their choice rather than committing to a choice option.

Bilingual Hong Kong Chinese participants completed some tasks, and the regulatory strategy they applied was observed. Importantly, some received an English version of the questionnaire, and others received a Chinese version. Briley et al. (2005) predicted that participants who experienced a Chinese language environment would use a prevention focus, applying a Chinese decision frame, and that those who experienced an English language environment would be less likely to do so. This was the case. In the Chinese (vs English) version, participants were more likely to select compromise options, endorse decision guidelines advocating compromise, and defer their selections altogether.

In summary, the way that the decision situation is presented can determine the goals to which the decision maker aspires. Presentational features that can have an influence include cues that prompt the decision maker to take the view of either an independent individual or a member of a group and, for bilinguals, the language used to communicate the decision problem.

Incidental events that are unrelated to the decision situation can influence goal pursuit as well, as discussed next.

Predecision exposure: Incidental events

Events that a person encounters before addressing a decision situation can affect the outcomes by influencing the accessibility of knowledge and motives that are brought to bear. Once knowledge is brought to the fore of the mind for this initial event, this knowledge is likely to remain highly accessible for the subsequent decision task and, therefore, to be applied (Wyer and Srull, 1989). This pattern of influence, often called "priming" effects, relies on the spread of activation across related constructs that are associated in the mind (Anderson, 1983).

Consistent with this line of thinking, Briley and Wyer (2002) suggest that decisions are likely to be affected by a prior event in which participants are encouraged to think of themselves as members of a group rather than as independent individuals. They predicted that individuals who experience an event that prompts a "group mindset" would be likely to adopt a prevention focus in subsequent decisions. In one of their studies, participants were offered two equally attractive types of candy. They could choose either two candies of the same type or one candy of each type. Those who were motivated by the desire to maximize positive consequences of their choice and who had a slight preference for one candy over the other should have chosen two candies of the preferred type. However, those with a disposition to avoid the negative consequences of their decision should have focused on what they stood to lose rather than what they might have gained. Because the choice of two candies of the same type would incur a loss of the attractive features of the alternative (not chosen) candy, they are likely to compromise by choosing one candy of each type.

Prior to selecting candies, participants took part in an ostensibly unrelated task that introduced the "group mindset" manipulation. They were assigned randomly to either an individual-focus or group-focus condition and told that they would be completing an anagram task to test their thinking skills. Those in group-focus conditions were told they would be performing the task in groups and, on this pretense, were assigned seats at five-person tables. To encourage group cohesiveness, participants were told that the group's performance on the anagram task would be evaluated as a whole. In contrast, participants in individual-focus conditions were told they would be performing the task individually and were seated at single-person desks separated by partitions.

Participants then completed the anagram task, were told that the experiment was over, and were offered two pieces of candy as a "thank you" for their participation. Two popular brands of candy bars were placed in separate bowls near the exit, and participants' candy selections were observed through a one-way mirror. As expected, participants were more likely to choose one candy of each brand when they had previously completed an activity in a group rather than individually.

Processing approach

Sometimes a person's approach to a decision problem can increase or attenuate the extent to which he or she draws on cultural knowledge. Cultural knowledge is more likely to inform decisions when people feel the need to justify their decisions (Briley et al., 2000) or devote limited cognitive resources to the decision-making process (Briley and Aaker, 2006a).

Choice justification

Research by Timothy Wilson and his colleagues shows that people who need to give reasons for their choices (referred to as "introspection") often make different selections than they would have otherwise (e.g., Wilson et al., 1995; Wilson and Schooler, 1991). Because people who are asked to report explanations after their decisions do not have access to the cognitive processes that led to the decision (Nisbett and Wilson, 1977), they generate reasons by accessing implicit theories or decision rules. These decision rules and related reasons then take control of the decision process, taking the place of associational processes that might otherwise have guided their decision making.

But what is the source of these decision rules? According to Nisbett and Wilson (1977, p. 248), many are conferred by the culture or sub-culture of the decision maker. Thus, one might expect that the need to provide reasons might elicit different patterns of choices for people of different cultures, through the types of reasons that people generate. That is, cultures could endow individuals with different rules or principles that provide guidance for making decisions, and the need to provide reasons could activate such cultural knowledge.

Briley and his colleagues (2000) test these propositions by examining Chinese and North American students' selections of compromise options. About half of the participants from each cultural group were asked to provide a reason for their selection before indicating their choice, and the other half were not asked to do so. As expected, Chinese and North American participants differed regarding their tendencies to select compromise options, but only when they were asked to explain their decisions. Chinese decision makers were more likely, and Americans less likely, to compromise when they provided reasons. A content analysis of the participants' reasons confirmed that cultural differences in the frequency of generating moderation-oriented reasons mediated the difference in choices. This pattern was replicated in a comparison of North American versus Japanese participants and in a comparison of European-American and Asian-American participants.

Cognitive resources

A person's cultural background influences which values-relevant constructs become highly accessible (Hong et al., 2000). These chronically accessible constructs can be activated by rather general stimuli, such as the need to make a judgment for which the construct is relevant (Higgins and King, 1981). Furthermore, the automatic activation of these highly accessible constructs can affect evaluative judgments (Bargh et al., 1986). Briley and Aaker (2006a) apply these ideas in the persuasion context, suggesting that an appeal is often assessed on the basis of whether the concepts presented fit with a person's highly accessible, culture-based knowledge. Important in their research, however, is the premise that the influence of cultural knowledge on judgments exerts its strongest effects when people give their immediate reactions to advertisements and its weakest effects when people deliberate when forming opinions.

They argue that judgments that arise through the former, "reflexive" mode reflect preferences that come to mind with minimal effort or introspection. Those that arise through the latter, "deliberative" mode take more time and resources, and are reflective and consciously monitored. These two modes describe a continuum. At the reflexive end, evaluations are fueled by automatic processes. They are based on initial impressions and formed on the basis of chronically accessible, commonly used constructs (e.g., cultural knowledge). On the other end of the continuum are more deliberate evaluations, which result from increasingly self-monitored processes. These evaluations involve thoughtful reasoning and more individuated personal knowledge, ultimately leading to an adjustment away from initial impressions.

Their studies support this conceptualization. Both Chinese and American individuals participated, and half of each group evaluated advertisements that emphasized prevention-oriented benefits, whereas the other half evaluated advertisements that emphasized promotion-oriented benefits. Another between-subjects manipulation instructed some participants to deliberate carefully to determine their judgment of the appeal and instructed others to give an initial, immediate judgment. The expected pattern of cultural differences in appeal evaluations (Chinese prefer prevention benefits, Americans prefer promotion benefits) occurred in conditions in which participants gave their initial reactions but disappeared in conditions in which they deliberated. This pattern of effects was replicated using other manipulations of participants' cognitive resources, such as limiting the available resources of some participants with a cognitive business task (Gilbert and Osborne, 1989).

Concluding comments

Research reviewed herein shows that cultural knowledge does not offer a stable, unwavering influence on people's judgments and decisions. Instead, the effects of this knowledge guide people in some but not other conditions. In particular, the motivational focus that people adopt in decision situations can shift on the basis of aspects of the particular decision situation encountered, incidental events to which people are exposed prior to decision situations, or factors related to the way in which the decision maker approaches and processes the decision problem. Each of these shifts can be explained by social cognitive principles (Wyer and Srull, 1989).

An implication of this body of research is that the norms and values that underlie many cultural differences in behavior may be situation specific. The search for general norms and values that account for cultural differences in decision behaviors, which was stimulated largely by Hofstede's work, may not be the most fruitful path of discovery. Consistent with the thesis of Douglas and Craig (this volume), research reviewed herein suggests that ongoing research examining cultural influence must endeavor to account for the context in which behaviors of interest occur. Culture's influence on behaviors derives from the complex interaction of people's socio-cultural experiences and training and the characteristics of the environment in which they find themselves. Research that fails to identify and take into account various forces that could reside in the particular situation or context in which a decision is made runs the risk of drawing inaccurate or incomplete conclusions.

An array of contextual variables can impact decision outcomes. Importantly, subtle forces that are not generally considered a part of the decision environment can influence decisions. Activities or events that a decision maker is exposed to before addressing decision situations can shift the person's mindset (Briley and Wyer, 2002) and influence the processing style used (Briley and Aaker, 2006a). Thus, it is important to think broadly about the decision environments that people experience and, specifically, consider the particular frame of mind a person has when addressing decision information.

A caveat regarding individuals' abilities to accurately report the particular values that drive their behavioral decisions should be noted as well. Cultural differences in decision making may often reflect socially learned response patterns that, once acquired, are performed with a minimum of mediating cognitive activity. These influences, which might occur spontaneously with a minimum of conscious cognitive deliberation (cf. Bargh, 1997), could constitute cognitive "productions" (Anderson, 1983; Smith, 1984, 1990) that are acquired through social learning and automatically activated when the situational features to which they have been conditioned exist. If the influence of cultural values on decision behaviors occurs through an automatic process such as this, rather than through conscious deliberation, individuals may not accurately report the values that guide their decisions.

The findings reviewed in the present chapter contribute not only to our understanding of culture but also to theory explaining the processes through which people construct preferences. Further research can elucidate both of these areas. More research is needed to understand the triggers and conditions that affect the ebb and flow of cultural inclinations. But equally as important, we can perhaps gain a much more thorough understanding of preference construction processes by bringing to bear ideas related to cultural influence.

References

Aaker, J. & Lee, A. (2001) "I Seek Pleasures, We Avoid Pains: The Role of Self Regulatory Goals in Information Processing and Persuasion," *Journal of Consumer Research*, 28 (June), 33–49.

Aaker, J. & Maheswaran, D. (1997) "The Effect of Cultural Orientation on Persuasion," *Journal of Consumer Research*, 24 (December), 315–28.

Aaker, J. & Schmitt, B. (2001) "Culture-Dependent Assimilation and Differentiation of the Self," *Journal of Cross Cultural Psychology*, 32 (September), 561–76.

Anderson, J. R. (1983) *The Architecture of Cognition*. Cambridge, MA: Harvard University Press.

Bargh, J. A., Bond, R. N., Lombardi, W., & Tota, M. E. (1986) "The Additive Nature of Chronic and Temporary Sources of Construct Accessibility," *Journal of Personality and Social Psychology*, 50, 869–78.

Bargh, J. A., Lombardi, W., & Higgins, E. T. (1988) "Automaticity of Person-Situation Effects in Impression Formation: It's Just a Matter of Time," *Journal of Personality and Social Psychology*, 55, 599–605.

Bargh, J. A. (1997) "The Automaticity of Everyday Life," in R. S. Wyer, Jr. (ed.) *Advances in Social Cognition, Vol. 10*. Mahwah, NJ: Erlbaum, 231–46.

Benet-Martínez, V., Leu, J., Lee, F., & Morris, M. W. (2002) "Negotiating biculturalism," *Journal of Cross-Cultural Psychology*, 33 (September), 492–516.

Bond, M. (1987) "Chinese Values and the Search for Cultural-free Dimensions of Culture," *Journal of Cross Cultural Psychology*, 18 (2), 143–64.

Briley, D. A. & Aaker, J. L. (2006a) "When Does Culture Matter?: Effects of Personal Knowledge on the Correction of Culture-based Judgments," *Journal of Marketing Research*, 43 (August), 395–408.

Briley, D. A. & Aaker, J. L. (2006b) "Bridging the Culture Chasm: Ensuring that Consumers are Healthy, Wealthy and Wise," *Journal of Public Policy & Marketing*, 25 (1), 53–66.

Briley, D. A., Morris, M., & Simonson, I. (2000) "Reasons as Carriers of Culture: Dynamic vs. Dispositional Models of Cultural Influence on Decision Making," *Journal of Consumer Research*, 27 (2), 157–78.

Briley, D. A., Morris, M., & Simonson, I. (2005) "Cultural Chameleons: Biculturals, Conformity Motives, and Decision Making," *Journal of Consumer Psychology*, 15 (4), 351–63.

Briley, D. A. & Wyer, Jr., R. S. (2001) "Transitory Determinants of Values and Decisions: The Utility (or Non-utility) of Individualism-Collectivism in Understanding Cultural Differences," *Social Cognition*, 19 (3), 198–229.

Briley, D. A. & Wyer, Jr., R. S. (2002) "The Effects of Group Membership on the Avoidance of Negative Outcomes: Implications for Social and Consumer Decisions," *Journal of Consumer Research*, 29 (3), 400–15.

Bruner, J. S. (1990) *Acts of Meaning*. Cambridge, MA: Harvard University Press.

Chiu, C.-Y. & Hong, Y.-Y. (2005) "Cultural Competence: Dynamic Processes," in A. Elliot & C. Dweck (eds), *Handbook of Motivation and Competence*. New York: Guilford, 489–505.

D'Andrade, R. G. (1984) "Cultural meaning systems," in R. A. Schweder & R. A. LeVine (eds) *Culture Theory: Essays on Mind, Self and Emotion*. Cambridge, UK: Cambridge University Press, 88–119.

Dawar, N. & Parker, P. (1994) "Marketing Universals: Consumers' Use of Brand Name, Price, Physical Appearance, and Retailer Reputation As Signals of Product Quality," *Journal of Marketing*, 58 (April), 81–95.

Dhar, R. (1996) "The Effect of Decision Strategy on Deciding to Defer Choice," *Journal of Behavioral Decision Making*, 9, 265–81.

Dhar, R. (1997) "Consumer Preference for a No-Choice Option," *Journal of Consumer Research*, 24, 215–31.

Gardner, W. L., Gabriel, S., & Lee, A. Y. (1999) "'I' value Freedom, but 'We' Value Relationships: Self-construal Priming Mirrors Cultural Differences in Judgment," *Psychological Science*, 10(4), 321–26.

Gilbert, D. & Osborne, R. E. (1989) "Thinking Backward: Some Curable and Incurable Consequences of Cognitive Busyness," *Journal of Personality and Social Psychology*, 57 (December), 940–49.

Han, S.-P. & Shavitt, S. (1994) "Persuasion and Culture: Advertising Appeals in Individualistic and Collectivistic Cultures," *Journal of Experimental Social Psychology*, 30 (July), 326–50.

Hassin, R. R., Uleman, J. S. & Bargh, J. A. (2004) *The New Unconscious*. Oxford, UK: Oxford University Press.

Heine, S. & Lehman, D. (1999) "Culture, Self-Discrepancies, and Self-Satisfaction," *Personality and Social Psychology Bulletin*, 25, 915–25.

Heine, S. J., Lehman, D. R., Peng, K., & Greenholtz, J. (2002) "What's Wrong with Cross-Cultural Comparisons of Subjective Likert Scales: The Reference-Group Problem," *Journal of Personality and Social Psychology*, 82, 903–18.

Hermans, H. J. M. & Kempen, H. J. G. (1998) "Moving Cultures: The Perilous Problems of Cultural Dichotomies in a Globalizing Society," *American Psychologist*, 53 (October), 1111–20.

Higgins, E. T. (1996) "Knowledge Activation: Accessibility, Applicability and Salience," in E. T. Higgins & A. E. Kruglanski (eds), *Social Psychology: Handbook of Basic Principles*. New York, NY: Guilford, 133–68.

Higgins, E. T. (1997) "Beyond Pleasure and Pain," *American Psychologist*, 55 (November), 1217–33.

Higgins, E. T. (1998) "Promotion and prevention: Regulatory focus as a motivational principle," in M. P. Zanna (ed.) *Advances in Experimental Social Psychology*, Vol. 30, San Diego, CA: Academic Press, 1–46.

Higgins, E. T. & King, G. A. (1981) "Accessibility of Social Constructs: Information Processing Consequences of Individual and Contextual Variability," in N. Cantor & J. F. Kihlstrom (eds) *Personality, Cognition, and Social Interaction*. Hillsdale, NJ: Lawrence Erlbaum Associates, 69–122.

Ho, D. Y. F. & Chiu, C. Y. (1994) "Component Ideas of Individualism, Collectivism, and Social Organization: An Application in the Study of Chinese Culture," in

U. Kim, C. Kagitcibasi, S. C. Choi, & G. Yoon (eds) *Individualism and Collectivism: Theory, Method, and Applications*. Thousand Oaks, CA: Sage, 137–56.

Hofstede, G. (1980) *Culture's Consequence: International Differences of Work-Related Values*. Beverly Hills, CA: Sage.

Hofstede, G. (1991) *Cultures and Organizations: Software of the Mind*. London, UK: McGraw-Hill.

Hong, Y.-Y., Morris, M. Y., Chiu, C.-Y., & Benet-Martínez, V. (2000) "Multicultural Minds: A Dynamic Constructivist Approach to Culture and Cognition," *American Psychologist*, 55 (7), 709–20.

House, R. J., Hanges, P. W., Javidan, M., Dorfman, P., & Gupta, V. (2004) *Culture, Leadership, and Organizations: The GLOBE Study of 62 Societies*. Thousand Oaks, CA: Sage.

Kahneman, D., Knetsch, J. L., & Thaler, R. (1991) "The Endowment Effect, Loss Aversion, and Status-Quo Bias," *Journal of Economic Perspectives*, 5, 193–206.

Kim, H. &, Markus, H. (1999) "Deviance or Uniqueness, Harmony or Conformity," *Journal of Personality and Social Psychology*, 77 (4), 785–800.

Kitayama, S., Snibbe, A. C., Markus, H. R., &, Suzuki, T. (2004) "Is There Any 'Free' Choice? Self and Dissonance in Two Cultures," *Psychological Science*, 15 (8), 527–33.

Lau-Gesk, L. (2003) "Activating Culture Through Persuasion Appeals," *Journal of Consumer Psychology*, 13 (3), 301–15.

Lee, A., Aaker, J., & Gardner, W. (2000) "The Pleasures and Pains of Distinct Self-Construals: The Role of Interdependence in Regulatory Focus," *Journal of Personality & Social Psychology*, 78 (June), 1122–34.

Leo, C., Bennett, R., & Härtel, C. (2005) "Cross-cultural Differences in Consumer Decision-making Styles," *Cross Cultural Management*, 12 (3), 32–62.

Lichtenstein, S. &, Slovic, P. (2006) *The Construction of Preference*. New York, NY: Cambridge University Press.

Loewenstein, G. (2007) *Exotic Preferences: Behavioural Economics and Human Motivation*. Oxford, England: Oxford University Press.

Lynn, M., Zinkhan, G., & Harris, J. (1993) "Consumer Tipping: A Cross-country Study," *Journal of Consumer Research*, 20 (December), 478–88.

Markus, H. & Kitayama, S. (1991) "Culture and the Self: Implications for Cognition, Emotion and Motivation," *Psychological Review*, 98, 224–53.

Markus, H. & Kitayama, S. (2004) "Models of Agency: Sociocultural Diversity in the Construction of Action," in V. Murphy-Berman & J. J. Berman (eds) *Nebraska Symposium on Motivation: Cross-Cultural Differences in Perspectives on the Self*, Vol. 49. Lincoln, NE: University of Nebraska Press, 1–57.

Morris, M. W., Menon, T., & Ames, D. (2001) "Culturally Conferred Conceptions of Agency: A Key to Social Perception of Persons, Groups, and Other Actors," *Personality and Social Psychology Review*, 5, 169–82.

Nisbett, R. E. & Wilson, T. D. (1977) "Telling More Than We Can Know: Verbal Reports on Mental Processes," *Psychological Review*, 84 (May), 231–59.

Oishi, S., Wyer, R. S., & Colcombe, S. (2000) "Cultural Variation in the Use of Current Life Satisfaction to Predict the Future," *Journal of Personality and Social Psychology*, 78, 434–45.

Padilla, A. M. (1994) "Theoretical and Empirical Examination," in R. Malgady & O. Rodriquez (eds), *Theoretical and Conceptual Issues in Hispanic Mental Health*. Malabar, FL: Krieger.

Phinney, J. S. (1996) "When We Talk about American Ethnic Groups, What Do We Mean?," *American Psychologist*, 51, 918–27.

Schwartz, S. (1999) "A Theory of Cultural Values and Some Implications for Work," *Applied Psychology: An International Review*, 48 (1), 23–47.

Schwartz, S. H. (1994) "Beyond Individualism-Collectivism: New Cultural Dimensions of Values," in U. Kim, H. Triandis, C. Kagitcibasi, S. Choi, & G. Yoon (eds) *Individualism & Collectivism: Theory, Method and Application*. Thousand Oaks, CA: Sage.

Steenkamp, J.-B. E. M., ter Hofstede, F., & Wedel, M.(1999) "A Cross-National Investigation into the Individual and National Cultural Antecedents of Consumer Innovativeness," *Journal of Marketing*, 63 (April), 55–69.

Simonson, I. (1989) "Choice Based on Reasons: The Case of Attraction and Compromise Effects," *Journal of Consumer Research*, 16, 158–74.

Smith,E. R. (1984) "Models of social inference processes," *Psychological Review*, 91, 292–413.

Smith, E. R. (1990) "Content and Process Specificity in the Effects of Prior Experiences," in T. Srull & R. S. Wyer (eds) *Advances in Social Cognition*. Hillsdale, NJ: Earlbaum, 1–60.

Srull, T. K. & Wyer, R. S. (1979) "The Role of Category Accessibility in the Interpretation of Information about Persons: Some Determinants and Implications," *Journal of Personality and Social Psychology*, 37, 1660–72.

Triandis, H. C. (1995) *Individualism and Collectivism*. Boulder, CO: Westview.

Watchravesringkan, K. & Yurchisin, J. (2007) "A Structural Analysis of value Orientations, Price Perceptions, and Ongoing Search Behavior: A Cross-Cultural Study of American and Korean Consumers," *International Journal of Consumer Studies*, 31 (3), 272–82.

Wilson, T., Hodges, S. D., & LaFleur, S. J. (1995) "Effects of Introspecting about Reasons: Inferring Attitudes from Accessible Thoughts," *Journal of Personality and Social Psychology*, 69 (July), 16–28.

Wilson, T. & Schooler, J. W. (1991) "Thinking Too Much: Introspection Can Reduce the Quality of Preferences and Decisions," *Journal of Personality and Social Psychology*, 60 (2), 181–92.

Wyer, Jr., R. S. & Srull, T. K. (1989) *Memory and Cognition in Its Social Context*. Hillsdale, NJ: Lawrence Erlbaum Associates.

Part V   Alternative Culture Frameworks and Perspectives

10
Shifting Perspectives: Multiple Cultures and Community Embeddedness in an Anglo-German MNC

Fiona Moore

Introduction

In management studies, the need is increasingly being felt for a model of culture in organizations that acknowledges the complexity of culture while still being usefully transferable from instance to instance. Using a case study of a British factory in an Anglo-German automobile manufacturing multinational corporation (MNC), and in particular an examination of the relationships that different subgroups in the organization cultivate with one another and with groups both in the surrounding area and at the national and global levels, I propose that firms are best conceived of not as bounded entities or fragmented cultures but as nexuses of internal subgroups with complex links to outside communities.

The challenge for researchers working in the area of cross-cultural management is to develop a usable, transferable model of culture that takes into account not only the fragmentation and multiplicity of culture in organizations but also the way in which the organization, and the various subgroups within it, have connections to outside cultures and discourses, while still remaining simple enough to be applied to management practice. This chapter argues, first, that we need to see culture in MNCs not as a matter of isolated or fragmented perspectives (such as "national" or "workplace" culture), but as a nexus of discourses, which simultaneously show fragmented and integrated characteristics. Second, we should view both management and MNCs as embedded in particular communities, contributing to internal and external discourses and being influenced by the same; to focus only on national culture and on managers in isolation from their wider context is to limit our abilities to analyze the full organization. Third, I contend that we need to work toward developing new perspectives on organizations that allow us to see them as incorporating multiple cultures simultaneously, perhaps by considering the organization as an interlinked nexus of integrated subcultures that have connections both with one another and with outside discourses, which are usable by practitioners.

Theoretical background

Theories of culture

As outlined by Sackmann and Phillips (2004), the literature on organizational culture was dominated for much of the 1980s and 1990s by Hofstede (1980) and other theorists adopting similarly functionalist, single-culture models (e.g., Trompenaars, 1992); Kirkman and colleagues' (2006) article, "A Quarter Century of *Culture's Consequences*: A Review of Empirical Research Incorporating Hofstede's Cultural Values Framework," gives some idea of the degree of penetration of Hofstedean theories in international business studies. These theories are based on the idea that organizational cultures are essentially unified, possessing definable and identifiable "traits." While these models can be developed to a high degree of complexity (e.g., Ghoshal and Nohria, 1989), they have come under criticism from a number of quarters for being reductionist, failing to take into account the diversity of multicultural societies and the interactions between national cultures and other sorts of culture (organizational, local, religious), as well as assuming, erroneously, that "culture" is commensurate with "nation" and/or "organization" (Martin, 2002; McKenna, 1998; McSweeney, 2002). The Hofstedean paradigm thus involves a model of the organization as having a single, unified culture, linked to national culture traits, which many would argue is an oversimplification.

A possible reason why this approach nonetheless continues to be popular is its simplicity and usefulness as a basic model that can be used to explain the workings of culture, particularly of the national sort, in organizations, giving it enduring appeal among practitioners (Sackmann and Phillips, 2004). However, as Joanne Martin (2002) notes, such studies are frequently too reductive to be genuinely useful, and as Lowe and colleagues (2007) argue, Hofstedean models are consequently a "heavy tool," which may cause more problems than they solve by virtue of their lack of adaptability. The challenge is thus to develop more complex models of culture, which are nonetheless simple enough to be useful to businesspeople.

Subsequently, more complex models of culture have been developed in theoretical circles. Sackmann and Phillips (2004) identify two significant developments, the intercultural interaction perspective, focusing on thick description and ethnographic perspectives, and the more analytic multiple cultures perspective, which assumes that "organizations may be home to, and carriers of, several cultures . . . individuals may identify with, and hold, simultaneous membership in several cultural groups" (Sackmann and Phillips, 2004, p. 378), which "may be separate from each other, overlapping, superimposed or nested, or interacting with each other." This perspective is illustrated by the recent work of Raz and Fadlon (2006) on organizational learning, which considers how the process of learning reveals, within a single workplace, a variety of interpretations, subversions of interpretations, and the construction and questioning of diverse ideologies. Another key writer in the field is Joanne Martin (2002), who argues that cultural issues are best viewed from triple, rather than single, perspectives—these perspectives being integration, differentiation, and fragmentation—which thus provides the necessary levels of complexity of analysis.

The problem, however, is that the complexity of these approaches means that they do not yield easily generalizable or practitioner-friendly models. Much of the theoretical work within the intercultural interaction and multiple cultures perspectives is based, either directly or indirectly, on ethnographic methodology, which is useful for developing a complex portrait of organizations that allows us to take the individual perspective into account (Morgan and Smircich, 1980; Sharpe, 2004). However, a number of researchers in business studies also express the concern that it might be *too* anecdotal and individual, making it difficult to develop generalizable theories (see Chapman, 1997; Hofstede, 1980). My own fieldwork experiences also suggest that many practitioners regard ethnography as something strange and esoteric, which has to do with the study of "primitive tribes." As Holden (2002, p. 20) notes, "would-be challengers [to Hofstede] face . . . the daunting prospect of . . . creating a model of more or less universal validity which renders Hofstede's famous model invalid and obsolete."

One possible alternative may be to follow the anthropological practice and differentiate international business studies into diverse subdisciplines focusing on a single MNC or sector. Both Kristensen and Zeitlin (2004) and Holden (2002) have tackled the issue of cultural complexity through eschewing simple models in favor of detailed case studies of a few field sites. However, this approach is of questionable utility to managers seeking to make use of academic research for their own ends, as well as making it difficult for researchers to develop more widely applicable models of organizational behavior, as Sackmann and Phillips (2004, p. 383) note:

> The other challenges for [the multiple cultures perspective] are . . . a consequence of its methodological focus, which requires extensive time for the research process, the training of researchers, and for publications. . . . The case-study approach yields rich data; however, it is limited in its range of applicability.

Martin's (2002) three-perspectives model goes some way toward providing a way of generalizing qualitative perspectives on organizations into something more usable; however, it is again a fairly descriptive model, and the question remains of whether it is actually possible, as she counsels, to view organizations simultaneously through three perspectives without some kind of integrating framework to bring them together. Complex perspectives on organizations are thus difficult to generalize into transferable models.

Cultural embeddedness of organizations

As well as through direct studies of culture in MNCs, studies of the MNC as a network have developed a more complex view of culture in MNCs. Such studies generally portray the organization as part of intricate flows of knowledge (see Birkinshaw and Hood, 1998; Doz et al., 2001). Kristensen and Zeitlin (2004) have developed a multilayered portrait of the firm as a product of different sorts of culture, history, legal proceedings, and other socio-cultural events and actors. By adding the network approach to the fragmented/multiple perspective, we gain an image of the cultures of firms as emerging from complex international networks.

Furthermore, such studies also acknowledge the embeddedness of firms in local contexts, as outlined by Andersson and colleagues (2001). Kristensen and Zeitlin's (2004) work challenges the traditional approach of viewing the MNC largely out of its immediate social and historical context, by taking a more complex, historical, long-term approach to the study of a single dairy-product MNC, looking at different branches of the company and how their different histories, relations with other local companies, management styles, and modes of acquisition make up different facets of their current culture and strategy. Andersson and colleagues (2001) consider how, by maintaining local links and connections to other groups around the world, MNCs are able to mobilize resources on many levels. These studies thus demonstrate how MNCs possess much more complex, shifting, and vague relationships with local communities than many had previously suspected.

Kristensen and Zeitlin's (2004) aim, at least in part, was to show how the different branches' interactions with local communities influence both the branch and the MNC as a whole in diverse ways. As a result of their findings, they argue that MNCs are not simply rivals for local companies but, properly run, are "potentially complementary to existing industrial districts" (Kristensen and Zeitlin, 2004, p. 2). They argue that "by tapping into a wide variety of regional economies, labour markets, and the institutional frameworks that underpin them, multinationals . . . could also create new opportunities for innovative cross-fertilisation in products and processes" (Kristensen and Zeitlin, 2004, p. 302).

This embedded description is also very much in keeping with the corporate social responsibility literature, particularly Frederick's (1998) naturological account of corporation–community relationships. This model

> defines the . . . organisation and surrounding community as a 'natural' system, existing in a symbiotic association that is subject to biological and physical principles. Such an ecological system (or ecosystem) consists of interconnected living 'organisms' with porous boundaries, suggesting that their daily existences as well as long-term survival are intimately tied to one another.
>
> (Frederick, 1998, p. 359)

The firm thus does not exist in a vacuum or in a one-to-one economic relationship with the community whereby, as Keim (1978) describes it, the community provides workers for the factory, the factory engages in philanthropic activities for the community, and both remain otherwise uncontaminated by each other. Rather, in Frederick's view, the firm cooperates and competes with other actors in the wider environment as part of an extensive system of negotiation and networking.

From this perspective, I postulate that the best way of moving beyond national and organizational paradigms, and integrating the advantages of an integrated and a fragmented perspective on culture, is to regard the organization as a nexus of interlinked subgroups connected to one another and to outside local and global cultures in diverse ways, which can be differentiated in different ways. The organization can, under this scenario, be seen as one of Holden's (2002) sites of "sense making," in which culture, and its traits and meanings, are negotiated, rather than an entity whose members show solidarity of culture and belief or

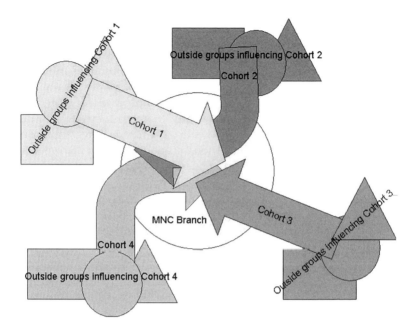

Figure 10.1   Cohorts and potential identities

as a collection of fragmented, disconnected cultures. Combining the integrated and fragmented perspectives into an interlinked perspective thus means that culture in organizations is less a matter of groups "possessing" cultures as of subgroups within organizations engaging in discourses with one another and with local and global interpretations of different cultural traits, which are constantly negotiated within the social site of the MNC and its branches. An illustration of this can be found in Figure 10.1.

Consequently, I would postulate the following theoretical perspective: *Organizations are not undifferentiated, bounded groups but are nexuses of subgroups that interact and are affected by others within the organization and outside of it, which share areas of cultural overlap.* We shall now consider this perspective with regard to a case study of the branch of a single MNC.

Methodology and background

In order to obtain a more organic, complex understanding of the firm and its community engagement, then, we shall turn, like Conley and Williams (2005), to anthropological/ethnographic research techniques.

This chapter is based partly on participant observation fieldwork at an Anglo-German automobile factory, here called AutoWorks UK, partly on interviews with employees, and partly on archival research with local historical collections. In 2003, I gained access to the company as part of a group of researchers affiliated with the Said Business School who had been asked to propose studies of the organization by top management; I was to conduct a study of gender diversity and staff retention among the workforce.

As part of my research, I spent three months on the line in the Final Assembly Area (more colloquially referred to as Assembly) of the plant, working as a temporary employee of the firm (known officially as an "associate") with the management's full knowledge and permission. Two tours were also taken of the entire plant as an outsider. Subsequently, I have spent about 12 months, intermittently, working with a group of managers from the Human Resources (HR) department on two projects, one involving the development of a management education program aimed at teaching managers how to use ethnographic techniques in their daily activities, and one aimed at assessing how the workforce feels about the plant's management style and working on ways of improving managerial practices. I was also able to follow up my research in Assembly by making a brief exploratory visit to one of the company's German plants. Until the end of 2003, I lived in the community described here and was affiliated with its resident university as a postdoctoral research associate (having completed a doctorate there the previous year).

Formal interviews were conduced with 13 staff members in total. Most were in white-collar managerial and/or coordination functions, though some were shop-floor managers. Most of the interviewees were associated with the Final Assembly Area, but there were also some involved with the Paint Shop or Body in White (the area where the unpainted car is assembled) sections as well. Most formal interviews were recorded, though in a few cases in which the interviewee was not comfortable with the presence of a tape recorder, shorthand notes were taken instead. In some cases, follow-up interviews were conducted, normally over the telephone. Informal, unrecorded discussions were held with workers on the line during the period of fieldwork, as well as with the HR managers with whom I worked on the two projects mentioned previously. While in Germany, I also interviewed five managers, all of whom had been involved with the change in ownership of the British plant, regarding their experiences as expatriates and the differences between the plants. The statistics used have been obtained from the firm, with permission.

The firm did not ask for confidentiality in publications; however, I have opted for partial confidentiality, disguising the identities of all interviewees and changing the name of the relevant company in the body of the text (while leaving references to it in the References undisguised). The interviews and observations that follow have been selected for what they reveal about the nature of relationships between groups in the firm; being a qualitative study, the data are intended to be impressionistic and evocative rather than focused on numerical data.

Although qualitative methodologies have been criticized for being too anecdotal and difficult to generalize (see Chapman, 1997), they have particular benefits that may be useful in investigating culture and social embeddedness. Conley and Williams (2005), for instance, speak in some detail on the benefits an ethnographic approach can bring to studies of culture studies, where what people say and what people actually do are often quite different things. Furthermore, qualitative methodologies are invaluable in situations where the data sought are not those that can be obtained through a quantitative approach aimed at tallying up known benefits obtained from known sources but involve more nebulous aspects of community engagement and its impact on a particular firm. We shall now consider the history of the plant under study, its subgroups, and its connections with external networks.

The plant: Lewis Motors/AutoWorks UK

The plant at which my study was conducted started out as a small domestic British car manufacturer, here called Lewis Motors, in the early 1910s (Newbigging et al., 1998) and remained more or less under the same ownership until the late 1960s. During this time, it rapidly became a focus of social activity for its workers, developing its own sports teams, bands, amateur dramatic societies, volunteer organizations, and social venues; examples cited by Newbigging and colleagues (1998) include football and cricket teams, ladies' hockey teams, and a workers' social club founded in the 1940s and still active at the time of my research. At least some of the people working at the factory at the time of fieldwork confessed to being second- or even third-generation factory workers (see Bardsley and Laing, 1999).

Although Lewis Motors prospered initially, amassing a large collection of satellite companies (Newbigging et al., 1998), and, indeed, was one of the success stories of the immediate post-World War II period (Whisler, 1999), the company was also hit by the decline that affected industrial Britain from the early 1960s onwards. Outcompeted by foreign companies and subject to questionable senior management decisions, it was

finally nationalized in 1968 and, when it continued to decline, was repri-
vatized in the 1980s, going from owner to owner before finally being
taken over by a German firm, known here as AutoWorks International.
German heavy industry had, in contrast to the British, expanded and
developed in the post-war period (Greenhalgh and Kilmister, 1993).

The surrounding community and its relationship with the factory

The presence of the Lewis Motors automobile factory in the area for
over 90 years meant that local people, even if they did not actually
work at the plant, described it as "our factory." The public outcry at
times when it seemed as if the plant were going to close was notable (see
Hayter, 1993; McCarthy, 1990), and the reason one particular previous
owner of the late 1980s was singled out for special scorn was usually
cited to me as that "they didn't care about the plant, they just wanted
to parcel it out and sell off the land," in the words of one worker; a manager put it similarly, saying that "all they wanted to do was asset-strip."
(Other owners, whose effect on the company's overall performance was
considerably more damaging, did not come in for such contempt; one
was even spoken of with praise for its attention to social relations with
the workers.) A factory worker whose father and grandfather had also
worked at the plant spoke nostalgically to me of the social events, "open
days," and children's Christmas parties for factory workers (implying
heavily as she did so that she did not expect the same community focus
from the present owners; but see subsequent discussion). Acquaintances
of mine who were not connected with the factory used occasionally to
refer to it as "the old Lewis plant," even though aware that the factory
had not used that name since the 1970s.

The town in which the field site is situated is one that historically
has been shaped by a strong social division between its industrial sector and its university population, referred to colloquially as Town and
Gown. Schofield and Noble (1993) argue that the establishment of the
Lewis Motors factory in the early twentieth century created a de facto
division between the northern quadrant and inner core of the town,
which were focused on the university, and the eastern and outer areas,
which were focused on the automobile plant. Although these divisions
were partly associated with social class—as Schofield and Noble (1993,
p. 258) dryly put it, "It was not hard to guess which part . . . housed
the football club [and] the dog track" (dog racing is a popular pastime
among the working-class Southern English)—the situation was more
complex. The university-associated group comprised not only academics and students but also support staff and those in the service sector

(cooks, housekeepers, cleaners, managers, marketing specialists, and so forth), and though the ethos of the university community was more multicultural than that of the workers, there was considerably more ethnic diversity in the east than in the north quadrant. Furthermore, the fact that housing in the eastern areas tends to be cheaper than that in the north meant that a number of university students and junior academic staff also live in the east, and more prosperous factory employees can buy houses in the north. There is thus not so much a social and geographical divide between Town and Gown as a complex series of interactions and discourses about class, ethnicity, and labor.

The community is also strongly multicultural. The presence of the factory attracted a number of labor migrants from the Indian subcontinent and the West Indies to the area in the 1950s; these migrants became assimilated into the local working class (Schofield and Noble, 1993). More recently, the presence of an immigration centre in the area has meant a rise in the factory's own diversity, as many migrants choose to work at the factory upon receiving their authorization to work, as it is a relatively well-paying job that does not require any particular qualifications, barring the ability to understand spoken and written English. This development has resulted in a strongly globally connected workforce.

Internal relations in the organization

Relations between managers

The managers in the factory were, as might be expected, divided along Anglo-German lines; however, rather than forming a simple ethnic division, this division took the form of a more porous, complex discourse between groups, shot through with power relations issues. While, as noted, there was relatively little animosity toward the new owner from the workers, the local managers were somewhat more ambivalent about it because, for them, the takeover had involved the departure of friends and superiors, changes to a familiar system, and having to deal with a different set of managers, with different priorities and from a different culture, with which their own cultural values were periodically in conflict. The managers thus expressed ambivalent and contradictory sentiments: Although they liked the prestige of working for a well-regarded company, and they were proud of the product, they also talked about tensions with the new regime and complained occasionally about measures that they felt were more in place for AutoWorks International's benefit than for the plant's. Implicitly, also, many resented the loss of

authority that came with the greater involvement of German expatriates in the branch's management. The managers thus did not develop
a simple opposition between British/local and German/expatriate, but
the two groups engaged in complex discourses that continually shaped
and transformed the company's culture.

The German managers came to the factory from an international/
German context, which informed the way in which they viewed
AutoWorks UK. Their main focus was on Head Office, whose style and
activities they viewed as transferable; one German manager, when asked
about national culture, replied that he did not think it had much impact
on the business, as the practice of making cars was universally transferable. Furthermore, the German managers at the UK plant were often
involved with an international management program that encouraged
them to move on after a few years, with consequences outlined by one
local manager:

> We are used to the German style of management, so it isn't an issue
> of nationality, but we know our German directors are only here for
> a few years; they are put into positions that are higher than this
> in Germany, and they don't have to live with the consequences,
> because they move every few years.

The German managers thus drew on external discourses from German
business and from their own identity as an international group when
defining themselves and engaged in discourse with local managers over
the degree of managerial contact needed.

The local managers, meanwhile, had developed an identity as an
embattled group of local keepers of forgotten knowledge; as one put it,
"This site has a history, good and bad, and all the qualities seem to have
been stripped away." This comment reflected discourses then current in
the British media about the British automobile industry, namely, that
the once-dominant automobile industry was now becoming a thing of
the past, its traditions and culture lost under foreign ownership and
factory closures (Jefford, 2000). While local managers acknowledged
that AutoWorks' takeover had prevented the company from failing
completely, there was still a sense that only the local managers, with
their local connections, "understood" the company. The managers of
the company thus do not come across as a group with solidarity and
unity around a particular corporate culture, but neither do they come
across as opposed and divided on all levels; rather, we see different
groups of managers engaging in mutual discourse of different sorts

within the organization and managing to get their voices heard with varying degrees of success.

Relations between managers and workers

While much of the literature on industrial action tends to paint manager-worker relations, particularly at automobile factories, as oppositional, the situation between managers and workers at AutoWorks UK was more complex. What I observed on the line was not so much direct action, as described in Thornett (1998), as an unspoken idea of a social contract: If the managers did not hold up their end of the bargain, they were subject to informal social sanctions. For instance, the harshest criticism was reserved not for the current owners but for a previous owner who engaged in "asset stripping." Other owners were, however, praised for sponsoring clubs or holding "open days" and Christmas parties for the workers. The workers regarded the factory not so much as a workplace but as a community member who should give back to the community, and they held the managers to this contract.

Conflict between managers and workers took place at more of a cultural than an industrial level. The company had a policy of engaging in nonfinancial reward practices, but the workers viewed gifts of company-branded merchandise (e.g., mugs, fleeces) as patronizing, while apparently regarding the sponsorship of activities, such as group visits to the dog track or car-racing sessions at a local racecourse, more positively. An attempt to hold a Christmas party for the workers one year also backfired: As one manager described the scene, "we have the managers dressed up and handing out cake, and you go down [to] the carpark and it's cake thrown all over." Again, other such events, such as a bonfire for Guy Fawkes' Night (a traditional English celebration held on November 5, involving fireworks and bonfires) and the family open day, had gone down much more positively with the workforce. The common denominator seemed to involve the exposition of cultural differences between managers and workers: Although both managers and workers said that they enjoyed working for the company, the managers expressed much more pride in the fact that they were working for a multinational with a global reputation for high-quality products, while the workers expressed pleasure in the high salaries and the social life that revolved around the plant ("good wages and good mates"). Relations between managers and workers thus indicate areas of negotiation about the nature of the company's identity and its role in the community.

The AutoWorks UK managers' view of the situation was, officially, that their community engagement made for positive social relations with their workforce and with their potential workforce in the wider community. Two British managers spoke to me of an incident during the recession of the 1970s in which the workers at one of the AutoWorks Germany plants took a temporary pay cut rather than see the company go under, evidence, the managers felt, of a tradition of trust between the company and its workers, which they were trying to maintain in the UK. The managers were keen to improve their community engagement activities, rethinking unsuccessful reward activities. The managers thus emphasized common points of connection with the workers and the presence of a shared identity.

However, from the workers' perspective, the messages were more mixed. Despite these activities, workers on the line frequently complained that they felt that the company "doesn't care" about them; though they were not on the whole discontented with their work, the lack of formal orientation and training programs at the time, and occasional attempts to speed up the line, were held as evidence that the company was only interested in the workers for their labor. The attempt by one line supervisor at a *kaizen* meeting (a quality-control session in which workers and managers were expected to discuss problems with and improvements to the factory processes) to point out that the workers benefited from the overall success of the company was subsequently derided by the workers as "taking the party line." Workers, even long-term joiners, felt no qualms about leaving the company if they felt their needs were not being met. The workers and managers thus were not part of an undifferentiated corporation but experienced the same workplace in different ways; moreover, power relations were not a simple equation of managers imposing their will on powerless workers.

As noted, however, the workers viewed the factory less as a prestige workplace than as a community asset. Many workers implied that they saw the factory as something they could "fall back on" when they needed work; a significant percentage of the workers were not long-term, permanent members of the workforce but people who worked for the company off and on (students working during the summer break or to fund pre-university travel, housewives earning "Christmas money" before the holidays, artists who did factory work between commissions) or who took on the factory job as a "stopgap" while waiting for a job more to their liking.

Seen from the perspective of inter-manager, and manager–worker, power relations, AutoWorks UK comes across less as a bounded, solidary entity with a unified culture and specific connections to the local national culture than as a nexus of discourses between different groups in the organization, which were a site of negotiation over what it meant to work for the company.

Relations with the wider community

Ethnicity and the local area

AutoWorks also, inevitably, became involved in local groups and discourses. The multiethnic nature of the workforce, for instance, both reflected, and contributed to, discourses about multiculturalism and immigration in the community over the years (Ward et al., 1993). While the prewar workforce at Lewis Motors was largely white and British, as discussed previously, migrants from overseas began to come to the community in the 1950s through the 1970s, drawn partly by the presence of the factory, though finding their access to jobs there initially blocked by racism and hostility from unions and management, they then turned to other industries in the area, as well as the establishment of small businesses, meaning that what can be seen as a hostile action by the factory wound up, ironically, benefiting other companies and sectors (Ward et al., 1993). By the mid-1960s, however, campaigning to lift the color bar had become one of the rallying points of the unions at Lewis Motors, who had by this point had adopted left-wing internationalist discourses (Ward et al., 1993).

By the time of my study, however, the discourses had changed to reflect more recent controversies related to immigration. At the time, there was a good deal of ambivalence regarding the presence of asylum-seekers in the UK, and also regarding economic migrants to the UK from Eastern Europe. As unskilled labor is an obvious option for new migrants and refugees to the United Kingdom, particularly in cases where their internationally obtained qualifications are not recognized in their new location, the factory had a number of recent migrants to the UK who fitted these descriptions. Also, with the British young adults increasingly viewing the service sector as more desirable employment, the factory would naturally draw on the pool of migrants to make up labor shortfalls. One consequence was that there was very little discussion on the shop-floor about people's antecedents and home countries, with conversation generally being limited to topics of cross-cultural interest (for men, sex, hip-hop music, and football; for women, sex, hip-hop music, and family). The workers in the factory were thus participating in British discourses about immigration and the provision of shelter to asylum seekers, through its hiring policies, and also through the tacit recognition of the controversy by the workers.

One other aspect of this study that is perhaps less immediately obvious is that, through building up local connections, the company in turn develops global links. The fact that the company pursued the policy of community support in Germany, the UK, and other branches as well (cf. Martin, 1997) meant that, at the same time as it was developing strong local connections, the branch was developing a sense of itself as a global entity. The international nature of the factory's workforce, and its ambivalent policies over the years toward them, meant that it has brought global connections on a working-class level to the community as well. AutoWorks' local activities generate global connections.

Class, gender, and work discourses

AutoWorks was also engaged in discourses regarding the role of class and gender in the British, European, and global workforces. The changing business culture of Britain in the post-Thatcher era meant that working-class young people in the town were just as likely, if not more so, to go and work for the service industries in preference to the factory, particularly since factory work was perceived as "hard work" as compared with office-temping, working for tour companies, and so forth; as a student at the local university a few years earlier, I had put my resume in at one of the temporary labor agencies that supplied the factory, but its agents never suggested to me that I might try factory work, instead putting me forward for office and service sector jobs. The factory's engagement with the university also did not extend to labor recruitment: While they did not discourage students from applying, most of the students whom I met at the factory were either from a working-class background, or, like myself, from non-British cultures where factory work is seen as suitable work for middle-class students. Nor does it necessarily ensure direct loyalty or support of the type that AutoWorks had enjoyed from its German workers in the 1970s; the workers at AutoWorks UK were quick to complain if they felt slighted or exploited and could sometimes be quite critical of the product even though they took pride in their work.

Furthermore, the factory workers did not all come from the local area. Recent plant closures in the Midlands and Southwest of England, plus the fact that AutoWorks UK had an unusual "concentrated" system of shifts (rather than running two, five-day-a-week, eight-hour shifts, as is usual, the factory ran three shifts, a day and night shift of four 10-hour days, followed by a weekend shift of three 15-hour days) and that the wages offered, as noted, were above average for unskilled labor in the UK, meant that an unknown (but noticeable) percentage of the workforce were "commuters," that is, workers from other parts of the UK who came in from their home communities elsewhere (an extreme case cited to me by a HR manager involved two men from Scotland who worked the three-day weekend shift: they would drive across the country on Thursday nights in a camper van, sleep in the van for two nights, and drive back on Sunday nights).

Finally, AutoWorks also contributed to, and was affected by, local discourses regarding gender and labor. Women did not initially work in the factory (aside from in auxiliary positions such as cooks in the canteen), but were brought in as substitute labor during the two World Wars and were for the most part encouraged to leave afterward; though some women continued in the factory, they were for the most part restricted to areas considered "women's work," such as upholstery sewing and fitting the interior panels (Sweeney, 1993). However, in light of British government initiatives in the early 2000s aimed at encouraging more women to participate in the workplace, the company was becoming more proactive in encouraging women to join the workforce; a condition of my being able to do fieldwork at the factory was that I should report on ways in which they could recruit and retain more women, and AutoWorks International was also engaging in wider initiatives aimed at encouraging women's presence in the auto industry. As with immigration, then, the company was affected by local, national, and global discourses on women in the workplace, and, in reacting to these, contributed to them.

The AutoWorks UK plant was thus not merely engaged in internal discourses between different groups in the organization, but these groups were also engaged in external discourses and groups that affected the factory.

Discussion: Toward a post-Hofstedean perspective?

The case study suggests that the perspective articulated at the start of this chapter may be a way of working toward the previously mentioned blend of fragmentation and integration, thus providing a way of considering culture that captures its complexity while still being generalizable enough for everyday use by practitioners. Under the interlinked perspective, we see a number of distinct groups, each with different connections to one another and with the outside world. These groups show different perspectives on the organization, and link to different outside groups, and yet also come from mutually compatible standpoints that allow communication. They also provide different perspectives on the same discourse: The German and British interviewees' perspectives on the same situation were visibly different, and yet these perspectives were not isolated from each other. The firm is thus seen as a nexus of groups interacting with one another and the outside world, to provide a variety of different interpretations that combine over time into constantly shifting meanings.

Furthermore, these discourses also indicate that one cannot properly analyze the firm without considering the cultures in which it is embedded. As the number of writers quoted on the subject indicates, discourses of national culture, class, and the nature of AutoWorks are going on in the outside world, and these perspectives are being brought into the system. Furthermore, these discourses do not simply feed into the organization, but the organization interprets discourses and feeds them back out into the environment through the activities of its members. This research thus supports Araujo and colleagues' (2003) contention that the boundaries of firms are complex and must be understood in relation to the firm's connection with other actors in its environment. The excerpts thus support the environmentally embedded model of the firm and develop it by adding the idea that the firm is linked to its environment, and the environment to the firm, through different subgroups in the organization.

More than this, however, the presence of different subgroups, with different relationships to outside groups and to each other, suggests that the firm should be understood by both researchers and managers not just in terms of its own connections with other actors but by its own internal actors' connections with other groups. The different subgroups are clearly connected to outside discourses, not just about nationality, but about class, gender, ethnicity, and local identity. Furthermore, the groups all deal with one another in different ways, and, significantly, some deal better than others, a fact that has implications for international business in general. The diversity of both the workforce and managers means that there is at least the potential for a variety of different discourses to take root in the organization, and for the organization to be seen less as a bounded, isolated entity than one of Doz and colleagues' (2001) global cultural networks, only fully understandable in terms of their diverse subgroups' connections to outside and inside cultures and subgroups (see Figure 10.2). Managers must therefore consider both internal and external influences on the organization when making human resource-related decisions.

These discourses also seem to involve the negotiation of the definition of the firm. The different groups define AutoWorks UK's situation

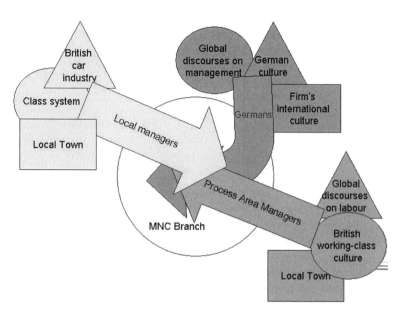

Figure 10.2   Cohorts and potential identities at AutoWorks UK

differently: the Germans as the bringers of a new international identity, the local managers as defenders of an embattled tradition, and the workers as the resigned recipients of the policies of the office managers. Culture here thus comes across not as a static property, but the meaning of what it is to be a member of the organization, British, German, or working or middle class, is a source of continued negotiation; once again, note that some groups are more successful in getting their message across than others. The boundaries of the firm, and of its subgroups, are also a source of constant negotiation.

The case study and analysis thus build up a picture of an organization that is both fragmented and integrated: a nexus of different, flexibly bounded subgroups, with different connections with one another and with outside groups, who are continually negotiating the meaning of the firm's culture over time, with greater and lesser degrees of success. Unlike the empirical perspectives discussed at the start of this chapter, the interlinked perspective allows us to take into account the cultural diversity and variety of inside and outside influences on organizations and acknowledges the background behind the cultural traits that different groups within the organization manifest. However, this perspective also improves on fragmented and multiple models of culture in that it acknowledges integration. It is also, again, one that can be adapted from firm to firm, providing a practitioner-friendly alternative to empirical models of culture.

Conclusions

The case discussed in this chapter has implications in a number of areas of research and practice, principally knowledge management, cross-cultural management, and human resource management. This model supports the image of the MNC as a kind of knowledge network developed, in the likes of Nonaka and Takeuchi (1995); however, it builds on Nonaka and Takeuchi's idea that firms should make use of the personal networks and connections of their employees as knowledge resources, suggesting that companies should be considering the social connections and influences upon their employees at all levels in greater detail. It also suggests that by focusing on the national level, cross-cultural management may be limiting itself unnecessarily, and the definition should be broadened to consider issues of class, sectoral, and other forms of culture as well. Moreover, it indicates that groups within organizations are not equal and that closer attention must be paid to the power dimension of relationships between groups in organizations. Finally, the practice of international HR management needs to be redeveloped to take into consideration the complexity of culture within MNCs, and the fact of their embeddedness in different national, local, and global discourses.

Further studies of firms from alternative perspectives may allow us to develop a more accurate picture of how culture affects organizations. We need more research that takes into account the complexity and multiplicity of culture (Kirkman and Shapiro, 2005), particularly articles that consider the whole organization rather than simply the managers or workers. More studies need to be done of MNCs situated in their cultural/historical contexts, and more cross-disciplinary studies. While a more longitudinal study was not possible in this case, the indications of cultural change that emerged in interviews and participant observations suggest that this is also an important factor. Finally, more studies need to be done that test the interlinked perspective on the organization, in order to refine and develop it into a more usable model of culture in MNCs.

A case study based around interviews with different types of managers at AutoWorks UK thus suggests that, in the post-Hofstedean era, both researchers and practitioners need to see culture in business not as a matter of national cultures in isolation from others but as something internally fragmented along various lines and embedded in external discourses, organizations as nexuses of subgroups with different connections to the outside world and different degrees of power and influence, with concurrent implications for research and management practice in cross-cultural management, knowledge management, and local and international HR management.

References

Andersson, U., Fosgren, M., & Holm, U. (2001) "Subsidiary Embeddedness and Competence Development in MNCs: A Multi-Level Analysis," *Organization Studies*, 22 (6), 1013–34.

Araujo, L., Dubois, A. & Gadde, L. (2003) "The Multiple Boundaries of the Firm," *Journal of Management Studies*, 40 (5), 1255–77.

Bardsley, G. & Laing, S. (1999) *Making Cars at Cowley: from Morris to Rover*. Stroud: British Motor Industry Heritage Trust.

Birkinshaw, J. & Hood, N. (1998) "Multinational Subsidiary Evolution: Capabilities And Charter Change In Foreign-Owned Companies," *Academy of Management Review*, 23 (4), 773–95.

Chapman, M. (1997) "Preface: Social Anthropology, Business Studies And Cultural Issues," *International Studies of Management and Organization*, 26 (4), 3–29.

Conley, J. M. & Williams, C. A. (2005) "Engage, Embed, and Embellish: Theory versus Practice in the Corporate Social Responsibility Movement," *Journal of Corporation Law*, 31 (1), 1–38.

Doz, Y. L., Santos, J., & Williamson, P. (2001) *From Global to Metanational: How Companies Win in the Knowledge Economy*. Cambridge, MA: Harvard Business School Press.

Frederick, W. C. (1998) "Creatures, Corporations, Communities, Chaos, Complexity," *Business and Society*, 37 (4), 358–89.

Ghoshal, S. & Nohria, N. (1989) "Internal Differentiation within Multinational Corporations," *Strategic Management Journal*, 10, 323–32.

Greenhalgh, C. & Kilmister, A. (1993) "The British Economy, The State And The Motor Industry," in T. Hayter and D. Harvey (eds) *The Factory and the City: The Story of the Cowley Automobile Workers in Oxford*. London: Mansell, 26–46.

Hayter, T. (1993) "Local Politics," in T. Hayter and D. Harvey (eds.) *The Factory and the City: The Story of the Cowley Automobile Workers in Oxford*. London: Mansell, 161–85.

Hofstede, G. (1980) *Culture's Consequences: International Differences in Work-Related Values*. London: Sage.

Holden, N. J. (2002) *Cross-Cultural Management: A Knowledge Management Perspective*. London: Financial Times/Prentice Hall.

Jefford, B. (2000) "In the Shadow of Longbridge," BBCi, May 2, 2000, available from http://news.bbc.co.uk.

Keim, G. D. (1978) "Corporate Social Responsibility: An Assessment of the Enlightened Self-Interest Model," *Academy of Management Review*, 3 (1), 32–40.

Kirkman, B. L. & Shapiro, D. L. (2005) "The Impact of Cultural Value Diversity on Multicultural Team Performance," in D. L. Shapiro, M. Von Glinow, & J. Cheng (eds) *Managing Multinational Teams: Global Perspectives*. London, UK: Elsevier Ltd., 33–67.

Kirkman, B. L., Lowe, K. B., & Gibson, C. (2006) "A Quarter Century of *Culture's Consequences*: A Review of Empirical Research Incorporating Hofstede's Cultural Values Framework," *Journal of International Business Studies*, 37 (3), 285–320.

Kristensen, P. H. & Zeitlin, J. (2004) *Local Players in Global Games: The Strategic Constitution of a Multinational Corporation*. Oxford, UK: Oxford University Press.

Lowe, S., Moore, F., & Carr, A. N. (2007) "Paradigmapping Studies of Culture and Organization," *International Journal of Cross-Cultural Management*, 7 (2), 237–51.

Martin, J. (1997) "Mercedes: Made in Alabama," *Fortune*, July 7.

Martin, J. (2002) *Organizational Culture: Mapping the Terrain*. London, UK: Sage.

McCarthy, Lord of Headington (1990) *The Future of Cowley: Report of the Independent Inquiry into the Rover Cowley Works Closure Proposals*. Oxford, UK: Oxford City Council.

McKenna, S. (1998) "Cross-Cultural Attitudes towards Leadership Dimensions," *Leadership and Organizational Journal*, 19 (2), 106–12.

McSweeney, B. (2002) "Hofstede's Model of National Cultural Differences and Their Consequences: A Triumph of Faith–A Failure of Analysis," *Human Relations* 55 (1), 89–119.

Morgan, G. & Smircich, L. (1980) "The Case for Qualitative Research," *Academy of Management Review*, 5 (4), 491–501.

Newbigging, C., Shatford, S., & Williams, T. (1998) *The Changing Faces of Cowley Works*. Witney: Robert Boyd Publications.

Nonaka, I. & Takeuchi, H. (1995) *The Knowledge-Creating Company*. Oxford, UK: Oxford University Press.

Raz, A. & Fadlon, J. (2006) "Managerial Culture, Workplace Culture and Situated Curricula in Organizational Learning," *Organization Studies*, 27 (2), 165–82.

Sackmann, S. A. & Phillips, M. E. (2004) "Contextual Influences on Culture Research: Shifting Assumptions for New Workplace Realities," *International Journal of Cross-Cultural Management*, 4 (3), 370–90

Schofield, A. & Noble, M. (1993) "Communities and Corporations: Rethinking the Connections," in T. Hayter & D. Harvey (eds) *The Factory and the City: The Story Of the Cowley Automobile Workers in Oxford*. London: Mansell, 256–74.

Sharpe, D. R. (2004) "The Relevance of Ethnography to International Business Research," in R. Marschan-Piekkari & C. Welch (eds) *Handbook of Qualitative Research Methods for International Business*. London, UK: Edward Elgar, 305–23.

Sweeney, A. (1993) "Women Making Cars, Making Trouble, Making History," in T. Hayter & D. Harvey (eds) *The Factory and the City: The Story of the Cowley Automobile Workers in Oxford*. London, UK: Mansell, 116–39.

Thornett, A. (1998) *Inside Cowley: Trade Union Struggles in the 1970s: Who Really Opened the Door to the Tory Onslaught?* London, UK: Porcupine Press.

Trompenaars, F. (1992) *Riding the Waves of Culture*. London: Nicholas Brealey.

Ward, S., Stuart, O., & Swingedouw, E. (1993) "Cowley in the Oxford Economy," in T. Hayter & D. Harvey (eds) *The Factory and the City: The Story of the Cowley Automobile Workers in Oxford*. London, UK: Mansell, 67–92.

Whisler, T. R. (1999) *The British Motor Industry, 1945–94: A Study in Industrial Decline*. Oxford, UK: Oxford University Press.

11
Using Mental Models to Study Cross-Cultural Interactions

Leigh Anne Liu and Claudia Dale

> It is extraordinary the way people, music and cultures develop. The paths and experiences that guide them are unpredictable. Shaped by our families, neighborhoods, cultures and countries, each of us ultimately goes through this process of incorporating what we learn with who we are and who we seek to become. As we struggle to find our individual voices, I believe we must look beyond the voice we've been assigned, and find our place among the tones and timbre of human expression.
>
> Yo-Yo Ma (2008)

The preceding quote illustrates the dynamic complexities of cultural development and convergence through individual experience and cognition. Cross-cultural interactions, including face-to-face and electronic communication, negotiation, conflict management, and teamwork, are critical components of today's global marketplace. In this chapter, from the lens of viewing culture as mental models and shared mental models, we advocate the need for using these cognitive networks to study and participate in intra- and intercultural interactions. We propose individual and shared mental models as a framework for evaluating cultural differences and navigating cross-cultural business interactions.

Cultural complexity and cross-cultural interactions

For almost three decades, since the publication of *Culture's Consequences* (1980), Hofstede's cultural values framework has been integral to international business research and practice. However, there are emerging problems with the framework for its country level of analysis and static perspective on individual cognition and experience (e.g., Earley, 1997; Fernandez et al., 1997; Hong and Chiu, 2001). Several scholars and practitioners have recognized a need to revisit or revise Hofstede's research on culture (e.g., Earley, 2006; Fernandez et al., 1997; Javidan et al., 2006; Smith, 2006). Smith (2006, p. 915) asserts that the study of culture as it applies in an international business context must move beyond dimensions toward a "more qualitative analyses of culture." Earley (2006, p. 925) argues for a different conception of culture that moves away from static values and toward dynamic meaning, "the meaning we attach to aspects of the world around us." Integrating meaning accounts for the differences that individuals may have within the same cultural context and allows for consideration of psychological and cognitive aspects of cultural identity (Earley, 2006).

Cultural dichotomies such as individualism–collectivism or high–low power distance are not sufficient to facilitate our understanding of the complexity of today's global marketplace: "cultural dichotomies do not and cannot meet the challenges raised by the process of globalization;" therefore, "We need an alternative approach that is sensitive to the process of cultural interchange, the complexities of social positions, and the dynamics of global interconnectedness" (Hermans and Kempen, 1998, p. 1112). Further, the interconnectedness of societies that globalization has given rise to makes the previous notion of cultures as "independent, coherent, and stable" irrelevant, evidenced by the interconnectedness found in multinational firms, regional entities, Internet communities, global institutions, and so on (Hermans and Kempen, 1998). Globalization, and the rise of multiculturalism, means that the view of culture as static no longer applies and that it is more constructive to view culture as a "dynamic open system that is spreading across space and changing over time," signaling the need for a paradigm shift (Hong and Chiu, 2001, p. 193).

Individuals as managers, leaders, negotiators, and communicators are the representatives of culture and presenters of cultural influence. Compared with static cultural value dimensions, unique personal experience and knowledge networks are much more telling when trying to predict behaviors and outcomes of interpersonal interactions in international and multicultural situations. The interaction between culture, domain, and context is complicated and cannot be explained by cultural differences alone; individual differences in experience and values are better explicators of cognitive processes (Conway et al., 2001). Conway and colleagues find that complexity is specific to the situation and depends on the individual's experience and values.

A cognitive approach to culture suits such increasing complexity. One particular aspect of the cognitive approach is the study of individuals' mental models, the cognitive representation of a situation. Given the social nature of cross-cultural interactions, knowing what is going on in the mind of each individual player is not enough to capture the interactive and dynamic process. Shared mental models provide a framework that seeks to capture the process by which a group will construct a collective understanding of a given situation.

Mental models and shared mental models

A mental model is a psychological representation of a domain or situation that allows an individual to understand, to explain, and to predict future states (Gentner, 2002; Holyoak, 1984; Johnson-Laird, 1983; Rouse and Morris, 1986). Mental models stand for the knowledge structures that help people make sense of and respond to a situation that they encounter. A mental model paints a picture in an individual's mind about what elements are in a situation and how the elements are related to one another, and as the situation changes, the relationship between elements is updated. In addition, mental models can be used to understand a new system based on what is known about another, analogically related system (Collins and Gentner, 1987). A mental model is one of many related concepts that address the knowledge structures individuals use to make sense of their surroundings. Examples include cognitive maps (Axelrod, 1976), scripts (Abelson, 1976), schemas (Fiske and Taylor, 1991; Neisser, 1976; Rumelhart, 1984), and belief or knowledge structures (Fiske and Taylor, 1991). These concepts all relate to the processes that facilitate an individual's ability to sort out information in his or her environment and use that information to further understanding. Cognitive maps are graphic representations of mental models. Scripts are concerned with event sequences in linear temporal order. Schemas are more general terms for mental models; mental models are more specific and situation-dependent than schemas. Knowledge structures emphasize the framework for organizing, relating, and retaining information (Mayer, 1992). The domains of these concepts are akin to mental models, though mental models are situation dependent and consider the interrelationship between cognitive elements.

Individual mental models compose the building blocks for social interaction. Shared mental models occur when the individual mental models held by members of a group change to reflect the group-level consensus during the group process. Shared mental models have attracted attention among researchers who study teams and groups and are used to refer to the group-level phenomenon of constructing similar (or at least complementary) individual mental models. Shared mental models are not the simple sum of individual mental models but include the synergistic effect of the communication process between individual mental models. In other words, in social interaction, people's individual mental models influence and are influenced by the social context, the people they communicate with, and the type of communication experienced. Due to this interdependence, it is not possible to look at shared mental models without understanding individual mental models, and vice versa.

Based on synthesizing previous works, we define a mental model in social interaction as *a cognitive network comprised of interrelated informational, relational, and emotional elements of knowledge*. Mental models help an individual to make sense of specific situations. There are three common characteristics of mental models in social interaction. First, mental models are situation specific. Second, depending on the specific situation and individual, the specific content of elements in one's mental model varies, but the elements themselves can be categorized as informational, relational, and emotional. Third, mental models recognize the patterns of interrelations between these elements and consider the situation holistically rather than as isolated factors or issues. The cartoon in Figure 11.1 depicts a mental model about the cognitive interrelationship of different element in a situation, which can include causal relations or decision-making strategies, such as how to get the ball off the table.

We define shared mental models in social interaction as *the degree of convergence between the individually held mental models*. Since mental models are defined as networks of perception and knowledge of the situation, the relational similarity between networks refers to the similarity in central elements and the similarity in the network structure. Here we emphasize two aspects of this definition of shared mental models. First, this definition and the proposed application of shared mental models in social interaction are at the individual and interpersonal level. We recognize that mental models and shared mental models do exist at the organizational and societal level. In this chapter, we examine the phenomenon of shared mental models at the individual and interpersonal level as a start to further our understanding of shared mental models in other levels of analysis. Second, shared mental models may exist at different points in the process of interaction, and the degree of convergence may vary and go through multiple rounds of iteration. We do

Figure 11.1 Cat thinks of a complex equation to get a ball off of a table
© *The New Yorker Collection 2001 Jack Ziegler from cartoonbank.com. All Rights Reserved.*

believe that mental model convergence will achieve relative stability toward the end of the interaction episode. The cartoon in Figure 11.2 illustrates that in social interactions, we not only exchange single isolated pieces of information such as the name and number of a street, but also how a certain address is structurally and spatially related to its context, like the neighboring streets and landmarks. Unshared mental models would lead to misunderstanding and miscommunication.

Mental models in interpersonal interaction

As does the concept of mental model in the generic term, individual mental models bear various names. Many works reviewed in this section do not explicitly mention the term mental models; they are included because the essences of the concepts are either closely akin to mental models or reflect important aspects of mental models. The works that treat mental models as informational, relational, emotional,

Figure 11.2 A policeman giving directions has a clear mental image of them, but the man receiving them has a very confused image

and comprehensive largely follow a natural timeline. Research on the cognitive and informational aspects of mental models first appeared in the 1980s and extends to the present. The few works on the relational and emotional aspects appeared in the 1990s, and the comprehensive approach has attracted attention only recently. Table 11.1 provides a summary of types of mental models and a brief list of works reviewed from the three approaches.

Informational approach

Kahneman and Tversky's (1979, 2000) prospect theory provides a theoretical base for the cognitive and informational approach to mental models in decision making. According to prospect theory, people value a certain gain more than a probable gain with an equal or greater expected value; the opposite is true for losses. The displeasure associated with the loss is greater than the pleasure associated with the same amount of gain. Therefore, people respond differently, depending on

Table 11.1 Summary of previous works on individual mental models

Types of mental models	Aspects of mental models	Reference
Positive and negative frames	Informational	Bazerman, Magliozzi, and Neale, 1985 Northcraft and Neale, 1986 Bottom and Studt, 1993 Lim and Carnevale, 1995 De Dreu and McCusker, 1997 Rachlinski, 1998 Guthrie, 2000
Fixed-pie perception Mental model	Informational	Thompson and Hastie, 1990 Van Boven and Thompson, 2003
Cognitive maps anchored by utility	Informational	Simons, 1993
Role	Relational	Friedman, 1994 Montgomery, 1998
Positive and negative affect	Emotional	Carnevale and Isen, 1986 Barry and Oliver, 1996 Forgas, 1998 Thompson, Nadler, and Kim, 1999
Name and label	Relational, emotional, and informational	Larrick and Blount, 1997 Ross and Ward, 1995
Metaphors	Relational, emotional, and informational	Gelfand and McCusker, 2002
Multidimensional frames	Relational, emotional, and informational	Pinkley, 1990 Gelfand et al., 2001
Five mental models		Thompson and Loewenstein, 2003

whether the choices are framed in terms of gains or losses. The concept of frame has informed much research related to the informational aspect of mental models.

Positive and Negative Frames. According to Kahneman and Tversky's (2000) research, negotiation disputants who frame outcomes in terms of potential loss will be risk-seeking, whereas those who frame the outcomes in terms of gains will be potentially risk-averse. In the context of interpersonal interaction, empirical evidence supports this argument that the negotiators' mental model, whether it is a positive/profit frame or a negative/loss frame, significantly influences the negotiators' behavior and the final outcome.

The Fixed-Pie Perception. Thompson and colleagues highlight the mental models that center on the perception that negotiation is a fixed pie.

Thompson and Hastie (1990) measure individual negotiators' perceptions of the negotiation structure and find that across various issues, most negotiators assume the negotiation is a fixed pie—the interests of the other party are completely opposite to those of their own. Van Boven and Thompson (2003) find that negotiators who reach optimal settlements hold an integrative mental model, while those who do not reach optimal settlements have a fixed-pie mental model. They also find that experienced negotiators have similar mental models to those who reach optimal settlements.

Cognitive Maps Anchored by Utility. Similar to Thompson's work regarding negotiator mental models around the fixed-pie perception, Simons (1993) studies negotiator mental models of the cognitive conceptualization of utility. He finds that negotiators' cognitive conceptualization of utility influences both the types of solutions reached and the negotiators' motivation for the task. Results suggest that the conceptualization of utility as a subjective preference promotes integrative solutions and does not reinforce the fixed-pie assumption.

Relational approach

Goffman's (1959, 1974) theories about frames and roles largely inform studies about the relational aspect of negotiators' mental models by emphasizing the social and interactional aspect. From a sociological perspective, Goffman's work on frame analysis argues that frames allow people to organize their social experience. He demonstrates that when human beings experience anything, we "frame" the experience. Goffman's theories offer opportunities for future exploration from both relational and emotional perspectives.

Following Goffman, Friedman (1994) examines the mental models of negotiators from the lens of their dramaturgical roles. From a symbolic interactionist perspective, the social interaction is viewed as a "performance," shaped by the environment and audience and constructed to provide the other party with "impressions" that are consonant with the desired goals scripted for the actors. Montgomery (1998) suggests that role theory might provide faithful representations of Granovetter's (1985) embeddedness of social relations in economic action. Montgomery constructs a repeated game model in which players are constrained to either the role of a profit-maximizing "businessperson" or the role of a "friend" who is expected to cooperate. He finds that in games with exactly the same economic structure, the "businessperson" acted more strategically than the "friend." The investigation of roles reflects the relational and interactional aspect of negotiators' mental models.

Emotional approach

Mental models related to emotion are also found to influence the results of interactions. Negotiators in positive moods are found to be more confident, trusting, and more likely to use collaborative strategies (Thompson et al., 1999). As Barry and colleagues find in their reviews, positive affect is significantly related to individual behavior, like information processing and creative problem-solving (Barry et al., 2004; Barry and Oliver, 1996). Investigating the benefits and costs of shared emotions, Thompson and colleagues (1999) indicate that when sharing with others, the emotional social-facilitation effect makes individuals experience their emotions more intensely. Emotions could also be contagious, and Thompson and colleagues (1999) argue that if the germ is negative emotions, there are potential costs of the contagion, and benefits for positive emotions.

Comprehensive approach

Works reviewed in this section represent comprehensive approaches to mental models that gauge the informational, relational, and emotional aspects implicitly or explicitly.

Names and Labels. How a game is named or labeled can trigger different responses and perceptions in a negotiator's mind. Ross and Ward (1995, p. 291) demonstrate that the way a game is labeled has a dramatic effect on the degree people cooperated and that the label creates an "impact on the way the game was constructed by the players, what they felt it was 'about,' and what kinds of real world situations came to mind as they made their choices." Based on a series of studies, Larrick and Blount (1997) find that depending on the name of the negotiation, ultimatum game or social dilemma game, negotiators differ in their level of cooperation, interpretation of fairness and selfishness, as well as in their determination of the rate of compliance of the other party.

Metaphors. Looking at the influence of culture, Gelfand and McCusker (2002) present a metaphor perspective on culture, believing that the psychological, social, and organizing functions of metaphors can help individuals structure problems, scripts, and feelings in comparable ways to cultivate stable and mutual understandings. For example, they argue that the cultural differences between the United States and Japan can be examined from the metaphors of American sports and the Japanese traditional household. These two metaphors resemble the people's mental models. In American culture, as in sports, people view conflict as normal and see conflict management as participating in a performance contest; therefore, task orientation, aggressive behavior, and sportsmanship are expected. In Japanese culture, as in their typical household, people see the need to foster harmony, be relationally oriented, avoid conflict, and save face, not only for themselves, but for everyone.

Multidimensional Frames and Mental Models. Pinkley (1990) suggests that owing to differences in framing, people can hold different interpretations of the same dispute situation. Pinkley develops three dimensions of conflict frames: relationship versus task, intellectual versus emotion, and compromise versus win. Disputants with a relationship frame concentrate on the need to maintain or build the relationship with the other party, while disputants with a task frame see little importance in relationships but emphasize the material benefits of the settlements. Disputants with an intellectual frame stress the facts and logic involved in the conflict, while disputants with an emotion frame emphasize feelings related to the conflict situation, such as anger, frustration, contempt, and so on. The disputant who holds a compromise frame would see the necessity for both parties to compromise to find a mutually agreeable solution, while the disputant with a win frame would see the conflict situation as zero-sum game, and the resolution would end with the parties either winning or losing.

Thompson and Loewenstein (2003) propose five negotiator mental models as paradigms for future descriptive, prescriptive, and theoretical research. Based on previous theoretical and empirical works, Thompson and Loewenstein provide descriptive perceptions of situation, key causal factors influencing behavior and outcomes, and key behavioral measures for each of the five mental models. Prescriptively on each mental model, they offer key advice to negotiators and suggest strategies. The multidimensionality of conflict frames and mental models comprehensively covers the informational, relational, and emotional aspects of mental models.

In summary, we have presented the extant literature that examined types of mental models from varying perspectives. Positive and negative frames, fixed-pie perception, and cognitive maps focused on the informational aspect of mental models; studies from the perspective of role theory focused on the relational and interactional aspects of mental models; and multidimensional frames and metaphors emphasized the informational, relational, and emotional aspects to arrive at a comprehensive approach. These studies provided constructive information about how individuals' mental processing of the situation, the others involved, and themselves would influence the outcome of the interaction. However, social interaction and interdependence between the socially interacting individuals have not been sufficiently explored.

Shared mental models and socially shared cognition

Although the notion of socially shared cognition has not been popular within traditional social psychology, it has informed studies about teams and organizations. In this section, we begin with social construction theory and then review the applications of socially shared cognition in organization theories and the social psychology of groups and teams. Social constructionism provides a theoretical foundation for work on shared mental models. Without denying the existence of an objective reality, social constructionists believe that social actors collectively construct meaning, and society is built in ways that depend on the interaction of members. Applying this idea to the way culture influences behavior, Morris and Gelfand (2004) argue that through socialization, social structure, and public symbols, culture affects the constructs that are available and chronically accessible, and thus forms the context that activates certain knowledge structures.

The study of social interactions is confluent with earlier works about sense-making or interpretation in organizational behavior and the interaction between an individual and his or her environment. Weick (1969) develops the concept of enactment to connote how an organism adjusts to its environment by directly acting upon and changing it. Weick discusses enactment in terms of active sense-making by individuals in organizations. The concept of enactment illuminates how agency and constructive cognitive processes are essential elements for understanding the interaction of individuals and their social context. Focusing on the interpretive aspect of cognitive processes, Daft and Weick (1984) argue that through enactment, individual cognition and action create the environment within which further cognition and action takes place.

Social psychologists who study group and interpersonal processes have suggested that shared knowledge allows team members to have more accurate expectations and compatible approaches for task performance (Cannon-Bowers and Salas, 2001; Cannon-Bowers et al., 1993; Klimoski and Mohammed, 1994). It is the interaction between one's disposition and the situation that determines behavior, and behavior can best be understood by considering it as a joint product of individual difference variables and environmental factors (Mischel, 1984). In the context of social interaction, there are "reciprocal" influences between the perceiver's beliefs and the target's behaviors (Snyder, 1984; Snyder and Stukas, 1999).

At the group/organizational level, Wegner (1987) introduces transactive memory to demonstrate the shared system for encoding, storing, and retrieving information. It is suggested that we learn others' domains of expertise through interaction and observation. As in friendships and romantic relationships, through shared memory, cognitive behaviors that classify, describe, and evaluate information can be more efficient and reach similarity. For example, Sondak and colleagues (1995) find that when the negotiators' relationships are long-term, the agreements they reach are more efficient. Similarly, studies find that close relationships (friends, dating couples) lead to more cooperative and committed performance (Jehn and Shah, 1997) and more shared information (Fry et al., 1983). Gruenfeld and Mannix (1996) find that groups with members who are familiar with one another are more efficient and more comfortable working together and expressing different opinions.

The notion of socially shared cognition has been applied in contexts of decision-making. Although not termed "mental models" specifically, Pinkley and Northcraft (1994) and Messick (1999) provide empirical evidence that negotiators or decision makers develop similar mental models. Pinkley and Northcraft (1994) find that disputants' conflict frames mutually influence and become similar to each other. Adapting March's (1995) theory of appropriateness, identity, and rule-based decision processes, Messick (1999) demonstrates that decision makers in social contexts become similar in their understandings of the situation, parties, and rules. More recently, Van Boven and Thompson (2003) showed that negotiators who reach optimal outcomes for joint gain share more similarity in their mental models than negotiators who do not reach optimal outcomes.

Theoretically, Pruitt and Canevale (1993; Pruitt, 1995) argue that in the dynamic system of social interaction, there are scripts that characterize working relationships, and rules that guide or coordinate the interaction between the negotiators. They also maintain that though scripts have been generally regarded as individual properties, they could become characteristics of the system when they are shared. At the group level, Brodt and Dietz (1999) examine the information-sharing and sense-making process among negotiators. They suggest that it is more important to establish "a mutual understanding of the situation" (Brodt and Dietz, 1999, p. 265) than to be concerned with dividing up resources, problem solving, and even reaching agreements. Further, they argue that parties' engaging in complex sense-making is a process of building a "collective construal" of the task, the situation, and the relationship.

Culture as mental models and shared mental models

In this section, we attempt to bridge the streams of research on individual and shared mental models and culture. Culture has an influence on members' way of thinking and organizing information and knowledge, their communication and comprehension. Culture leads to different ways of thinking (Faure, 2002), and there are cross-cultural differences in how people perceive, reason, and organize the world around them (Conway et al., 2001). The social differences between cultures affect the ways in which people understand the nature of the universe, determine what constitutes knowledge, and the nature of cognitive processes (Nisbett et al., 2001). Thus, there are similarities between culture and mental models, which we have defined as knowledge structures that help people understand new situations.

Triandis (1994, p. 22) defines culture as "a set of human made objective and subjective elements that in the past have increased the probability of survival and resulted in satisfaction for the participation in an ecological niche, and thus became shared among those who could communicate with each other because they had a common language and they lived in the same time and place." Hofstede (1997) claims that each individual carries patterns of thinking, feeling, and potential acting that were learned within their social environments. In fact, Hofstede's conception of culture as "mental programs" that are shared among participants finds correspondence in the idea of culture as a shared mental model. An important difference is the dynamism inherent in a mental model that can be context and situation dependent and adaptable to new situations and environments.

One of the major arguments about cross-cultural differences is that different national cultures have different assumptions about social interactions (cf. Hofstede, 1980; Triandis, 1995). A large number of studies have found empirical evidence of cultural differences in negotiation and conflict management (e.g., Adair et al., 2001; Gelfand and Realo, 1999; Triandis, 1995). Individuals have culture-specific preferences for various behaviors, hold different perceptions regarding which behaviors may be appropriate or preferred, and perceive the same conflict situation differently (Gelfand et al., 2001). Therefore, culturally different assumptions in social interactions correlate with different preferences, which in turn lead to different central components in individuals' mental models across cultures.

Previous research shows that individuals in different cultural environments may exhibit different behaviors. For example, Adair and colleagues (2001) find that Americans exchanged information directly and avoided influence when interacting both intra-culturally and interculturally, while Japanese exchanged information indirectly and used influence when interacting in intracultural deals but adapted their behaviors in intercultural situations. In Chapter 8 of this book, Adair, Buchan, and Chen develop a framework for classifying cultures in terms of the form in which communication and social interaction occur. The framework is dynamic, being "a function of how people relate to others, perceive their social context, and process information within it."

The question of how context affects mental models is intriguing. Different components of an individual's mental model may be triggered by specific events or environmental factors. Morris and Gelfand (2004) argue that culture affects the knowledge structure by providing available and accessible constructs and forms the context that activates certain knowledge structures. Further, Briley, in Chapter 9 of this book, finds that context can activate certain cognitions that in turn inform people's preferences. If we conceive of culture as a mental model, we can consider context as an agent that may act upon the components of an individual's mental model, making certain features more or less prevalent depending on the situation.

Gulliver (1988, p. 253) summarizes the goal of cross-cultural analysis as to "conceptualize the pattern of a basic universal process applicable to all kinds of situations at whatever societal level (from interpersonal to international), in whatever socio-cultural context and irrespective of the issues in contention . . . [is] useful to the extent it can facilitate cross-cultural comparison and the identification of fundamental features and processual interactions." Whether one interacts with a member of her own culture or with a member of a different culture may also have moderating effects on the individual and shared mental models.

Hong and Chiu (2001) argue that individuals in a culture have access to shared cognitive tools that are relied upon to guide judgments and reactions to situations. Shared mental models are one such cognitive tool. Lau and colleagues (2001) assert that social representations, shared knowledge, and beliefs are central to culture, and within-culture communication gives rise to culturally shared social representations. These shared representations, too, have similarities with shared mental models. Leung and colleagues (2005) propose that cultural differences may be more easily mediated if the mental processes associated with national culture can be made fluid so as to be influenced by different situations. Shared mental models, because they are context dependent, are more malleable in terms of responding to situations.

Implications

Using the mental models approach to study cross-cultural interactions gives rise to the potential to navigate cross-cultural business situations in new and more effective ways. By transforming abstract, static cultural characteristics into actionable, flexible mental models, more successful inter- and intracultural interactions may be achieved. The mental models framework allows for a more dynamic and adaptable cognitive approach.

The mental models framework is applicable to international business research and practice in many areas. Here, we provide a summary of implications of mental models in areas of communication, conflict management, negotiation, organizational identity, partnerships, and multicultural teams. While far from complete, this summary serves to illustrate the challenges and opportunities implied by the existing literature and the potential value of the mental models framework for deciphering complexity in cross-cultural interactions, as well as identifies topics for further research.

Communication

Communication is central to every facet of human life, not least to the realm of business. Lau and colleagues' (2001, p. 366) research on communication finds that people modify their individual conceptions during communication and reach a common understanding by the end of the communication; "in communication, participants strive to establish a shared reality." Mental models help communicators by facilitating such shared representations. In terms of managers' communication with a multicultural workforce, the mental models framework enables greater understanding of individual employees' values that could influence mutual comprehension. According to Fernandez and colleagues (1997, p. 52), "managers should make an effort to determine the values currently prevailing and not rely on classifications or labels placed on cultures by researchers." Mental models serve as the knowledge structures that allow for a multidimensional construct of individual and cultural characteristics for communication.

Conflict management

In addition to aiding with understanding conflict, mental models mitigate the negative effects of conflict. Leung and colleagues (2005) posit that cognitive constructs, such as mental models, are useful for understanding cross-cultural differences in conflict behaviors. Because intercultural conflict may be worsened by "hidden assumptions" that one culture group has about another (Weisinger and Salipante, 1995, p. 148), a cognitive approach may alleviate the dangers of assumptions based on culture. In their research on using scenarios to study conflict situations, Weisinger and Salipante (1995) find that presenting participants with real-life multicultural conflict situations results in improved intercultural understanding with regard to interpreting behaviors and actions. Scenarios, while distinct from the previously discussed approaches to mental models, nonetheless share the aspect of situation specificity. Establishing a link between scenarios and mental models in conflict management is an area for further research.

Negotiation

A natural match between mental models and negotiation is that analogical reasoning, which involves making comparisons and transferring knowledge from a previous situation to a new situation, helps negotiators distinguish between relevant and irrelevant information to apply to the negotiation at hand (Gillespie et al., 1999). Our review of research on negotiators' use of mental models summarizes the ways in which different types of mental models can impact negotiation outcomes. Intercultural negotiation presents increased opportunity for misunderstanding, both in terms of how the parties view the negotiation itself and the proceedings and content of the negotiation. At the same time, Faure (2002) finds that negotiation becomes even more useful as global interdependence increases the likelihood of conflicts in various settings. Different cultures have different concepts of negotiation, and culture affects how the individual parties view the negotiation (Faure, 2002). As we have seen how cultural differences may be illuminated by mental models, intercultural negotiation presents an opportunity for mental models to be used in order to increase mutual perception of both the negotiation itself and the cultural factors impacting the parties in the negotiation.

Shared mental models are also significant for negotiation. When negotiators seek to find a common basis by starting with cultural differences and moving to shared understandings, the relationship benefits (Faure, 2002). Shared meaning systems allow negotiation participants to map from one domain to another, thus creating a shared reality and common definitions for the negotiation, its purpose, actions, and outcome (Gelfand and McCusker, 2002).

Organizational identity

For shared mental models within industry, organizations in which individuals' mental models have common core elements give rise to organizational coherence (Hodgkinson and Johnson, 1994). Where there is cognitive diversity among individuals, the organization may use political pressure or symbolic activity and routines to mediate diversity. Cornelissen's (2005) research on metaphor in organization theory strongly suggests the significance of metaphor for organizational theory and research, particularly organizational identity and the learning organization. As a type of mental model, the importance of metaphor in organization theory suggests a place for mental models as well, as additional research may demonstrate.

Partnerships

International business partnerships occur with more frequency, and the globalization of business continues. Graen and Hui (1996) write that cross-cultural partners must seek to understand cultural differences to manage partnerships effectively. Graen and Hui (1996, p. 65) propose the creation of "third culture" that is a bridge between two different cultures and a means of "transcending" the differences. Several researchers have found that a particular culture affects how its members think as well as behave (e.g., Hofstede, 1997; Hong and Chiu, 2001; Leung et al., 2005; Nisbett et al., 2001). Mental models, by providing structures for understanding cultural and cognitive differences, may be useful in partnerships to facilitate greater recognition of differences.

Multicultural work groups/teams

Shared mental models find application in multinational and multicultural work groups and teams. Several researchers have studied individuals' interactions in groups as affected by culture. Thomas (1999) shows that individual group members' sociocultural norms affect the way in which culturally diverse groups function. National culture significantly impacts the way in which individuals think and act in a group (Hambrick et al., 1998); specifically, nationality (national culture) affects personal characteristics of values, cognitive schema, demeanor (outward behavior), and language.

Individuals' mental models overlap with each other in team situations, allowing for shared understanding. Millhous (1999) finds that in multicultural work groups, there is a tendency for groups to arrive at shared understandings; this process can mitigate barriers of cultural differences. Banks and Millward (2000) propose that instead of duplicating a certain model, shared mental models should be distributed between team members for improved performance. The shared mental model concept suggests that teamwork and performance is improved through members' sharing of mental models. However, there are more complex pros and cons of sharing mental models: If individuals' models don't overlap, there can be a lack of common expectations and coordinated action; if models overlap too much, there can be duplication of work (Banks and Millward, 2000).

To summarize, we have briefly examined different areas of international business for which mental models may be useful. Mental models allow for improved communication by providing a means of approaching and understanding differences. Similarly, in conflict situations, mental models mitigate the danger presented by assumptions that individuals from one culture may make about another. In negotiation, individual and shared mental models help parties arrive at a mutual perception of the negotiation and mutually beneficial outcomes. Mental models are relevant for organizational theory and research. Opportunities for further research are present in these as well as other areas of social and intercultural interaction and cultural complexity.

Conclusion

We encounter cultural complexity in all manner of social interactions. The effects of globalization are not only to multiply the opportunities for intercultural interactions in all areas of business and society but also to give rise to an interconnected society in which cultural identity, never completely static to begin with, is subject to further complexity at both the individual and cultural levels. To meet the challenge of increasing cultural complexity, a new framework, one that goes beyond linear dichotomies, for approaching cross-cultural interactions is needed. In this chapter, we have advocated using the more dynamic system of mental models for research of and participation in intra- and intercultural interactions, with specific reference to international business interactions. Individual and shared mental models may serve as such a framework for evaluating cultural differences and navigating cross-cultural business interactions in complex situations.

At the same time, the implications of a dynamic view of culture for international business research and practice have not been sufficiently explored. Leung and colleagues (2005, p. 367) suggest that cultural differences may be easier to overcome than previously assumed if mental processes "are relatively fluid, and can be changed and sustained by appropriate situational influences." We hereby offer mental models as a framework for realizing such fluidity.

References

Abelson, R. P. (1976) "Script Processing in Attitude Formation and Decision Making," in J. S. Carroll & J. Payne, (eds) *Cognition and Social Behavior.* Hillsdale, NJ: Erlbaum.

Adair, W. L., Okumura, T., & Brett, J. M. (2001) "Negotiation Behavior When Cultures Collide: The United States and Japan," *Journal of Applied Psychology,* 86, 371–85.

Axelrod, R. (1976) *Structure of Decision: The Cognitive Maps of Political Elites.* Princeton, NJ: Princeton University.

Banks, A. P. & Millward, L. J. (2000) "Running Shared Mental Models as a Distributed Cognitive Process," *British Journal of Psychology,* 91, 513–31.

Barry, B., Fulmer, I. S., & Van Kleef, G. A. (2004) "I Laughed, I Cried, I Settled: The Role of Emotion in Negotiation," *The Handbook of Negotiation and Culture.* Stanford, CA: Stanford University Press, 71–94.

Barry, B. & Oliver, R. L. (1996) "Affect in Negotiation: A Model and Propositions," *Organizational Behavior and Human Decision Processes,* 67, 127–43.

Bazerman, M. H., Magliozzi, T., & Neale, M. A. (1985) "Integrative Bargaining in a Competitive Market," *Organizational Behavior and Human Decision Processes,* 35, 294–313.

Bottom, W. P. & Studt, A. (1993) "Framing Effects and the Distributive Aspect of Integrative Bargaining," *Organizational Behavior and Human Decision Processes,* 56, 459–74.

Brodt, S. E. & Dietz, L. E. (1999) "Shared Information and Information-Sharing: Understanding Negotiation as Collective Construal," in R. J. Bies & R. J. Lewicki (eds) *Research in Negotiation in Organizations,* Vol. 7. Stamford, CT: JAI, 263–83.

Cannon-Bowers, J. A. & Salas, E. (2001) "Reflections on Shared Cognition," *Journal of Organizational Behavior,* 22, 195–202.

Cannon-Bowers, J. A., Salas, E., & Converse, S. (1993) "Shared Mental Models in Expert Team Decision Making," in J. N. J. Castellan (ed.) *Individual and Group Decision Making: Current Issues.* Hillsdale, NJ: Erlbaum, 221–46.

Carnevale, P. J. & Isen, A. M. (1986) "The Influence of Positive Affect and Visual Access on the Discovery of Integrative Solutions in Bilateral Negotiations," *Organizational Behavior and Human Decision Processes,* 37, 1–13.

Collins, A., & Gentner, D. (1987) "How People Construct Mental Models," in D. Holland & N. Quinn (eds) *Cultural Models in Language and Thought.* Cambridge, England: Cambridge University, 243–65.

Conway, L. G., Schaller, M., Tweed, R. G., & Hallett, D. (2001) "The Complexity of Thinking Across Cultures: Interactions between Culture and Situational Context," *Social Cognition,* 19, 228–50.

Cornelissen, J. P. (2005) "Beyond Compare: Metaphor in Organization Theory," *Academy of Management Review,* 30, 751–64.

Daft, R. L. & Weick, K. E. (1984) "Toward a Model of Organizations as Interpretation Systems," *Academy of Management Review,* 9, 284–95.

De Dreu, C. K. W. & McCusker, C. (1997) "Gain-Loss Frames and Cooperation in Two-Person Social Dilemmas: A Transformation Analysis," *Journal of Personality and Social Psychology,* 72, 1093–106.

Earley, P. C. (1997) *Face, Harmony, and Social Structure: An Analysis of Organizational Behavior across Cultures.* New York, NY: Oxford University.

Earley, P. C. (2006) "Leading Cultural Research in the Future: A Matter of Paradigms and Taste," *Journal of International Business Studies*, 37, 922–31.

Faure, G.-O. (2002) "International Negotiation: The Cultural Dimension," in V. A. Kremenyuk (ed.) *International Negotiation: Analysis, Approaches, Issues*, 2nd edn. San Francisco, CA: Jossey-Bass, 392–415.

Fernandez, D. R., Carlson, D. S., Stepina, L. P., & Nicholson, J. D. (1997) "Hofstede's Country Classification 25 Years Later," *Journal of Social Psychology*, 137, 43–54.

Fiske, S. T. & Taylor, S. E. (1991) *Social Cognition*, 2nd edn. New York, NY: McGraw-Hill.

Forgas, J. P. (1998) "On Feeling Good and Getting Your Way: Mood Effects on Negotiator Cognition and Bargaining Strategies," *Journal of Personality and Social Psychology*, 7, 565–77.

Friedman, R. A. (1994) *Front Stage, Backstage: The Dramatic Structure of Labor Negotiations*. Cambridge, MA: MIT Press.

Fry, W. R., Firestone, I. J., & Williams, D. J. (1983) "Negotiation Process and Outcome of Stranger Dyads and Dating Couples: Do Lovers Lose?," *Basic and Applied Social Psychology*, 4, 1–16.

Gelfand, M. J. & McCusker, C. (2002) "Metaphor and the Cultural Construction of Negotiation: A Paradigm for Research and Practice," in M. J. Gannon & K. L. Newman (eds) *Handbook of Cross-Cultural Management*. New York, NY: Blackwell, 292–314.

Gelfand, M. J., Nishii, L. H., Holcombe, K. M., Dyer, N., Ohbuchi, K. I., & Fukuno, M. (2001) "Cultural Influences on Cognitive Representations of Conflict: Interpretations of Conflict Episodes in the United States and Japan," *Journal of Applied Psychology*, 86, 1059–74.

Gelfand, M. J. & Realo, A. (1999) "Individualism-Collectivism and Accountability in Intergroup Negotiations," *Journal of Applied Psychology*, 84, 721–36.

Gentner, D. (2002) "Mental Models, Psychology of," in N. J. Smelser & P. B. Bates (eds) *International Encyclopedia of the Social & Behavioral Sciences*. Amsterdam, Netherlands: Elsevier, 9683–7.

Gillespie, J. J., Thompson, L., Loewenstein, J., & Gentner, D. (1999) "Lessons from Analogical Reasoning in the Teaching of Negotiation," *Negotiation Journal*, 15, 363–71.

Goffman, E. (1959) *The Presentation of Self in Everyday Life*. Garden City, NJ: Doubleday.

Goffman, E. (1974) *Frame Analysis: An Essay on the Organization of Experience*. Cambridge, MA: Harvard.

Graen, G. & Hui, C. (1996) "Managing Changes in Globalizing Business: How to Manage Cross-Cultural Business Partners," *Journal of Organizational Change Management*, 9 (3), 62–72.

Granovetter, M. (1985) "Economic Action and Social Structure: The Problem of Embeddedness," *The American Journal of Sociology*, 91, 481–510.

Gruenfeld, D. H. & Mannix, E. A. (1996) "Group Composition and Decision Making: How Member Familiarity and Information Distribution Affect Process and Performance," *Organizational Behavior & Human Decision Processes*, 67, 1–15.

Gulliver, P. H. (1988) "Anthropological Contributions to the Study of Negotiations," *Negotiation Journal*, 4, 247–55.

Guthrie, C. (2000) "Framing Frivolous Litigation: A Psychological Theory," *The University of Chicago Law Review*, 67, 163–216.

Hambrick, D. C., Davison, S.C., Snell, S. A., & Snow, C. C. (1998) "When Groups Consist of Multiple Nationalities: Towards a New Understanding of the Implications," *Organization Studies*, 19, 181–205.

Hermans, H. J. M. & Kempen, H. J. G. (1998) "Moving Cultures: The Perilous Problems of Cultural Dichotomies in a Globalizing Society," *American Psychologist*, 53, 1111–20.

Hodgkinson, G. P. & Johnson, G. (1994) "Exploring the Mental Models of Competitive Strategists: The Case for a Processual Approach," *Journal of Management Studies*, 31, 525–51.

Hofstede, G. (1980) *Culture's Consequences, International Differences in Work-Related Values*. Beverly Hills, CA: Sage.

Hofstede, G. (1997) *Cultures and Organizations: Software of the Mind* (Revised ed.). New York: McGraw-Hill.

Holyoak, K. J. (1984) "Mental Models in Problem Solving," in J. R. Anderson & S. M. Kosslyn (eds) *Tutorials in Learning and Memory*. New York, NY: W. H. Freeman, 193–218.

Hong, Y. Y. & Chiu, C. Y. (2001) "Toward a Paradigm Shift: From Cross-Cultural Differences in Social Cognition to Social-Cognitive Mediation of Cultural Differences," *Social Cognition*, 19, 181–96.

Javidan, M., House, R. J., Dorfman, P. W., Hanges, P. J., & de Luque, M. S. (2006) "Conceptualizing and Measuring Cultures and their Consequences: A Comparative Review of GLOBE's and Hofstede's Approaches," *Journal of International Business Studies*, 37, 897–914.

Jehn, K. A. & Shah, P. P. (1997) "Interpersonal Relationships and Task Performance: An Examination of Mediating Processes in Friendship and Acquaintance Groups," *Journal of Personality and Social Psychology*, 72, 775–90.

Johnson-Laird, P. N. (1983) *Mental Models*. Cambridge, MA: Harvard.

Kahneman, D. & Tversky, A. (1979) "Prospect Theory: An Analysis of Decision under Risk," *Econometrica*, 47, 263–91.

Kahneman, D. & Tversky, A. (2000) *Choices, Values, and Frames*. New York, NY: Russell Sage Foundation.

Klimoski, R. & Mohammed, S. (1994) "Team Mental Model: Construct or Metaphor?," *Journal of Management Studies*, 20, 403–37.

Larrick, R. P. & Blount, S. (1997) "The Claiming Effect: Why Players Are More Generous in Social Dilemmas than in Ultimatum Games," *Journal of Personality and Social Psychology*, 72 (4), 810–25.

Lau, I. Y.-M., Chiu, C.-Y., & Lee, S.-L. (2001) "Communication and Shared Reality: Implications for the Psychological Foundations of Culture," *Social Cognition*, 19, 350–71.

Leung, K., Bhagat, R. S., Buchan, N. R., Erez, M., & Gibson, C. B. (2005) "Culture and International Business: Recent Advances and their Implications for Future Research," *Journal of International Business Studies*, 36, 357–78.

Lim, R. G., & Carnevale, P. J. (1995) "Influencing Mediator Behavior Through Framing," *International Journal of Conflict Management*, 6, 349–68.

Ma, Y.-y. (2008) "A Musician of Many Cultures," *This I Believe*. Washington, DC: National Public Radio.

March, J. G. (1995) *A Primer on Decision Making*. New York, NY: Free Press.

Mayer, R. E. (1992) *Thinking, Problem Solving and Cognition*. New York, NY: W. H. Freeman.

Messick, D. M. (1999) "Alternative Logics for Decision Making in Social Settings," *Journal of Economic Behavior & Organization*, 39, 11–28.

Millhous, L. M. (1999) "The Experience of Culture in Multicultural Groups—Case Studies of Russian-American Collaboration in Business," *Small Group Research*, 30, 280–308.

Mischel, W. (1984) "Convergences and Challenges in the Search for Consistency," *American Psychologist*, 39, 351–64.

Montgomery, J. D. (1998) "Toward a Role-Theoretic Conceptions of Embeddedness," *American Journal of Sociology*, 104, 92–125.

Morris, M. W. & Gelfand, M. J. (2004) "Cultural Differences and Cognitive Dynamics: Expanding the Cognitive Tradition in Negotiation," in M. J. Gelfand & J. Brett (eds) *Culture and Negotiation: Integrative Approaches to Theory and Research*. Palo Alto, CA: Stanford.

Neisser, U. (1976) *Cognition and Reality: Principles and Implications of Cognitive Psychology*. San Francisco, CA: W. H. Freeman.

Nisbett, R. E., Peng, K. P., Choi, I., & Norenzayan, A. (2001) "Culture and Systems of Thought: Holistic Versus Analytic Cognition," *Psychological Review*, 108, 291–310.

Northcraft, G. B., & Neale, M. A. (1986) "Opportunity Costs and the Framing of Resource Allocation Decisions," *Organizational Behavior and Human Decision Processes*, 37, 348–56.

Pinkley, R. (1990) "Dimensions of Conflict Frame: Disputant Interpretations of Conflict," *Journal of Applied Psychology*, 75, 117–26.

Pinkley, R. & Northcraft, G. B. (1994) "Cognitive Interpretations of Conflict: Implications for Dispute Processes and Outcomes," *Academy of Management Journal*, 37, 193–205.

Pruitt, D. G. (1995) "Networks and Collective Scripts: Paying Attention to Structure in Bargaining Theory," in R. M. Kramer & D. M. Messick (eds), *Negotiation as a Social Process: New Trends in Theory and Research*. Thousand Oaks, CA: Sage, 37–47.

Pruitt, D. G. & Carnevale, P. J. (1993) *Negotiation in Social Conflict*. Belmont, CA: Brooks/Cole.

Rachlinski, J. J. (1998) "A Positive Theory of Judging in Hindsight," *The University of Chicago Law Review*, 65, 571–625.

Ross, L. & Ward, A. (1995) "Psychological Barriers to Dispute Resolution," *Advances in Experimental Social Psychology*, 27, 255–303.

Rouse, W. B. & Morris, N. M. (1986) "On Looking into the Black Box: Prospects and Limits in the Search for Mental Models," *Psychological Bulletin*, 100, 349–63.

Rumelhart, D. E. (1984) "Schemata and the Cognitive System," in R. S. Wyer & T. K. Shrull (eds), *The Handbook of Social Cognition*, Vol. 1. Hillsdale, NJ: Erlbaum, 161–88.

Simons, T. (1993) "Speech Patterns and Concept of Utility in Cognitive Maps: The Case of Integrative Bargaining," *Academy of Management Journal*, 36, 139–56.

Smith, P. B. (2006) "When Elephants Fight, the Grass Gets Trampled: The GLOBE and Hofstede Projects," *Journal of International Business Studies*, 37, 915–21.

Snyder, M. (1984) "When Belief Creates Reality," *Advances in Experimental Social Psychology*, 18, 248–305.

Snyder, M. & Stukas, A. A. J. (1999) "Interpersonal Processes: The Interplay of Cognitive, Motivational, and Behavioral Activities in Social Interaction," *Annual Review of Psychology*, 50, 273–303.

Sondak, H., Neale, M. A., & Pinkley, R. (1995) "The Negotiated Allocation of Benefits and Burdens: The Impact of Outcome Valence, Contribution, and Relationship," *Organizational Behavior and Human Decision Processes*, 64, 249–60.

Stevenson, J. (1976) "Direct," *New Yorker*, February 16, 38 (ID: 42716 at cartoon-bank.com).

Thomas, D. C. (1999) "Cultural Diversity and Work Group Effectiveness: An Experimental Study," *Journal of Cross-Cultural Psychology*, 30, 242–63.

Thompson, L. & Hastie, R. (1990) "Social Perception in Negotiation," *Organizational Behavior and Human Decision Processes*, 47, 98–123.

Thompson, L. & Loewenstein, J. (2003) "Mental Models in Negotiations," in M. A. Hogg & J. Cooper (eds) *Sage Handbook of Social Psychology*. Thousand Oaks, CA: Sage.

Thompson, L., Nadler, J., & Kim, P. H. (1999) "Some Like It Hot: The Case for the Emotional Negotiator," in L. L. Thompson & J. M. Levine (eds) *Shared Cognition in Organizations: The Management of Knowledge*. Mahwah, NJ: Erlbaum, 139–62.

Triandis, H. C. (1994) *Culture and Social Behavior*. New York, NY: McGraw-Hill.

Triandis, H. C. (1995) *Individualism and Collectivism*. Boulder, CO: Westview.

Van Boven, L. & Thompson, L. (2003) "Mental Models of Negotiators," *Group Processes and Intergroup Relations*, 6, 387–404.

Wegner, D. M. (1987) "Transactive Memory: A Contemporary Analysis of the Group Mind," in B. Mullen & G. R. Goethals (eds) *Theories of Group Behavior*. New York, NY: Springer, 185–208.

Weick, K. E. (1969) *Social Psychology of Organizing*. New York, NY: McGraw Hill.

Weisinger, J. Y. & Salipante, P. F. (1995) "Toward a Method of Exposing Hidden Assumptions in Multicultural Conflict," *International Journal of Conflict Management*, 6, 147–70.

Ziegler, J. (2001) "Cat," *New Yorker*, Nov 26, 52 (ID: 46752 at cartoonbank.com).

Part VI Reflexive Considerations

12
Reflexive Considerations of Culture Theories in Global Marketing

Cheryl Nakata

Culture theories have long been used to explain and predict a host of global marketing phenomena, such as cross-cultural responses to advertising (Alden et al., 1993), global consumer persuasion appeals (Aaker and Maheswaran, 1997), and national product development processes (Song et al., 2000). Despite their increasing application to global marketing issues, culture theories tend to be narrowly construed, of weaker conceptual forms, and dominated by the Hofstedean paradigm (see Chapter 4 by Nakata and Izberk-Bilgin). Similar observations have been drawn by other researchers (see Chapter 2 by Earley, and Chapter 3 by Taras and Steele in this book). Consequently, insights into culture and its implications for global marketing have been severely restricted.

To begin to redress this situation, I embark on a reflexive study of culture writings from the social sciences to expand the understanding of culture beyond interpretations in global marketing. I then apply this broader understanding to delineate a new course for culture theories. In the following sections, I describe my approach to selecting culture writings, propose a structure for examining these works, summarize what they convey about culture—as juxtaposed with the views of culture offered by Hofstede and others—and discuss how culture theories may be developed and applied in the future to address vital global marketing concerns. Because this book is concerned with culture in relation to both marketing and management, I note that much of what this study shows and the direction outlined for global marketing also applies to global management.

Methodology

I do not claim to examine all writings on culture in the social sciences. Such a claim would ring false by virtue of the immense volume of recorded ruminations on culture over several centuries. Since ancient times, poets, kings, soldiers, and ordinary men and women have remarked on the distinctive customs and characteristics of various peoples (Gorer, 1955; Kroeber and Kluckhohn, 1952). In modern times, culture has been an interdisciplinary magnet, drawing the attention of historians, political scientists, and philosophers, among others (Poole, 1999). Thus, for practical reasons, I delimit the literature, emphasizing the social sciences most closely associated with the subject, namely, anthropology and sociology, and sample classical as well as contemporary works on culture from these fields.

To structure the reading, I focus on works that elaborate the ontology and epistemology of culture. Ontology is the metaphysics of being, and epistemology is the study of knowledge. I look specifically for what these works say about culture's ontological traits, epistemological structure, and epistemological philosophy. The first refers to the essential attributes of culture. The second is the larger gestalt of culture and, by implication, the means to study it. The last are core beliefs about how knowledge of culture is produced. I examine these three dimensions because they are fundamental elements of all culture theories (Hunt, 1991). I note how the leading culture theories in global marketing, especially Hofstede's, describe each dimension, and I compare these views with those in the social sciences. I deliberately attempt to expand the understanding of culture in global marketing by exploring the range of ontological and epistemological properties presented about culture in writings by sociologists, anthropologists, and authors in related fields.

Findings

Ontological traits

The culture theories most often featured in global marketing literature are those by Hofstede, Hall, and Triandis. Hofstede's theory is, however, far and away the most prevalent culture framework in global marketing (see Chapter 4 of this book), as it is in management and international business (see Taras and Steele in this book). These leading theories indicate that culture has four ontological traits. I present each attribute, and then discuss complementary and contrasting views articulated in the social sciences.

Culture Is Cognitive

Hofstede (1980, p. 13) argues that culture is the "collective programming of the mind," a statement that has gained veracity by being so often quoted. Accordingly, culture is cognitive—it is what people think. Thoughts that are more commonly shared, packaged as values or desired states, characterize a society. For example, Americans on average believe in and value autonomy highly, so their culture is said to be individualistic. Triandis (1989) makes a similar assertion, arguing that in individualist cultures, cognitions about the private self as separated and distinct from others are encouraged, whereas in collectivist cultures, cognitions about the self as attached to others are reinforced. Hall (1966, 1976) shares the view that culture has a strong mental component. He elaborates that culture filters what individuals pay attention to, directing their information processing and communications. Culture is so deeply internalized that it is synonymous at times with the mind itself.

Similar to these interpretations, culture is formulated as a mental good in many social science writings. This conceptualization is not new (Derne, 1994; Harris, 1999). Classical sociological and social anthropological works often refer to culture as "the values, norms, beliefs, and attitudes of the entire population or subgroups within the population" (Crane, 1994, p. 2). An exemplar is Parsons's (1937) theory of social action, which frames culture as a paramount value system that embeds itself in a diversity of social and political structures. The value system consists of patterned variables, such as universalism–particularism, achievement–ascription, and affectivity–neutrality, with societies differing on which ends of these value-anchored continua they fall.

The notion of culture as a mental good continues to have great appeal in the social sciences. As explained by Swidler (1986), because researchers want to determine culture's causal significance, drawing linkages to action, they gravitate toward cognitions that offer such links. Over the last half century, however, the idea has come under attack (Bidney, 1944; Blake and Davis, 1964; Shweder, 1984). The main reason relates to the assignment of more power to thought than may be warranted, ignoring the roles of habit, practice, language, symbols, meaning, and emotions in social lives. Consequently, culture theories that diminish the role of cognition are appearing in the social sciences. An example is the theory of tastes, a poststructuralist paradigm offered by the sociologist Pierre Bourdieu (1984). Bourdieu argues that ways of feeling and practice are as much attributes of culture as ways of thinking, together forming a complex milieu that reinforces class distinctions and other social constructions. What Bourdieu's work and others like it suggest is that culture is not purely or even mostly cognitive; rather, it is a mix of cognitive and non- or less cognitive dimensions.

Culture Is Bounded

The leading culture theories in global marketing assume culture is geographically bounded and most often by national borders. Hofstede

(1980, 2001) is the most explicit in this regard when he defines culture as national culture. Each country has a unique culture reflected in central tendencies on four universal values. Hall (1966, 1976) is less explicit but discusses high- versus low-context cultures almost exclusively in terms of the propensities of countries and their citizenry. Triandis (1989) does not equate culture with nation per se but typically operationalizes individualism and collectivism by comparing dispositions of persons from one country and with those of another (Trafimow, Triandis, and Goto, 1991).

The idea that members of a nation are culturally distinctive is long-standing in the social sciences. Anthropologist Ruth Benedict, whose seminal work *The Chrysanthemum and the Sword* (1946) initiated the formal study of national character, posited that nations have a discernable psychic unity. Some social scientists have maintained this assumption because of the continuing relevance of the nation state. Among them are the sociologist Immanuel Wallerstein (1997, p. 92), who calls nation states "our primary cultural container," and the philosopher Ross Poole (1999, p. 15), who observes that the "nation is a specific cultural object." They make cogent arguments that the nation state, admittedly a geographical and political artifact, has asserted itself over other cultural forms. They observe that nations use language policy, formal education, mass media, civil religion, and meta-narratives to coalesce the identity and loyalty of their citizens. Benedict Anderson (1991, pp. 5, 16) refers to a country as an "imagined community," wherein strangers are knit together by cultural apparatuses to form a "deep, horizontal comradeship."

Yet in more recent years, there has been vigorous debate about whether culture can be contained (James, 1996; Schudson, 1994). Even those who advocate the culture-as-country position recognize that there are multiple ways to circumscribe culture. Culture can be defined at levels above and below that of the nation. Richard Jenkins (1997), for instance, analyzes cultures in one country, the United Kingdom, by region (Wales vs Northern Ireland), religion (Protestant vs Catholic), ethnicity (Irish vs Scot), and language (Gaelic vs English). Similarly, culture can move up in scope, referring to a continent (Africa), region (Southeast Asia), trading bloc (European Union), hemisphere (Southern), and, broadest of all, a universal phenomenon (the global culture).

The primary criticism lodged against the culture-as-country assertion is that the nation may be a "problematic social and historical construction" (Schudson 1994, p. 21). National borders change and are traversed. The last century witnessed radical political reconstitutions, such as the reemergence of Estonia and the dismantlement of the USSR. Borders, even when temporarily fixed, are highly permeable: Through immigration and economic zones, people—the possessors, creators, and messengers of culture—are moving across borders in unprecedented numbers. For this reason, concepts of culture that are less geographically determined are emergent in the social sciences. An example is Samuel Huntington's (1996) theory of civilizations. Huntington proposes that civilizations are meaningful culture constructs for political, economic, and historical analyses. Civilizations, which are religiously rooted, cut across nation-states, and multiples can coexist within one country, such as Hindu and Islamic civilizations in India.

Culture Is Immutable

A third ontological trait described by the leading culture theories in global marketing is immutability or constancy. Hofstede (1980, 2001) describes how shared values are reinforced by institutions and environmental factors. All three elements combine to create a homeostatic system that maintains cultural patterns across generations. Hofstede (1980, 2001) does not claim that culture is completely static but that change is glacial. Hall echoes this perspective, elaborating that ways of thinking and communicating become inculcated after centuries of practice. The result is a pervasive, hidden culture that is "quite stable and long-persisting" (Hall, 1976, p. 52). Triandis (2000; Triandis and Suh, 2002) does not directly address the issue of cultural constancy but implies his position in descriptions of culture as generationally transferred. He says societies develop enduring conventions over time to improve their functional effectiveness in certain ecologies.

The immutability of culture is assumed in many of the writings from social sciences. It is for instance found in *The Division of Labor* (1984), Emile Durkheim's seminal sociological study. Durkheim addresses large questions such as consequences of the division of labor on the solidarity of societies and how to reconcile tensions between individual autonomy and the disciplined regulation of modern life. He argues that stable social bonds are requisite for the functioning of societies, which otherwise decay under the fracturing tendencies of individualism (Durkheim, 1984, p. 233).

Although some contemporary social scientists are adhering to this assumption, others are not. Change has become the primary interest of historical sociologists and ecological anthropologists who are investigating how culture on its own or in conjunction with other social structures fuels dynamism (Crane, 1994; Morawska and Spohn, 1994). Accordingly, culture is en route, constructing or deconstructing, but rarely standing still. Illustrating this point, Michael Carrithers (1992) describes in his anthropological studies of the Jain minority in India that while certain aspects of this 2400-year culture have survived intact to this day, others have disappeared or been radically transformed.

A major reason put forth for rejecting the static picture is that no culture is isolated, and without isolation, permanence is impossible. Historian Eric Wolf (1982) argues that no society is completely local and unaffected, pristine and untouched. He demonstrates through historical analysis how each region in the Western world, starting from about AD 1400, was greatly affected by and intertwined with others, such that every culture, however peculiar it seems, is in reality epiphenomenal or a derivative of another. Another reason for rejecting the idea of culture as more or less fixed is that, when time is considered, cultures do change. Ignoring historicity means that insights on cultures are at best provisional. Historian Thomas Sowell (1994, p. 254) provides a good illustration in his discussion of the British:

> "The British" were the world's leading slave traders in the 18th century—and the most implacable and relentless enemies of slave trading in the 19th and 20th centuries. These facts do not contradict each other, or cancel each other, nor is it necessary to attempt a net balance for "the British." Both facts are realities of history and it is only our use of a single inter-temporal abstraction called "the British" for a changing collection of people with changing ideas and commitments that make the facts seem inconsistent.

Social scientists are consequently constructing more evolutionary theories of culture. An example is Thompson and colleagues (1990), who propose that culture is composed of cultural biases, social relations, and ways of life. Ways of life are represented in differing degrees in each society at a given moment, and dynamism occurs through continuous rivalry among the five ways, which compete for adherents.

Culture Is Coherent and Unified

Coherence and unity are other ontological traits of culture reflected in the leading paradigms in global marketing. These attributes are pronounced in Hofstede's framework, wherein a set of values represents the totality of culture. Hence France's *sui generis* character high individualism, power distance, and uncertainty avoidance, combined with low masculinity (Hofstede, 2001). Hall's and Triandis's theories are even more integrated interpretations of cultures: Societies are either high or low in context, individualistic or collectivist in disposition. Although Hall (1976) acknowledges that no society resides exclusively on one end or the other of the context range, he generally places each in a single category. Triandis advances similar notions: Certain people favor self-oriented cognitions and understand themselves as autonomous (e.g., British), whereas other persons are outwardly oriented and conceive of themselves as members of groups (e.g., Russians) (Triandis, 2000; Triandis et al., 1995).

The annals of anthropology and sociology are filled with references to culture as coherent and integrated. Culture is described by Sapir (1917, p. 442) as "the mass of typical reactions"; by Benedict (1934, p. 176) as the "coherent organizations of behaviour"; and by Herskovits (1945, p. 28) as "patterned reactions." Such concepts of discernable cultural wholes were popular not only in the past but are also widely accepted in the present. Trompenaars (1994), Schwartz (1992), and House and colleagues (2004), among others, describe cultures as discrete, coherent, incommensurable dimensions, such as neutrality versus emotionalism.

However, critics have charged that framing culture as cohesive is more ideology than reality, noting the lack of convincing evidence that culture is a neat, orderly, and consistent package (Crane, 1994; Wagner, 1981; Wolf, 1982). They point to signs of culture's indeterminate and contestable nature, such as violent resurrections of long-dormant religious and ethnic animosities in places like Russia and Iraq (Herzfeld, 1997; Morawska and Spohn, 1994). Culture is paradoxical, in that it is both an integrative and a disintegrative force (Carrithers, 1992; Smith, 1995): It bonds certain individuals together (the in-group), while distinguishing and pushing aside others (the out-group). This dynamic can lead to a blending and borrowing, or hybridization, of cultures, whereas in other cases, the results are chasms of separation and open displays of hostility.

Not surprisingly, theories that portray culture as fractured and discontinuous are appearing in the social sciences. Among them is Ann Swidler's (1986) paradigm in which culture is a "tool kit" of symbols, stories, rituals, and worldviews that people use in varying configurations to solve problems and organize time. Individuals develop "strategies of action," or ways of ordering activities, to accomplish different life goals. These strategies depend on habit, mood, sensibility, and other contextual factors. Culture is not a unified system that pushes people in a consistent direction but rather offers them a repertoire to select from to construct lines of action. This leaves room for variation as well as interjects fluidity.

In summary, the ontological assumptions of culture as cognitive, bounded, immutable, coherent, and unified—assumptions held of culture by Hofstede, Triandis, and Hall and thus descriptive of culture as framed in global marketing—find support as well as opposition in traditional and modern works in the social sciences. To broaden our understanding of culture, we can consider the alternative perspective found in the social sciences, namely culture as loosely settled, contradictory, varied or heterogeneous, and under negotiation.

Epistemological structure

Idealized–Superorganic Epistemology

Stepping back from the ontological attributes allows us to see the underlying shape or whole of culture, or its epistemological structure, much like how the subject of a pointillism painting comes into view when examined from a distance. When culture is considered as cognitive, bounded, immutable, coherent, and unified, its whole is an idealized, abstract entity with strong causal force. It is idealized in that it upholds certain modes of living over others; it is abstract in that it is derived or inferred rather than directly observed; and it is causal in that it triggers and demands a response from people. I name this epistemology the idealized–superorganic structure and represent it with Figure 12.1. The word superorganic captures how culture exists above the level of individuals and groups. It plays a stabilizing and integrating role, sanctioning certain modes of

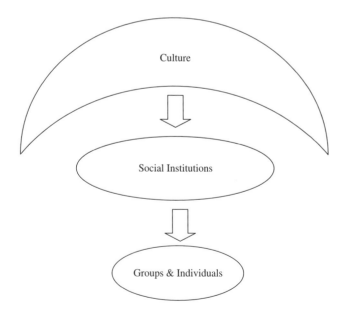

Figure 12.1   Idealist–superorganic epistemological structure

living and dissuading others. Its effects are mediated and reinforced by social institutions, including religion, education, language, media, and the government. I review the selected social sciences writings to examine this and other epistemological structures reflexively.

According to social sciences literature, the idealized–superorganic view of culture originated in the eighteenth century and reigned through much of the twentieth century. Notable expositors were Emile Durkheim, Alfred Louis Kroeber, and Leslie White. Durkheim (1966) was quite emphatic in his works about the coercive power of culture to force people into "ecstatic submission," assigning culture a considerable influence over daily lives and actions. The label "superorganic" was first applied by the anthropologist Kroeber (1917), who drew the distinction between the individual "organic" level of existence and the larger "superorganic" system known as culture. Like Durkheim, Kroeber advocated a transcendent view, articulating that culture exists apart from biological agents (people) who contribute to its perpetuation (Norbeck, 1976). Perhaps the clearest expressions of this epistemology were given by anthropologist Leslie White in a series of writings, starting in the 1940s. White (1959) proposed that culture is not a mere summation of individual psychologies but an extrasomatic phenomenon that has a will of its own and can be apprehended without taking human organisms into account.

As Kroeber and White were forwarding this epistemology, others such as anthropologists Franz Boas and A. R. Radcliffe-Brown were dissenting. One issue raised by dissenters was reifying culture. The epistemology effectively disembodies culture by separating it from its organic source (Carrithers, 1992; Hanson, 1975). Another issue was denying the autonomy of people and their ability to defy culture, that is, their agency. In this epistemology, people are passive cultural robots pushed around by a monolithic force that tells them how to think, what to do, which way to live (Swidler, 1986). Yet defiance, even of a partial nature, is routine in communities. Finally, there was concern about framing culture as highly deterministic. The superorganic view ignores the intervention of accident, intent, and the commingling of circumstances (Wolf, 1982). Historians are most sensitive to this possibility, noting the vicissitudes of time and the convergence of factors much beyond culture that transform a society.

Realist–Organic Epistemology

If culture is weakly bounded, changeable, unsettled, disjunctive, and more than cognitive—an ontology present in the social sciences literature, as described previously—culture possesses a more complex and

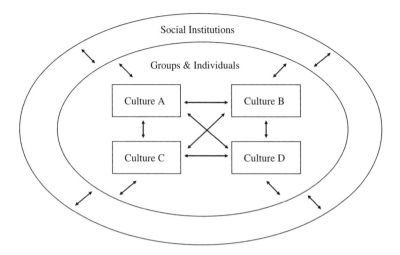

Figure 12.2   Realist–organic epistemological structure

dynamic makeup than that typically portrayed. This structure, which I call the realist–organic, represents an alternative epistemology and is depicted in Figure 12.2. It bears several marks. One is that culture is organic, existing at the level of actual persons rather than as a cosmic unity hovering above. This shifts the emphasis from a metaphysical impersonal force to a thoroughly social dialectic among humans. A second mark, one resulting from the first, is that culture is directly observable as customs, artifacts, actions, and symbolates instead of indirectly through surrogate constructions such as values, ideals, and personality. Another mark is that, given traits such as mutability and discontinuity, culture is an evolving complex of ideas, actions, and beliefs. Closer examination reveals not a tight homogeneous whole but a loose heterogeneity; there are subcultures, a federation of sorts, all interacting, imprinting, and affecting one another. A fourth distinction is that individuals impact culture. This is not a one-way street, and effects go both ways to and from people and the larger culture. Given this, culture has both stabilizing and destabilizing effects (Eisenhardt, 1992). Social institutions act as material intermediaries, as in the idealized–superorganic structure, but permit influences in both directions.

The realist–organic position is assumed in past as well as current works on culture in the social sciences. Edward Tylor and Margaret Mead (1928) argued that culture consists of acquired capabilities, habits, or customs and that culture is best described as human social behavior rather than as an independent and immaterial life force (Bidney, 1944). Similarly, A. R. Radcliffe-Brown contended that people and their processes of social interaction are all important and that studying culture as an abstraction is apt to be misleading (White, 1959). In recent years, researchers have put forth several culture theories rooted in this epistemology. In his sociality theory, Michael Carrithers (1992, pp. 34–5) emphasizes that culture is about how "people do things with, to, and in respect of each other" and acknowledges "that humans in the first instance relate to each other not to the abstraction of culture." Bernardo Bernardi (1977) describes how people are culture makers rather than passive carriers, able to assimilate, appropriate, or refuse aspects of their culture. He articulates individuals are "living interpreters of culture," such that culture is a temporal phenomenon (Bernardi, 1977). Steve Derne (1994) observes that values are socially contested, that culture users interpret symbols in diverse ways, and that even shared values do not necessarily result in similar actions. And Thompson and colleagues (1990) detail that ways of life are periodically dislodged and that change and modification are paradoxically essential for a culture to survive.

In summary, both the idealized–superorganic and realistic–organic epistemologies are actively discussed in the social sciences. As with their corresponding ontologies, they are complements that together represent a wide range of theoretical understandings about the essential nature of culture.

Epistemological philosophy

The final aspect of culture I examine reflexively is epistemological philosophy. By epistemological philosophy, I mean fundamental tenets about the nature of truth, and specifically how the truth about culture is apprehended. The leading culture theories in global marketing are rooted in certain tenets: (1) knowledge is objective and rational; (2) there is a single reality, or truth, to be discovered; (3) phenomena operate according to universal laws applicable across time and space; and (4) the scientific method of experimentation and falsification guides the progression of knowledge.

The first tenet is observable in Hofstede's work (1980, 2001), insofar as culture is said to possess a logical, impartially observable structure. The culture values of individualism, uncertainty avoidance, and so on are discrete and linear, as derived through statistical analyses of survey data. There is little ambiguity about the values (what they refer to, their characteristics, how they are manifest) or how much they are present in a specific society (standardized indexes indicate their exact intensities in each country). Triandis's theory exemplifies the second tenet. Triandis (2000, p. 146) acknowledges that culture is complex and diffuse, but that it is "best conceptualized as different patterns of sampling information in the environment." In other words, the truth about culture is rather singular: It is how much a society prefers individualistic versus collectivistic thoughts. Culture is not multiplex, contradictory, or debatable. The third tenet can be seen in Hall's writings. Hall (1976) argues that humans have developed acuities to certain forms of messaging. Sensory receptors and the brain's neocortex have adapted to environmental and group demands over several millennia according to the principles of evolution and biology. Culture is thus governed by universal forces. Finally, reflecting the fourth tenet, Hofstede and Triandis emphasize the importance of adhering to the scientific method to produce, test, and refine their theories. Although Hall articulates this point far less, all three researchers have a high regard for empirical evidence to support their ideas.

Modernism

The four tenets are captured by the philosophy of modernism. Modernism's origins are in the Enlightenment. Voltaire, Rousseau, Bacon, and others favored reason because it demystifies the world by breaking the hold of tradition and religion. Modernism today signifies secularism in human thought; science as the basis of knowledge; the search for metaphysical, transcendent truths; knowledge as complete yet progressive; the capacity and power of human creativity; and the pursuit of objective understanding (Hunt, 1991; Venkatesh et al., 1993).

Modernism is reflected in classical as well as contemporary works on culture. An example is Karl Marx's conceptualization of class struggle (Marx and Engels, 1967). According to Marx, the bourgeoisie, using private ownership and capitalism, extract surplus value from the labor of the proletariat class. Increasing their wealth and power, the bourgeoisie sow the seeds of dissension and alienation, and are inevitably overthrown by the underclass, which establishes a new order based on shared need rather than exploitation. The theory is very much a modernist vision in that it stresses scientific thought, human creativity, and historical progress. A more contemporary example of modernism is Stace Lindsay's work on cultural mentalities. Lindsay (2000) observes that economic progress is impeded or facilitated by mental models used by a country's elite. Models resistant to development are rooted in paternalism and hierarchicalism, whereas models promoting advancement integrate flexibility and a focus on knowledge capital. The Cartesian logic of Lindsay's theory, use of scientific research methods, and faith in intellectual solutions for entrenched issues like global poverty are consistent with modernism.

Postmodernism

While continuing to be a popular epistemology for culture theories in the social sciences, modernism has been confronted by an alternative philosophy known as postmodernism. Postmodernism can be traced to a movement in art and architecture in the 1920s. It diffused across the intellectual landscape, forwarded by poststructuralist thinkers such as Jean-François Lyotard, Roland Barthes, Jacques Derrida, and Michel Foucault (Brown, 1995; Waugh, 1992). It has made significant inroads into disciplines as divergent as economics, history, and linguistics (Brown, 1995; Firat et al., 1994).

Different ideas have fallen under the rubric of postmodernism (Docherty, 1993; Jencks, 1992), but the following appear to be its major concerns. First, it purports that reality is socially or self-constructed. Contrary to the emphasis in modernism on a single, objective, and external truth, postmodernism sees truth as dependent on the observer and context of observation, resulting in multiple understandings of equal legitimacy with no fixed ontology (Firat et al., 1994; Firat and Schultz, 1997). Second, postmodernism argues for particularism, looking at the subject in relation to its setting. Thus variation and exception rather than uniformity and constancy are observed across time and space. What are viewed as global and permanent from a modernist perspective become local and temporary, shifting and reconstituting, in a postmodernist frame (Nooteboom, 2001). Third, the philosophy focuses on the fragmented, often contradictory, aspects of a phenomenon. Unified grand schemas and narratives are discounted because the human condition is itself juxtapositional and disassembled, a montage of not-all-together coherent experiences and qualities (Venkatesh et al., 1993).

Postmodernism has led to new culture theories in the social sciences. Among these is a theory by Jean Baudrillard (1981). He argues that signs—images and symbols—have become central to the human experience in lieu of the actual entities they represent, as in the case of consumers. Advertising and the display of goods in fantasy formats play on a logic of signs, creating and recreating meaning, such that these meanings are valued as much as, and perhaps more than, the products themselves. It is a thoroughly postmodern perspective in that the dream or hallucinatory world has a greater reality than the material basis. Another postmodern culture theory is Jonathan Friedman's (1994) panorama of cultural strategies. Friedman posits that the principal theme in contemporary global transformations is the decline of Western hegemony, along with the corresponding rise of postmodern values in some geographies and resurgence of religious, ethnic, and nationalistic ties in others. The results are five cultural strategies present around the world: modernism (emphasis on progressive evolution, democratic solutions, and moral and modern governance), postmodernism–consumptionist (cultural distancing, unanchored identity, and narcissistic dependency on consumption), traditionalist–religious–ethnic (failure of the modernist project and promise of success and mobility vis-à-vis traditional religious–ethnic identities), third world (centrality of the state-class ranking system, consumption as symbol of modernity and prestige), and fourth world (cultural movements focused on repressed lifestyles and rejection of universal development). The five strategies comprise a fragmented world system characterized by frenetic adaptation to changing conditions.

Turning to culture writings in the social sciences, we see an astonishing range of perspectives on philosophical epistemologies. On the one hand, there are modernist interpretations of culture, such as those of Marx and Lindsay; on the other hand, there are postmodern understandings, such as by Baudrillard and Friedman. The culture theories of Hofstede, Triandis, and Hall, dominant in global marketing, however, reflect only one end of the range, the modernist philosophy.

Discussion

Culture is of increasing interest to help explain and predict a variety of global marketing phenomena. Yet the frameworks used to understand culture, predominantly Hofstede's, are limited in their ability to generate insights and implications. To address this limitation, I sought directions from the social sciences. I selected writings on culture from both classical and contemporary streams in the social sciences, and then reflexively examined them to expand the understanding of culture used in global marketing.

The primary finding from this reflexive study is that outside of global marketing, culture is a wide and competitive terrain. The perspectives of sociologists, anthropologists, historians, and other social scientists are highly diverse yet commonly indicate the potency of culture to illumine perplexing social phenomena. Consequently, the culture theories they describe reflect a range of ontological and epistemological properties, as shown in Figure 12.3. In terms of ontological traits, some theories present culture as cognitive, bounded, fixed, coherent, and unified (the "A" end of this range); others show culture as cognitive and non-cognitive, permeable, changeable, indeterminate, and fragmented (the "B" end). With respect to epistemological structure, certain theories imply that culture's gestalt is a metaphysical force imprinting tendencies on to individuals (the idealized–superorganic structure or "A" end), while others portray it as a person-to-person dialectic, with actions,

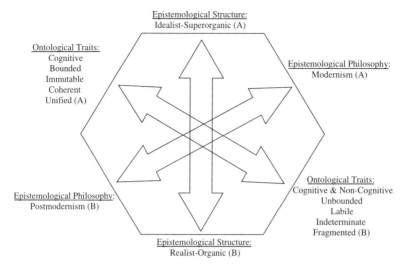

Epistemological Structure:
Idealist-Superorganic (A)

Ontological Traits:
Cognitive
Bounded
Immutable
Coherent
Unified (A)

Epistemological Philosophy:
Modernism (A)

Epistemological Philosophy:
Postmodernism (B)

Ontological Traits:
Cognitive & Non-Cognitive
Unbounded
Labile
Indeterminate
Fragmented (B)

Epistemological Structure:
Realist-Organic (B)

Figure 12.3　Culture theory properties

ideas, and beliefs forming an evolving complex among individuals, groups, and larger social structures (the realist–organic structure or "B" end of the range). Finally, the theories encompass contrasting epistemological philosophies about the nature of truth and how to apprehend it, extending from modernist assumptions ("A" end), such as the operation of universal laws, to postmodernist ones ("B" end), where truth is said to be constructed, particularistic, and incomplete.

I draw several conclusions. First and perhaps most obvious is that the leading culture theories in global marketing mirror some deeply held convictions about culture within the social sciences ("A" ends of Figure 12.3), and therefore, these and similar frameworks ("Pure A" theories) represent a viable path for culture theories in global marketing. Put another way, the ontological and epistemological suppositions of the leading theories appear in and are thus validated by external culture writings. This finding suggests these frameworks are capable of producing genuine and useful insights on culture for global marketing. At the same time, the near exclusive use of Pure A theories in global marketing suggests the conceptual base is quite narrow. As noted in commentaries on international business, the embrace of a narrow vision or premature constriction of theories should be avoided (Sullivan, 1998; Sullivan and Weaver, 2000). It is preferable to allow distinct theories to compete openly with one another, thereby generating larger leaps of knowledge. Diversification contributes to this important end by inserting competing logics, which in turn generate discourse on culture theories and tests of their relative merits.

This perspective leads to the second conclusion: The opposing perspective on culture is also validated by the social science writings ("B" ends of Figure 12.3), so theories with B properties ("Pure B" theories) represent another viable and complementary route for culture theories in global marketing. Whether it is Bourdieu's (1984) paradigm of culture capital, Geertz's (1988, 2000) articulation of culture as context-laden, or Mead's (1928) exposition of culture as existing at the level of daily human interactions, theories in the B form have undoubtedly shed light on the nature and workings of culture in the social sciences and offer to do the same in global marketing. Pure B theories are not significantly present in the global marketing literature (see Chapter 4 by Nakata and Izberk-Bilgin) and thus represent more potential than actuality.

The final and main conclusion, which is deduced logically from the first two, is that for culture theories to advance the discipline of global marketing—helping meet the field's long-standing need for stronger theoretical underpinnings—Pure A, Pure B, and hybrid forms (which mix ontological and epistemological properties from the "A" and "B" ends) should be actively and *concurrently* pursued. This goal represents the future course for the development and application of culture theories in global marketing. I also suggest by extension that it offers a future course of culture theories for global management (see Chapter 2 by Earley, and Chapter 3 by Taras and Steele in this book). My reflexive examination identifies the presence of both A and B properties in the selected culture writings. Culture theories on both ends of the ontological and epistemological ranges have been created and used by social scientists. While theories of the B persuasion are more recent, those of the A variety have by no means been abandoned. The two coexist, representing legitimate approaches and vibrant streams of work. By forming a broader, richer, and complementary landscape of ideas, theories representing A *and* B polarities (rather than A *or* B) promise to invigorate culture studies in global marketing as they have in the social sciences. To illustrate how Pure A, Pure B, and hybrid theories may be directed to critical global marketing concerns, I provide a few illustrations. Given space constraints, other examples are given in Table 12.1.

Pure A culture theory application

A promising theory of the Pure A form is Fons Trompenaars's (1994) culture paradigm. Like Hofstede, Trompenaars operationalizes culture as the mean tendencies within a nation. Similarly, he measures these

Table 12.1 Illustrations of Pure A, Pure B, and Hybrid culture theories applied to global marketing issues

Global marketing domain	Culture theory (author)/ theory form	Culture theory's propositions	Sample global marketing issue	Sample research question
Marketing management/ organization	Culture types (Trompenaars, 1994)/Hybrid	There are seven national culture dimensions, each represented by a pair of opposing propensities toward people, time, and the environment. An example of a propensity is particularism vs universalism.	Culture-based approaches toward marketing planning	In multinational firms, subsidiaries develop country-specific marketing plans, which must then be integrated into a coherent global or regional marketing plan. How might this process be affected by distinct cultural propensities among marketing managers, such as analytical vs intuitive, and what can be done to optimize the process?
Consumer behavior	Cultural tool kit (Swidler, 1986)/Pure B	Culture is a tool kit, from which people select and apply certain items (symbols, practices, stories, knowledge) in order to resolve dilemmas. The choice of tool depends on circumstances, personal preference, and mood, and thus outwardly appears idiosyncratic.	Fragmentation of consumption in transitional vs non-transitional economies	Does the cultural tool kit theory help explain fragmented consumption habits? For instance, is the inconsistency of consumption habits (e.g., driving a Mercedes-Benz but shopping at Wal-Mart) predictable based on this theory? How might these behaviors differ or be similar between transitional and non-transitional economies (e.g., China and Sweden, respectively)?

(Continued)

Table 12.1   (Continued)

Global marketing domain	Culture theory (author)/ theory form	Culture theory's propositions	Sample global marketing issue	Sample research question
Import/export	Social identity theory (Jenkins, 1997)/Pure B	Social and individual identities co-exist and dialectically interact. The processes by which identities are produced, re-produced, and changed are essentially social. Identities are constructed through interactions with others and are thus subject to change.	Social identities of exporters and importers	How are social identities of exporters and importers constructed in relation to one another? Can superordinate identities result from intense social interactions? What may be the moderating roles of resources (e.g., organizational slack, foreign market knowledge), and functionalism (e.g., assuming importer is an order-taker rather than an equal partner) in the effectiveness of social identity formation and export performance?
License/franchise	Self Perceptions (Markus and Kitayama, 1991)/Pure A	Culture has two dimensions: (1) the extent people view themselves as interdependent with others; (2) the extent people see themselves as autonomous from others. Interdependence and independence are orthogonal constructs.	Strength of ties in international licensor-licensee relationships	International licensing arrangements can fail due to geographic distance and other complexities. Does culture (interdependence/independence of licensees and licensors) influence strength of ties and thereby the success of an international licensing arrangement?

Non-equity strategic alliance	Cultural typology of economic development (Grondona, 2000)/Pure A	Societies are girded by deeply inculcated, cultural values that promote or resist sustained creation of economic wealth. There are 20 cultural values, including positive vs negative competition, and utilitarianism vs idealism (or cosmovisionary).	Global strategic alliances	Global strategic alliances can bring together competing firms from different countries to collaborate on large, risky projects over an extended time period. Can the cultural typology be used to identify more optimal cultural combinations of partner firms that are congruent with the long-term wealth-producing vision of global strategic alliances?
Product	Interpretive theory of culture (Geertz, 2000)/Pure B	Culture is a "historically transmitted pattern of meanings embodied in symbols, a system of inherited conceptions . . . by which men communicate, perpetuate, and develop their knowledge about and attitudes toward life" (Geertz, 1973: 89). Culture is not a force but a context to be thickly described and semiotically understood.	Foreign brand image and attitudes	Do images of and attitudes toward foreign brands change in relation to (1) shifting geo-political conditions, and (2) ambiguity of country of origin? What are the specific dynamics? For instance, some American brands (e.g., Starbucks) are suffering from negative reactions in foreign markets since the Iraq War; however, American brands with more amorphous identities (e.g., Visa and Kleenex) have not been affected.

(Continued)

Table 12.1   (Continued)

Global marketing domain	Culture theory (author)/ theory form	Culture theory's propositions	Sample global marketing issue	Sample research question
Pricing	Culture as signs (Baudrillard, 1981)/Pure B	Culture is a commodification of signs (images and symbols), which are central to the human experience and sometimes valued more than the actual entities they represent. Referents can be substituted by signs that take on a life of their own.	Pricing of global luxury goods	Are prices for global luxury goods consumed as signs? If so, how does this process occur and what can marketers do to perpetuate it as a value-generating activity? Prices do not necessarily correspond with the material worth of products, but can act as symbolates. Prices carry this function especially for global luxury goods. For example, when BMW prices a model at $150,000, is it selling *the dream* of penultimate wealth as much as the actual vehicle or driving experience?

| Distribution | Universal culture values (Schwartz, 1992)/Pure A | Culture is a set of shared values (e.g., mastery vs harmony) reflecting a society's response to three universal issues. | Global supply chain management | Is formal, contractual-based global supply chain management tied to the cultural preference for mastery? Conversely, is informal, relation-based global supply chain management tied to the cultural preference for harmony? Respective exemplars of the two types of supply networks are American and Japanese. How are global supply chains that are composed of multiple cultures and firms best formed and managed? |
| Markets and marketing structures | Cultural capital (Bourdieu, 1984)/Pure B | Social classes are distinguished by the degree they possess and ways they express cultural capital (taste, cultural knowledge). Distinctions are maintained through consumption, dress, speech, décor, and aspects of people's habitus. | Global market segments | In what ways is the emergence of global market segments, such as elites or cosmopolitans, explained by a common desire for culture capital? How can and do marketers leverage this desire in global marketing campaigns? |

(Continued)

Table 12.1 (Continued)

Global marketing domain	Culture theory (author)/ theory form	Culture theory's propositions	Sample global marketing issue	Sample research question
Political–legal–ethical environment	Means/end social theory (Merton, 1938)/Hybrid	All societies (1) set cultural goals that human actors seek to achieve, and (2) sanction the means to get them. However, because social systems limit access to opportunity structures, individuals with lesser access will seek creative and/or criminal ways to fulfill those goals. Societies with greater limits on access will produce higher levels of unethical behaviors.	Cross-cultural marketing ethics	Which societal-level correlates mark or identify foreign markets with weaker or stronger marketing ethics? If a market emphasizes achievement but severely restricts opportunities, Merton's theory says unethical marketing behaviors prevail. Therefore possible correlates or predictors of unethical marketing are high social need for achievement, large income disparities, low levels of compulsory education, and endemic racial divides.

tendencies through large-scale international surveys of business professionals (nearly 15,000 respondents in 47 countries). Trompenaars also projects the same ontology and epistemology on to culture as did Hofstede (e.g., culture as a potent life force and subject to scientific inquiry). Distinctive, however, is Trompenaars's notion that culture represents ways of resolving essential and universal dilemmas regarding people, time, and the environment. The ways are expressed as preferences on seven dimensions: universalism vs particularism, individualism vs collectivism, neutrality vs emotion, specificity vs diffuseness, achievement vs ascription, sequential vs synchronic, and internality vs externality. Several of these dimensions overlap with those outlined by Hofstede, Hall, or Triandis, but the ones that differ are worthy of exploration in global marketing studies.

One potential area of application is the development of multinational marketing strategies. A global firm typically has subsidiaries in several countries, each of which develops a marketing plan in consultation with regional or corporate headquarters. Difficulties can arise in this process because of differences among managers and analysts on how to interpret market conditions, arrive at solutions to improve market performance, and translate these thoughts into a useful plan of action. Studies have shown that information-based tasks are culturally influenced (e.g., Gurhan-Canli and Maheswaran, 2000), so it may be helpful to examine the role of culture in marketing planning. Specifically, how does culture affect the process and outcomes of marketing planning in multinational organizations? Trompenaars's paradigm may be applied to this question. Universalism–particularism is an especially interesting and relevant culture dimension. It refers to the degree to which rules or relationships govern a society. In universalistic countries like the United States, there is a clear preference for generating and abiding by explicit and shared principles. In contrast, particularistic countries like Russia place a higher priority on maintaining strong personal relationships. Rules, while not completely ignored, are meant to be flexibly interpreted to accommodate unique circumstances. Trompenaars's paradigm suggests that subsidiaries in universalistic cultures lean toward rationally derived marketing plans with measurable objectives, whereas subsidiaries in particularistic cultures produce marketing plans intuitively and informally, with subjective goals that change depending on market conditions. This idea can be formulated into a research hypothesis and tested in a comparative study of international subsidiaries. Hypotheses can also be tested for other cultural dimensions in the Trompenaars's framework, such as sequential versus synchronic approaches to tasking.

Based on the findings, implications can be drawn for proceeding more effectively with marketing planning and execution across complex transnational organizations.

Pure B culture theory application

An example of a Pure B theory is Ann Swidler's (1986) paradigm of culture as a tool kit. Swidler, a sociologist, proposed that culture is a collection of shared symbols, stories, and rituals that people have at their disposal. To achieve life goals, people use elements from this collection in varying combinations, just as they apply items from a tool kit to accomplish tasks. Ontologically, the paradigm is polar from Pure A theories in that culture is portrayed as malleable and indeterminate. It is malleable in the sense that the tool kit evolves as elements are incorporated, eliminated, or altered in response to external events and shared experiences. Swidler notes that in periods of social transformation, people add new elements and dislodge old ones. Culture is also indeterminate in that, while it is widely available, people apply its elements selectively depending on circumstance, habit, mood, and sensibility. People's behaviors can thus appear idiosyncratic and unpredictable. In addition, Swidler's paradigm contrasts with Pure A theories in terms of epistemology: It does not characterize culture as an omnipresent force that pushes people around as cultural dopes (the idealized–superorganic view). Instead culture is a repertoire from which individuals choose items to construct lines of action. In this realist–organic frame, people are active and skilled culture users, not takers. Swidler's paradigm also reflects a postmodern sensibility through an emphasis on particulars (e.g., allowing for individual choices) and fragmentation (e.g., inconsistencies between lines of action).

To illustrate how Swidler's paradigm specifically and Pure B theories generally can be applied to global marketing, I now describe a possible study. Global marketers are faced with the challenge of satisfying customers who are not entirely consistent in their purchase and consumption practices. While segmentation to a degree tackles that issue, even within segments, critical inconsistencies arise. For example, in the worldwide segment known as global elites or cosmopolitans, there is considerable variation in values, personal goals, and living standards. An individual in that segment can exhibit contradictory behaviors: shopping at a discount store one day and making high-end purchases at a luxury boutique another day. If these variations are assumed away, as is often done when income is the chief or only parameter for segment definition, the marketing task is simple. But if these distinctions are acknowledged to increase a global marketing program's efficacy or exploit paradoxical consumption behaviors, the task becomes complex. Swidler's paradigm may offer guidance. A study can be done to explore whether and how the paradigm explains fragmented and contradictory consumption practices within global segments. Swidler's notion of individuals selectively appropriating cultural elements in response to differing personal and public conditions may illumine the motivations and lines of action for conflicting purchase patterns. The findings can be used to formulate marketing strategies by global marketers such as Wal-Mart and LVMH. Contrary to assumptions, both draw the well heeled, along with the less monied. Prior to now, most research on global segments has focused on intragroup homogeneity, perhaps owing to the lack of a robust theory explaining the plausibility and reasons for heterogeneity.

Hybrid theory application

One hybrid theory that has generated enormous attention in political science is Samuel Huntington's conceptualization on civilizations. In *The Clash of Civilizations and the Remaking of World Order*, Huntington (1996) forwards the thesis that "world politics is being reconfigured along cultural lines," unlike the ideological entrenchments of the Cold War. He predicts future wars will occur along cultural fault lines, such as in the Ukraine and Sudan. The work has been prescient since its publication, identifying political hotspots around the world before their eruption. Huntington equates culture with civilization, which is an overall way of life that has endured over thousands of years. Examples of civilizations are Sinic and Orthodox. Huntington's framework is anchored on the A end epistemologically, specifically in the idealized–superorganic structure (e.g., culture as a deterministic life force) and modernist philosophy (e.g., culture as scientifically observable). Where Huntington diverges from the A anchor is in ontology. Huntington asserts that culture is not well bounded, geographically or politically. A large and complex country like Indonesia can have multiple civilizations, which spill beyond national borders into other regions of the world.

I now illustrate how Huntington's framework, representing hybrid culture theories, can be used in global marketing research. Promotions have been designed and executed on national, subnational, and supranational (i.e., global) bases. While these bases appear orthogonal, capturing all possibilities, Huntington's theory raises the prospect of one other approach: civilizational. It is well understood that promotions must be congruent with the target culture to be effective. However, international marketers face a dilemma. On the one hand, adapting promotions to a culture increases buyer appeal and thereby generates more sales. On the other hand, producing a unique promotion for each culture or subculture is resource-consuming. Conversely, marketers can disregard cultural differences and produce uniform promotions to save time and costs; yet the promotions may not be sufficiently tailored to persuade individuals to hand over their euros, yen, or pesos to purchase the advertised items. The dilemma reflects the difficult tension between customization and standardization. Perhaps one way to move beyond the impasse is to investigate whether both customization and standardization can be accommodated simultaneously through promotions directed at civilizations. Such promotions are culturally adapted but offer greater efficiencies than national-based forms because the targets are civilizations, which are large populations dispersed across several countries and/or regions. A study may be done to explore the efficacy of civilization-based promotions. Take one civilization, the Sinic-Confucian, as an example. Rooted in China, the civilization has experienced a diaspora into much of Southeast Asia and the Pacific Rim over the last two centuries. Promotions can be developed for this civilization, incorporating Confucian values such as frugality and filial piety, and tested against other promotional forms. Marketers appear already to be experimenting with civilizational promotions. Tsingtao Brewery has executed advertising for its namesake beer aimed at Chinese living in the United States, Taiwan, and elsewhere. The advertising recognizes the existence of borderless yet culturally specific markets.

Conclusion

To enlarge the frame of possible culture theories for global marketing, I have turned to classical and contemporary culture studies in the social sciences. I juxtapose the culture theories found in these works against the primary paradigms in global marketing, comparing their ontological and epistemological features. This reflexive exercise leads to recognizing the wide range of assumptions that has been made about culture in the social sciences, a range not equally well reflected in global marketing. Therefore, I conclude that more of this range needs to be represented in future global marketing studies to ensure understanding of culture and how it matters in the global context. More specifically, I argue for the simultaneous pursuit of Pure A, Pure B, and hybrid culture theories, as together they will collectively enhance knowledge for global marketing purposes.

This argument is not for theoretical variety for its own sake. Rather, it advocates the exploration of theories representing equally legitimate assumptions about culture (Hofstede's assumptions constitute just one set among several), then allowing these theories to compete vigorously with one another and thereby enrich intellectual discourse and strengthen knowledge generation. This approach is likely to bear more fruit in the long run than confining research narrowly to one or a handful of culture theories, however valuable they appear to be. Doing the latter may bring to a premature close the fascinating, and often frustrating, quest to fathom cultural phenomena.

The recent discussion in the *Journal of International Business Studies* regarding the GLOBE dimensions and their similarities and differences with Hofstede's framework and methodology is a fine example of the kind of intellectual vigor that is needed in global marketing and management culture research (Leung, 2006). Ultimately, culture theories promise to build a more rigorous conceptual foundation for this research—potential that waits to be fully exploited. I hope other researchers will join me in tapping this potential. My recommended path is to traverse a broader, richer theoretical terrain, employing a variety of culture frameworks. This path may appear long, indirect, or circuitous, but it will help us arrive at the desired destination, namely, a more assured grasp of how culture theories forward the study and practice of global marketing.

References

Aaker, J. L. & Maheswaran, D. (1997) "The Effect of Cultural Orientation on Persuasion," *Journal of Consumer Research*, 24 (December), 315–28.

Alden, D. L., Hoyer, W. D., & Lee, C. (1993) "Identifying Global and Culture-Specific Dimensions of Humor in Advertising: A Multinational Analysis," *Journal of Marketing*, 57 (April), 64–75.

Anderson, B. (1991) Imagined Communities: Reflections on the Origin and Spread of Nationalism, 2nd edn. London, UK: Verso.

Baudrillard, J. (1981) *For a Critique of the Political Economy of the Sign*. St. Louis, MO: Telos Press.

Benedict, R. (1934) *Patterns of Culture*. Boston: Houghton Mifflin.

Benedict, R. (1946) *The Chrysanthemum and the Sword*. London, UK: Routledge and Kegan Paul.

Bernardi, B. (1977) "The Concept of Culture: A New Presentation," in B. Benardi (ed.), *The Concept and Dynamics of Culture*. Chicago, IL: Mouton Publishers, 75–88.

Bidney, D. (1944) "On the Concept of Culture and Some Cultural Fallacies," *American Anthropologist*, 46 (1), 30–44.

Blake, J. & Davis, K. (1964) "Norms, Values and Sanctions," in R. L. Faris (ed.) *Handbook of Modern Sociology*. Chicago, IL: Rand-McNally, 456–84.

Bourdieu, P. (1984) *Distinction: A Social Critique of the Judgement of Taste.* Cambridge, MA: Harvard University Press.

Brown, S. (1995) "Postmodernism, the Wheel of Retailing and Will to Power," *International Review of Retail, Distribution and Consumer Research*, 5 (3), 387–414.

Carrithers, M. (1992) Why Humans Have Cultures: Explaining Anthropology and Social Diversity. Oxford, UK: Oxford University Press.

Crane, D. (1994) "Introduction: The Challenge of the Sociology of Culture to Sociology as a Discipline," in D. Crane (ed.) *The Sociology of Culture: Emerging Theoretical Perspectives.* Oxford, UK: Blackwell, 1–20.

Derne, S. (1994) "Cultural Conceptions of Human Motivation and Their Significance for Culture Theory," in D. Crane (ed.) *The Sociology of Culture: Emerging Theoretical Perspectives.* Oxford, UK: Blackwell Publishers, 267–87.

Docherty, T. (1993) *Postmodernism: A Reader.* New York, NY: Columbia University Press.

Durkheim, E. (1966) *The Rules of Sociological Method*, 8th edn. New York, NY: Macmillan.

Durkheim, E. (1984) *The Division of Labor in Society*, W. D. Halls, trans. New York, NY: The Free Press. (Originally published as *De la Division du Travail Social: Étude sur l'Organisation des Sociétés supérieures*, 1893. Paris, France: Alcan).

Eisenhardt, S. N. (1992) "The Order-Maintaining and Order-Transforming Dimensions of Culture," in R. Munch & N. J. Smelser (eds) *Theory of Culture*. Berkeley, CA: University of California Press, 64–87.

Firat, A. Fuat, Sherry, J. F., Jr., & Venkatesh, A. (1994) "Postmodernism, Marketing and the Consumer," *International Journal of Research in Marketing*, 11, 311–16.

Firat, A. F. & Schultz, C. J., II (1997) "From Segmentation to Fragmentation: Markets and Marketing Strategy in the Postmodern Era," *European Journal of Marketing*, 31 (3/4), 183–207.

Friedman, J. (1994) *Cultural Identity and the Global Process*. Thousand Oaks, CA: Sage Publications.

Geertz, C. (1973) *The Interpretation of Cultures: Selected Essays.* New York, NY: Basic Books.

Geertz, C. (1988) "Thick Description: Toward an Interpretive Theory of Culture," in P. Bohannan & M. Glazer (eds) *High Points in Anthropology*, 2nd edn. New York, NY: McGraw-Hill.

Geertz, C. (2000) Available Light: Anthropological Reflections on Philosophical Topics. Princeton, NJ: Princeton University Press.

Gorer, G. (1955) "The Concept of National Character," in C. Kluckhohn & H. A. Murray (eds) *Personality in Nature, Society, and Culture*, 2nd edn. New York, NY: Alfred A. Knopf.

Grondona, M. (2000) "A Cultural Typology of Economic Development," in L. E. Harrison & S. Huntington (eds) *Culture Matters: How Values Shape Human Progress*. New York, NY: Basic Books, 44–55.

Gurhan-Canli, Z & Maheswaran, D. (2000) "Cultural Variation in Country of Origin Effects," *Journal of Marketing Research*, 37 (August), 309–17.

Hall, E. (1966) *The Hidden Dimension.* New York, NY: Anchor Books.

Hall, E. (1976) *Beyond Culture.* New York, NY: Anchor Books.

Hanson, F. A. (1975) *Meaning in Culture*. London, UK: Routledge and Kegan Paul.

Harris, M. (1999) *Theories of Culture in Postmodern Times*. Walnut Creek, CA: Altamira Press.

Herskovits, M. J. (1945) "The Processes of Cultural Change," in R. Lindon (ed.) *The Science of Man in the World Crisis*. New York, NY: Oxford University Press.

Herzfeld, M. (1997) Cultural Intimacy: Social Poetics in the Nation-State. New York, NY: Routledge.

Hofstede, G. (1980) Culture's Consequences: International Differences in Work-Related Values. Beverly Hills, CA: Sage Publications.

Hofstede, G. (2001) Culture's Consequences: Comparing Values, Behaviors, Institutions and Organizations Across Nations. Thousand Oaks, CA: Sage Publications.

House, R. J., Hanges, P. J., Javidan, M., Dorfman, P., & Gupta, V. (2004) *Culture, Leadership, and Organizations: The GLOBE Study of 62 Societies*. Thousand Oaks, CA: Sage Publications.

Hunt, S. D. (1991) Modern Marketing Theory: Critical Issues in the Philosophy of Marketing Science. Cincinnati, OH: South-Western Publishing.

Huntington, S. (1996) The Clash of Civilizations and the Remaking of the World Order. New York, NY: Simon & Schuster.

James, P. (1996) Nation Formation: Towards a Theory of Abstract Community. London, UK: Sage.

Jencks, C. (1992) *The Post-Modern Reader*. London, UK: Academy Editions

Jenkins, R. (1997) Rethinking Ethnicity: Arguments and Explorations. London, UK: Sage.

Kroeber, A. L. (1917) "The Superorganic," *American Anthropologist*, 19 (2), 163–213.

Kroeber, A. L. & Kluckhohn, C. (1952) *Culture: A Critical Review of Concepts and Definitions*. Papers of the Peabody Museum of American Archaeology and Ethnology, Harvard University, Vol. 67, No. 1.

Leung, K. (2006) "Editor's Introduction to the Exchange Between Hofstede and GLOBE," *Journal of International Business Studies*, 37, 881.

Lindsay, S. (2000) "Culture, Mental Models, and National Prosperity," in L. E. Harrison & S. P. Huntington (eds), *Culture Matters: How Values Shape Human Progress*. New York, NY: Basic Books, 282–95.

Markus, H. R. & Kitayama, S. (1991) "Culture and the Self: Implications for Cognition, Emotion, and Motivation," *Psychological Review*, 98, 224–53.

Marx, K. & Engels, F. (1967) *The Communist Manifesto*. London, UK: Penguin.

Mead, M. (1928) Coming of Age in Samoa: A Psychological Study of Primitive Youth for Western Civilisation. New York, NY: W. Morrow.

Merton, R. K. (1938) "Social Structure and Anomie," *American Sociological Review*, 3 (5), 672–82.

Morawska, E. & Spohn, W. (1994) "Cultural Pluralism in Historical Sociology," in D. Crane (ed.) *The Sociology of Culture*. Cambridge, MA: Blackwell Publishers, 45–90.

Nooteboom, B. (2001) "A Postmodern Philosophy of Markets," *International Studies of Management and Organization*, 22 (2), 53–76.

Norbeck, E. (1976) "Introduction: Cultural Anthropology and Concepts of Culture," in F. C. Gamst & E. Norbeck (eds) *Ideas of Culture: Sources and Uses*. New York, NY: Holt, Rinehart, and Winston, 1–17.

Parsons, T. (1937) *The Structure of Social Action*. New York, NY: The Free Press.

Poole, R. (1999) *Nation and Identity*. London, UK: Routledge.

Sapir, E. (1917) "Do We Need a Superorganic?" *American Anthropologist*, 19, 441–7.

Schudson, M. (1994) "Culture and the Integration of National Societies," in D. Crane (ed.) *The Sociology of Culture: Emerging Theoretical Perspectives*. Oxford, UK: Blackwell, 21–44.

Schwartz, S. H. (1992) "Universals in the Content and Structure of Values: Theoretical Advances and Empirical Tests in Twenty Countries," in M. Zanna (ed.) *Advances in Experimental Social Psychology*, Vol. 25, New York, NY: Academic Press, 1–65.

Shweder, R. A. (1984) "Preview: A Colloquy of Culture Theorists," in R. A. Shweder & R. A. Levine (eds) *Culture Theory: Essays on Mind, Self, and Emotion*. Cambridge, UK: Cambridge University Press, 1–26.

Smith, A. D. (1995) *Nations and Nationalism in a Global Era*. Cambridge: Polity Press.

Song, X. M., Xie, J., & Dyer, B. (2000) "Antecedents and Consequences of Marketing Managers' Conflict-Handling Behaviors," *Journal of Marketing*, 64 (January), 50–66.

Sowell, T. (1994) *Race and Culture: A World View*. New York, NY: Basic Books.

Sullivan, D. P. (1998) "Cognitive Tendencies in International Business Research: Implications to the Matter of a Narrow Vision," *Journal of International Business Studies*, 29, 837–63.

Sullivan, D. P. & Weaver, G. R. (2000) "Cultural Cognition in International Business Research," *Management International Review*, 40 (3), 269–97.

Swidler, A. (1986) "Culture in Action: Symbols and Strategies," *American Sociological Review*, 51 (April), 273–86.

Thompson, M., Ellis, R., & Wildavsky, A. (1990) *Cultural Theory*. Boulder, CO: Westview.

Trafimow, D., Triandis, H., & Goto, S. (1991) "Some Tests of the Distinction between the Private Self and the Collective Self," *Journal of Personality and Social Psychology*, 60 (May), 649–55.

Triandis, H. C. (1989) "The Self and Behavior in Differing Cultural Contexts," *Psychological Review*, 96 (July), 506–52.

Triandis, H. C. (2000) "Culture and Conflict," *International Journal of Psychology*, 35 (2), 145–52.

Triandis, H. C., Chan, D. K. S., Bhawuk, D. P. S., Iwao, S., & Sinha, J. B. P. (1995) "Multimethod Probes of Allocentrism and Idiocentrism," *International Journal of Psychology*, 30 (4), 461–80.

Triandis, H. C. & Suh, E. M. (2002) "Cultural Influences on Personality," *Annual Review of Psychology*, 53, 133–60.

Trompenaars, F. (1994) Riding the Waves of Culture: Understanding Diversity in Global Business. Burr Ridge, IL: Irwin Professional Publishing.

Venkatesh, A., Sherry, J. F., Jr., & Firat, F. (1993) "Postmodernism and the Marketing Imaginary," *International Journal of Research in Marketing*, 10, 215–23.

Wagner, R. (1981) *The Invention of Culture*. Chicago, IL: University of Chicago Press.

Waugh, P. (1992) Practicing Postmodernism, Reading Postmodernism. London, UK: Edward Arnold.

Wallerstein, I. (1997) "The National and the Universal: Can There Be Such a Thing as World Culture?," in A. D. King (ed.) *Culture, Globalization, and the World-System*. Minneapolis: University of Minnesota Press, 91–106.

White, L. A. (1959) "The Concept of Culture," *American Anthropologist*, 61 (2), 227–53.

Wolf, E. (1982) *Europe and the People without History*. London, UK: University of California Press.

Index